WHAT THE HORSE WHISPERS

A Deeper Understanding of the Horse's Mind and Heart

Ditte Young

Printed in the United States of America

ISBN Paperback: 979-8-9951881-0-0

ISBN eBook: 979-8-9951881-1-7

Contents

"When we learn to understand that examples of unusual human potential (such as genius-level creativity, telepathy, psychokinesis, precognition, and memories of past lives) do occur in some people, we begin to realize that this ability lies dormant in all human beings. In other words, these are skills that can be developed and enhanced. The consequences for the human race, if such abilities are possible to attain, are overwhelming!"
— Eben Alexander, MD

Introduction

Being *Different* is Also a Strength

Today, there's a name for what I am. It's called *highly sensitive*. I have always felt different. Partly because I am adopted from South Korea, and when I started school, I entered a world full of people who didn't look like me. But mainly because I have some special abilities that I have kept to myself since early childhood. As the years have passed, I no longer feel that my abilities are so unusual. I've come to understand that I've learned to sense the world more deeply. And in that sensitivity, I feel everything much more intensely.

What is special about my abilities is that I have taught myself to channel all my energy and power into one place and shut off my thoughts. In an encounter with another soul, I receive energy and release it in an intense, loving way. A love that is pure and without noise, and that has one direction. A love that can only be achieved and experienced when I am fully present in the moment. That's what makes it powerful. Some days, this ability feels like a curse to me, because being so *sensitive* can be really hard. However, most of the time, I view my sensitivity and deep-rooted love as my greatest strength: to be a channel and interpreter for the animals I help or the spiritual world. Interpreting for animals is called telepathy. One of the terms that describes it beautifully is *non-verbal communication.*

It occurs in a meeting, an exchange of energy between two souls, whether they are human or animal. A meeting without words, without grand gestures or body language. But with a delicate sense *of* and *for* each other. It's an energy that feels like a piece of silk landing softly on my face and over my body. It's a sensation of something unfamiliar yet gently brushing my face as we meet. And the art lies in learning to dance in sync, so two pieces of silk meet and play in the wind, without ever losing their connection. It's an energetic connectedness and a respect for being allowed to be as we are. And yet, we belong together in that very *now*, for just a moment, when we share thoughts and feelings. When I *talk with the animals*, it requires me to remove all the layers around me. Layers made up of defense mechanisms, interpretations, opinions, and prejudices. It requires me to turn off my rational brain. To stop thinking and just be open. To make myself available, to listen in silence, both inwardly and to the outer world, so I can sense what information is rushing toward me.

And so, I can make sense of it, without being overwhelmed by the many impulses blowing my way. This is part of being spiritually aware. If you're one of those who wish to understand your animal on a deeper level, I hope this book will also take you on a journey that allows you to understand *yourself* on a deeper level. I believe this ability exists within you, within me, within the animals, and within all souls. But it requires that you listen. That you become so still within yourself that you can sense and hear even the subtlest sensations, vibrations, and whispers in your inner ear.

The Path That Led Me Here

The journey has taken me many years, and I am grateful for each day that begins with new energies around me. I am thankful for my life as it is today, both personally and in my work as an animal telepath, therapist, and clairvoyant. Growing up, I often asked my school friends, *"Have you ever thought about how different I look?"* They all responded, each in their way, that they had never even thought about it. To them, I was, and still am, just Ditte.

But I felt different, both on the outside and inside. I felt *over-sensi-*

tive in some way, and back then, I thought that feeling too much was something negative. My inner world has always revolved around the fact that I felt everything much more deeply than most people. I could sense an entire room the moment I walked into it. I heard everything people said, and even what they didn't say. I could feel who was struggling, who had just gone through a divorce, who was dealing with addiction, who had an eating disorder, who was being unfaithful to their partner, who was unhappy at work, and much more. I just *knew*, and I still do today.

In every building, I saw the spirit world. I saw the deceased, and they spoke to me. I saw old energy imprints everywhere I went, like a horse-drawn carriage passing through a square, even though parking spaces now covered the spot I stood on. I thought it was just my imagination. At that time, I hadn't yet developed clairvoyant vision, so I saw the spirits as impressions inside my mind, like when you sit in a dark room and look out a window and sense someone on the other side, even if you can't see them clearly. They whispered to me, they spoke out loud, and sometimes they shouted. The spirits had messages they wanted me to pass on to their loved ones, but I didn't know what to do with them. They were still there, right in front of me, but on a frequency that was still unfamiliar to me. It's challenging to have abilities that allow you to hear, see, and feel things that others don't pick up on. The challenge, for me, was eventually finding balance, learning to shut out a great deal. I had to learn to shut down. I had to learn to accept that there are many things I cannot communicate, either because no one asked, or because I need to protect myself, or because I sense that the recipient isn't yet ready to receive all the insight I've been given.

Today, I've turned this into a strength. I can listen, see, and feel, and I can also shut it off. I now view the ability to close off as the most essential part of my work. It is also the most vital form of protection for me, given that I live in this spiritually open state constantly.

There are so many episodes in my life where I've been left wondering, especially when I was little, before I even knew what I could do. One rainy day on the bus to school, I looked at a little boy standing in the aisle and thought, *"He's going to fall."* The very next second, he fell when the bus braked suddenly. I was startled because it happened and frightened by my abilities, questioning why I had that thought in the first place. Where had the thought come from? I looked around the bus, and everyone else seemed completely unfazed by what I had just experienced. To them, it was just a boy who hadn't held on properly, right?

Another time, back in elementary school, I dreamed that one of my classmates' little brothers would drown. I didn't know how or when. I just *knew* that he would. A week later, I was told that he had drowned. Fortunately, he survived, but he was very close to death, and everyone was deeply affected by the incident. I was scared because many of the things I had dreamed of or seen came true. I didn't know it was an ability, what's now known as precognition or foresight. I had no idea what to do with it, so I ignored it for many years. As time went on, I couldn't attend social gatherings without receiving information and messages about the people I was with. It wasn't like someone would come over and whisper something in my ear. Out of nowhere, I'd get a thought in my mind followed by a strong emotion of either joy, sorrow, anger, anxiety, and so on.

At first, I thought I just had a vivid imagination. However, I soon discovered that I had a sense which was often confirmed later when I spoke with people. I never mentioned what I had sensed. Instead of feeling validated in my abilities, I just felt sad. I felt lonely, and didn't know what to do with what I was sensing. What was I supposed to do with information like that? When I felt that the girl I was looking at was self-harming, or that a woman's husband was cheating on her? These questions and the pressure that I felt from receiving all this information became a major foundation in the journey that brought me to where I am today, a path of continuous development, self-insight, and a desire to understand.

I have always been a helper. Even as a little girl, I wanted to be a psychologist or a therapist when I grew up. And I did become a licensed therapist. Today, I still navigate through an *energetic world*, in the sense that I see and feel everything as energy. This is a place where I want to help, without compromising my well-being in the process. And I have a feeling that most *sensitive souls* will recognize this inner conflict: wanting to help yourself first, without feeling selfish, disloyal, or like you're a bad person.

As I neared the end of my teenage years, I talked with some of my friends about whether it was possible to shut down my abilities. Eventually, I decided to contact a clairvoyance school. This school was located in a small city near Copenhagen, one of my friends was enrolled there at the time I started becoming interested in training myself. I didn't know you could *train* to become clairvoyant. Wasn't that just an ability reserved for a chosen few? And what could I possibly learn at such a school?

I decided to apply, not knowing what I was getting myself into. I was nervous, but I was determined to learn how to shut down these thoughts and feelings that felt uncontrollable to me. Since I'm someone who likes to stay in control, even though I'm constantly trying to let go, this was important to me: to regain control over the thoughts, images, and feelings within me.

Building a Bridge Between Heaven and Earth

I laughed out loud when my future teacher, Gjertrud Berlon, the founder of the Clairvoyance School of Denmark, told me that I could communicate with animals and that one day I would become nationally and internationally renowned for this work. At that time, I didn't have any animals of my own, and I still don't. I didn't want to subject them to my constantly busy lifestyle. I had never ridden or owned a horse, and it wasn't until my late 30s that I finally got the courage to take up dressage lessons: a course that taught me about horsemanship, handling horses, facing my fear of these majestic animals, while learning the basics of riding.

I've always been a little afraid of horses. That fear stems from when one of my childhood friends got her nose kicked off at a racetrack and nearly died. She had plastic surgery, and today you'd never know her nose isn't real, but I clearly remember the fear I felt from witnessing the sheer force of a horse.

I grew up with boxer dogs. I loved the smell of newspaper on the floor and the unique scent only a puppy has. I also loved having chickens in the backyard of my childhood home. We had chicks, collected fresh eggs, and fed them leftovers from dinner; potato peels, carrot skins, and more saved in a bucket for their meals. My sister and I each had budgies in our rooms, I quickly tamed mine. As a child, I loved the feeling of my budgie sitting in my hair or perching on my thin glasses frames while I did my homework. But as I grew older and these animals passed away, either naturally or through euthanasia and I began to shut down my deep emotions toward them. I grieved for days whenever I woke to find one of my budgies had fallen to the floor. I held funerals for them in the garden, planted flowers, and cried rivers of tears, and a piece of me died with them. That deep bond and love I had for them, as my best friends and confidants, was too much for me. The pain of losing them cut so deeply into my soul and heart. Most likely because I am adopted and carry abandonment as one of the core themes of my life. But also, because I couldn't bear saying goodbye to an animal. I was convinced, after we no longer had budgies, that I would never again become so attached to an animal. That's why it was both ironic and anxiety-provoking to hear Gjertrud's words predicting my coming path. I felt afraid of opening up to animals. *"What if I get sad? What if they don't want to talk to me? What if I see dead animals and they haunt me in my already strange dreams?"*

I had numerous thoughts and questions as I tried to sit calmly and smile at this woman, who was still a stranger to me during our initial meeting. She looked at me with deep seriousness, yet with a gentleness and a smile, and I could feel that she was proud of the information or images she saw with her inner eye in connection with me. Gjertrud told me that one day I would build a bridge between heaven and earth. She told me that one day I would have a son who would inspire me to give many lectures and public speeches, and that one day, I would even provide speeches *with* him.

I sat there, a giant question mark, completely confused by what she was saying or where these messages were coming from. *"That sounds exciting, but how on earth am I supposed to do that? How is it even possible? And what does heaven have to do with animals?"* I thought.

It was the year 1999, and I was sitting on Gjertrud's green velvet couch in her small apartment in a small city in Copenhagen, sipping coffee. I was at an entrance interview, where Gjertrud *tuned in* to me to see whether I had the clairvoyant abilities necessary to join her training program.

I've always had vivid dreams, and in 1999, they became more intense and overwhelming. I began training myself to record my dreams while still half-asleep. In the beginning, I wrote down only keywords, whatever I could remember. The next morning, when I looked at my notes, something would stir within me, but it still felt like being in a fog, far from my conscious awareness. Over time, I got better at turning those key words into complete sentences. Some mornings, I would wake up to what resembled a short essay; five to ten pages of detailed accounts from my dreams. And over the years, I discovered that these were precognitions, predictions, and premonitions that came to me in my sleep, when my physical body was at rest, but my mind was still working in a layer or frequency I didn't yet understand. The things I dreamt would happen later, and the dreams became increasingly frequent. There were nights when I was afraid to fall asleep, out of fear of what I might see. I was exhausted from lack of sleep, but I stubbornly persisted because I wanted to understand. I began reading about dream interpretation, and later, during my four-year study as a psychotherapist, I became deeply engaged in dream work. I explored the meaning and connection between psychoanalysis, Gestalt therapy, existentialism, and processing the unconscious *versus* spirituality and prophecy. I was hungry for more. I was curious about understanding the spiritual world and the concept of spirituality itself. At the core, I was hungry to understand myself, the abilities I possessed, and couldn't control or understand at all.

Before I left the first meeting at the Clairvoyance School, Gjertrud gave me a few exercises and tools to help me balance my chakras. First, I didn't even know what chakras *were*! And I was nervous, what if I did the exercises wrong? What could happen if I make a mistake? What was I tampering with—within myself, my sensitivity, and my abilities? Even though I felt burdened by having these so-called abilities, I didn't want them to disappear forever. I wished to learn how to control them.

Despite really liking Gjertrud as a person, I also felt some skepticism inside me. I thought: *"I wonder if she's just saying all these things to make me feel special, so I'll join a course she profits from?"* Instead, I chose to focus on the joy of having been accepted into her training. I decided that if I was going to invest money in education over the next six months, I needed to be open to what I could learn. I had said A, now I had to say B. So, I sat down diligently in my apartment in a small town in Copenhagen, with the piece of paper Gjertrud had given me. I began practicing *that thing* with the chakras, even though I had no idea what I was doing. But I followed the instructions on the paper carefully and didn't tell anyone about the exercises. I sat alone in silence, practicing.

With all my discipline and restraint, I showed up nervous and the training began. A course that ran one whole weekend each month for half a year. It was a training that changed my life.

Chapter 1

The Horse's Voice

How I Learned to Communicate with Animals

As the first weekend of the course approached, I grew increasingly nervous. I was on the verge of backing out. But there was a voice inside me that almost screamed that I had to explore this. I was the youngest in the group, and I felt so stupid, naive, unintelligent, and blank. It felt like the other students knew much more than I did. They nodded along with the spiritual terms being thrown around the room, such as *aura*, *affinity*, *ether body*, and many more. For me, there was the body of Christ, and that was a wafer you ate during communion in church. But *ether*? I didn't get it! Still, I knew there was more living inside me that I sincerely wanted to understand. I eventually *surrendered* and chose to go a layer deeper into myself. It felt like surrendering because I had spent so many years fighting it. I let go of my fear of also feeling different on the course, and instead, I accepted that there were so many things I didn't know, and that was perfectly okay.

About The Education

As mentioned, I attended the clairvoyance school on weekends alongside my full-time job. A job that pulled me in the complete opposite direction, in a stressful TV production environment where there was no time at all to feel anything. In school, we were given a lot of great exercises designed to help us open up to our abilities, but also to learn how to shut them down again. We received a large binder full of papers covering auras, chakras, mental bodies, astral bodies, cosmic consciousness, spiritual work, protection, telekinesis, possession, angels, shielding, and many other topics. And I was still scared when I looked at those pages because it all seemed so incredibly occult to begin with. *Protection from what? Evil forces?"* I didn't want to be anywhere near that! *See dead people?* That was not an ability I wanted developed any further than it already was.

I had heard that if you gained full clairvoyant sight, you wouldn't be able to tell the difference between the living and the dead. I had seen the dead before, but it was more like shadows or a reflection in a dark window, as I've described earlier. That I could handle. But not if I couldn't tell the difference. I've never been a fan of horror movies, and as a child, I was terrified of getting shocked. I always had this horror scenario that whenever I walked past a mirror, I'd see a dead face in it. I remember that fear in my nervous system. Often when I went to the bathroom at night, I kept the light off because I was terrified that if I turned it on, someone would be standing next to me, out of nowhere. As a kid, I was also afraid that someone was hiding under my bed and would suddenly grab my feet if I put them on the floor. I often imagined them as trolls who just laughed at me. Beings, which I now know exist and are called *lower entities,* but which I wasn't consciously aware of back then.

Even as a small child, I was unconsciously aware that there were beings who could influence me, or that there were people who were no longer alive, and that someone might be able to see them. I still had no idea what to do with them when I encountered them. I hoped, despite my fear, that someone like my teacher Gjertrud Berlon could help me with precisely these things.

The Training

I recall some of the first exercises I did at school. Most of them involved constant visualization, seeing images before us. It could be the chakras, which are part of the aura or colors and much more. We had to meditate, learn to breathe correctly, and reconnect with ourselves. Because only through connecting with ourselves can we connect with something else, something I still didn't fully understand at that time. But they called it *The Universe.* It was quite a challenge for me and very difficult. I had spent most of my teenage years shutting down my feelings, as a way of protecting myself, my sensitivity, my abilities, and just as part of the typical adolescent process. I was into clothes, makeup, boys, parties, and fun. And I had become one of those *tough girls* who always had a witty remark and could own a whole room because I knew I was good at commanding attention. Back then, I didn't even think about it. It was a way to feel safe in the world, to feel loved, as the popular girl I was in the schools I attended. But I had also learned not to feel too much, to maintain that facade.

During training, we were told that we had to *feel*. And imagine, there I was, afraid to feel anything. I was also scared others might feel into *me*. What if they could read me like an open book? See all my flaws? All my secrets? My facade? We were taught that the most challenging part of delivering messages was getting the first word out of your mouth. We had to learn to let go of control and stop worrying about how our words might affect the person we were helping. It was such a vulnerable place to be, as the helper I was, and still am. Have you ever heard of, or dreamt of showing up naked at school or work, and once people start laughing at you, you realize you're not wearing any clothes? That's exactly how it felt for me the first time I had to deliver a message to someone. Because what if I made them sad? Either by making up some random story in my head, or by receiving a message that would touch something painful inside them. *How could that possibly be helpful?* I thought.

One of the exercises was to stand up, walk over to a person in the room we felt drawn to, and begin speaking, saying what we felt. I still remember how overwhelming that was. I had performance anxiety. *"What if nothing came to me? And what was even supposed to come? What if I said something that made the person sad? What if they couldn't relate to anything I said?"* I remember my heart racing and my palms sweating.

I approached a man in the group. He was much taller than I and older, too. Suddenly, I just began to speak. The first words that came to me, I let them out. I was nervous that it would be wrong. But the words kept repeating in my head until I surrendered and spoke them aloud. I felt awful. I felt sad. I interpreted that as *his* pain, and I began to cry, because I felt his emotions inside my own body and system. I put words to everything I was feeling, together with the thoughts that kept flooding my mind. A battle and doubt about whether what I felt were my feelings or his. Was this clairvoyant messaging, or just my imagination running wild? I didn't understand back then that it was *his* sorrow I was feeling, and it overwhelmed me completely. I felt like throwing up. I got dizzy and my vision blurred. The feeling was so intense I couldn't control or manage it. And I got scared because I didn't understand what was happening.

When I was done crying and feeling what this man was going through, my teacher explained to me that this was what it was like to receive messages from *the other side*. It would be overwhelming the first few times. Later, the messages wouldn't be so intense, and I learned to control the tears when I sensed someone else's sorrow. I also discovered that this type of exercise is referred to as *platform work*.

It's common in mediumship, where a medium or clairvoyant stands on stage or the floor in front of a group of people. It was very popular for a while in churches all over the country, and it's still widely practiced in England, where spiritualism is much more accepted than in Denmark. At many of these platform sessions, spirits come through with messages, and it's up to the medium to deliver accurate information to the right person in the audience, even if there are 50–300 people there.

Conversely, when some of my fellow students practiced on me, I found it both strange and, over time, increasingly natural to be *read*. I let go, and I gave in, and it was an immense relief and liberation for me to be seen, exactly as I am and was, by another human being. This despite the fact that we barely knew each other privately. Being mirrored and understood just as I was had the effect of teaching me to stand on my own and be who I am fully, with everything that this gift entails. Through that mirroring, I began to love myself again. Something I believe I did when I first arrived in this world, before I ever questioned my existence. But through childhood, life experiences and soul wounds I acquired, I came to interpret that I wasn't always good enough. Being read and mirrored in that way made me feel less alone. It has always been difficult for me to feel alone and to view loneliness as part of the human experience for all of us. Both with my abilities, but also feeling different because of how I looked, gave me a sense of loneliness earlier in my life.

What I eventually learned was that in a clairvoyance session, one connects with the spiritual guides of the person being helped, also known as *The Guides*. There can be anywhere from one to several, for example, four guides beside a person. There will typically be one guide who has been by your side since birth. We call that soul *The Gatekeeper*. It is therefore rare that a grandparent would be your spiritual guide if you grew up with them in this life. Your guides are very highly spiritually evolved and are here for one purpose: to be there for YOU in your life. That's why they only want what's best for you. The messages I receive from them as a clairvoyant medium are always from a place of love. They tell you what you, as the client, need to know at that specific point in time when you're sitting with someone like me. They know there's a greater plan for you. They know you have a life purpose. And through their messages, they hope to help you move toward that life purpose, with love and respect for who you are. The messages I receive can relate to their personality, financial challenges, health, relationships, children, past, future, or present. It can also be information from a past life that is relevant to the life you are living today. That's what's known as *Regression Therapy.* As a practitioner, it's essential to assess what the client should and should not be told, and also to remember that we, as clairvoyants, must never direct a client's choices. That's why I always try to open several doors for the clients I sit with. For example, if you choose door number 1 in the future, it will look like this. If you choose door number 2, your future looks like that. As the client, you always have the free will to do and choose precisely what you want. Your karma will always follow you, no matter which door you open. Karma is the learning you have chosen to go through in this lifetime on Earth, and not necessarily a negative punishment for something you did in your past life.

I believe in reincarnation, that there is life after life, and a life between lives.

And that also means, to put it very simply, that we make agreements *on the other side,* you might call it *Heaven,* to return to live as human beings and learn something.

What we choose to learn is entirely individual.

What we want to learn will give us a feeling of resistance, or *a theme* in our life that keeps repeating itself until we've learned how to handle it and face it. This is also known as a *core wound.* A theme might include learning about betrayal, trust, loss, and so on. That theme is what, in spiritual work, is referred to as *karma.*

During the clairvoyance training, we learned, among other things, to give clairvoyant readings for both living and deceased individuals using jewelry or objects they had worn or were carrying. We learned to help others clairvoyantly while blindfolded, ensuring that none of us could *cold read* the people we were sitting with, but would instead communicate only what came through energetically. To *cold read* means that, as a practitioner, you rely more on reading body language and the client's reactions or facial expressions than on actual messages received. Cold reading has nothing to do with clairvoyance. It's more akin to being an excellent judge of character or being able to manipulate someone in a direction you want based on the reactions you observe in them.

I had so many questions throughout my training. I doubted myself and my abilities, often wondering how all of this could even be possible. My mind refused to understand that any of this could be real. I often thought, *Wouldn't these messages apply to just anyone?* But time and time again, I experienced detailed messages being delivered to me, by me, or by my fellow students to one another in a steady flow.

Bringing it into Practice

During my training as a clairvoyant, it was a requirement from Gjertrud that all students practice on 60 test subjects who volunteered so that I could train and prepare for my exam with an external examiner. I had grown curious about whether I was capable of communicating with animals. I didn't know thousands of animal owners, and I didn't think it was realistic to travel all over the country in search of opportunities to speak with animals.

At first, I considered all kinds of animals, simply because I was curious to see if I could do it. I thought about farm animals, including pigs, horses, sheep, cows, dogs, guinea pigs, and goats, among others.

However, I quickly concluded that I needed feedback from the animal's owner to be convinced that communication with animals was even remotely possible. Otherwise, I'd have to assume that I was making up the wildest stories in my head, and then decide whether I was either a genius or downright crazy.

Early in the course, Gjertrud had told me that I could communicate with animals simply by looking at a picture of them. I nearly fell off my chair laughing. I didn't understand anything anymore! Didn't I at least have to be physically present in the same room as the animal? However, as the training progressed and the theory became more complex and intense, I also came to understand that energy always finds a way, regardless of whether we are physically present or not. I soon discovered remote practices.

In addition to the 60 people I practiced on, I also worked with 40 animals, either by being physically present with them or by asking for a photo of them. During the time I was practicing with the 40 animals I had committed to, I had the opportunity to work with some horses in North Zealand. I visited, among other places, Holte Riding Club, located north of Copenhagen, where the horse owner openly acknowledged that she was using my services. I was allowed to practice, but I could also feel the skepticism and strong resistance to my mere presence from others passing me in the stable corridor. I remember it was a cold winter day, at first, I couldn't find the horse's stall, and I was surprised to see a riding club for the first time in my life. There was a lot of noise and a hectic energy, as many people were going in and out or leading horses to and from their stalls—something I had never experienced before. A radio was playing in the background, adding even more noise and distraction. Years later, this environment has become routine for me, and I no longer find it quite as overwhelming. Still, I find it difficult to concentrate on telepathy if the radio is on while I'm working. That's because, when I work with energy, and thus with frequencies, the radio's frequency can drown out the information I receive telepathically. I observed the hustle and bustle at the riding club and then quietly walked in, tuning into the energy inside. The ceilings were high. There were people around, but not down at the far end of the stable. So, I walked down there, and the horse I was supposed to *speak* with was standing right there. I felt relieved not to have to stand in the middle of everything with people constantly walking past. I remember thinking those horses must get a bit stressed from all the chatter and traffic going back and forth past them, but at the time, I didn't ask them what they thought of the commotion. It was fascinating for me to enter a world I knew nothing about as an outsider. I felt exposed, unwelcome, and entirely out of place and again, I felt different. But it wasn't enough to stop me from trying to communicate with that horse. I was curious, and by then I was eager to know more about what these abilities might reveal to me. I stood in front of a large chestnut mare. She felt very big to me, and I was a bit afraid of her. The owner was someone I trusted, and she reassured me, telling me I could take all the time I needed. I had tried this many times with people by now, so it had to work the same way. I performed the exercises I had learned at school, where I visualized something in front of me, spun objects counterclockwise, and attempted to control my pulse to a different rhythm than the music I was listening to. I saw colors around me and breathed deeply until I entered a trance-like state, one familiar to me from my school days. A state where the space around me faded away. And in that space, I could feel and see only the person, or the animal, standing in front of me, even if other students were watching me while I worked. Still to this day, when I work clairvoyantly, I feel that everything vibrates rapidly around me as if the air itself is humming at a higher frequency than my physical body. In that moment, standing in the riding club, I discovered, for the first time, that there was no change in vibration. The air didn't shift around me, or between me and the horse. I was instantly overcome with performance anxiety and thought, *Now everything has shut down. I can't do this.* It felt so different from giving a clairvoyance reading.

I could hear the radio the entire time and began focusing on that instead. I noticed that my breathing became heavy. I felt a heaviness in my right leg, and I started to feel increasingly calm. I felt the urge to raise my head and carry myself with more nobility, like a royal. Yes, perhaps more like a princess or a queen. I looked at the owner, who was standing there waiting for me to say something, and I suddenly felt this deep love for her as if I was profoundly grateful to her for taking me in. I had a strong desire to go outside with her and be with her, and for her to always keep her eyes on me, a kind of attention-seeking behavior. And *then* it hit me. These weren't my thoughts!

It was the mare I was standing in front of. It was her energy and her inner world I was sensing. Her needs, desires, and longings were flowing into me and through my body.

For a couple of hours, I spoke with the mare and sensed what it felt like to be her; both mentally and physically. It was such a *trippy* experience. Instead of hearing, seeing, or sensing *about* the person I was usually sitting across from, I now experienced it *in* my own body, utterly different from how I worked clairvoyantly. Yes, I had felt things intensely and deeply before, especially when picking up on a fellow student's sorrow back at school, but that had felt more like a form of empathy. Naturally, in many of the animal sessions that followed, I kept suspecting myself of simply making something up. I must have a wildly creative imagination, because I honestly couldn't grasp how this was even possible.

There wasn't, and still hasn't been, a single time where I didn't ask my guides for help in doing my very best for the one standing in front of me, whether horse or human. I always prayed for clear messages and to be as detailed as possible, so that they would make sense to the person I was trying to help. It felt natural to me, and also logical, that humility was, and still is, an essential part of this work. I know now that if one becomes overconfident or superior, one is bound to fall. This ability is not meant to be used with ego or arrogance. The greater the humility, the greater the heart and purity in using one's ability as an interpreter. It felt right for me to be a kind of helper. I forced myself to keep any thoughts of needing to convince others that I was *right* as a practitioner. That way, I also prevented performance anxiety from taking over the session. And in that very second, the information came pouring in. Thanks to the riders, the animal owners, and the people I helped through clairvoyance, I received feedback on the things I was shown, sensed, felt, and verbalized. And everything I received was something the people I was working with could recognize. I grew more confident and began practicing with an increasing number of horses. As the sessions continued, I began to see a pattern emerge, one that was different from how I worked clairvoyantly, yet closely aligned with it. I realized that horses don't have spiritual guides or helpers with them at all times, unlike humans. I had to be that for them, because I could understand them. And my most important task became to help them with pure love. My heart nearly broke at the thought that they didn't receive the same help as we humans did. Horses, I learned, were partly placed in the world to help us. And because they came into this world as a herd species, their sense of *we-connection* was more developed by default than ours as humans. That was a theory, and a message, I received, although I didn't fully understand it the first time my spiritual guides brought it to my attention.

In the months that followed, while I was practicing with every animal I could, I began to hear horses speak to me in my inner ear. It felt like my own thoughts being gently whispered into my ear, and that sometimes confused me because those thoughts came in my voice, just like when I was thinking and reflecting.

Over time, I realized the difference between my thoughts and theirs. I was receiving thoughts that I could never have come up with myself, not even in my wildest imagination. I saw images in my mind's eye, and I felt pain in my body that, at first, I didn't understand was being transmitted by the horses. In this telepathic work, I also became overwhelmed. I cried, and I even felt nauseous in the beginning. It was unbelievable to take in, but I tried to accept that I *could* do it, even if I didn't understand *how*. I suddenly found myself able to help horses get into trailers, because the horses told me why they were afraid of being loaded. I listened to them, to their fear, anxiety, and past bad experiences, and I saw how they became calmer and more cooperative after they had shared their thoughts.

I couldn't help but think that it was exactly like when humans go to a psychologist or therapist. The changes I observed required only an hour-long conversation. It surprised me how little it could take for an animal to change its behavior. I grew increasingly brave and even began leading the horses into the trailers myself, despite my fear of these large animals. I felt like I knew where I had them, and yet, I didn't. I had never worked with horses before, except as their interpreter.

After graduating from the Clairvoyance School, which I thankfully passed with top marks, I felt both proud and terrified. One thing was practicing in a safe and closed environment at school, surrounded by other students and classmates who were just as *crazy* as I was. But stepping out into the *real world* and working with actual clients was extremely anxiety-inducing for me.

I continued practicing for quite some time. I didn't charge any money for it because I wanted to be sure that the work I did would one day be worth charging for. As I practiced, word began to spread quietly that *"Ditte Young talks with animals."*

During the telepathic sessions with horses, I tested whether I was practicing clairvoyance on the humans or truly telepathic with the horses. What I discovered was that during clairvoyant sessions, other helpers would come down and convey messages, including spiritual guides or helpers, repeatedly. During the telepathic sessions, no such helpers appeared, except when I specifically asked for them to step in. When I used telepathy, and still do today, I saw the horses blink, yawn, smack their lips, become sleepy, and show clear signs that they were undergoing a treatment and releasing something. The owners didn't become tired or show signs of being treated.

The horses spoke about things the owners weren't aware of, but they made sense to the owners later. They called me for feedback and were stunned. For me, that was proof that I was in communication with the animal. It also showed me just how spiritually aware and incredibly intelligent these large animals were and still are. I asked for pictures of guinea pigs, rabbits, budgerigars, parrots, fish, cats, dogs, everything I could get my hands on to practice with, and I discovered their worlds, seen through their eyes. When I communicated with budgerigars, I would suddenly be looking out through a cage and into the owners' apartments, hearing the sounds, seeing the people who came into the home, and even smelling the scents of their household. All of this I would describe to the stunned owners: moved, surprised, laughed, and much more. It was so life-affirming. The more animals I got to practice with, the clearer it became to me that the ones I most wanted to work with were cats, dogs, and horses. The reason for this was, and still is, that they are much more direct, and you can see the results of the behavioral changes as I worked with them. For me, that made the idea of working as an animal telepath far more motivating, something to pursue in the future. Back then, it also gave me a chance to prove to all the skeptics who had laughed at me that I was capable of something. I now saw this brave new world of animals, and the spiritual world before me. At the same time, I encountered massive skepticism, which I knew I would have to help soften over the years.

It was a massive eye-opener for me to realize that I could help horses change their behavior. It moved me deeply because these large animals, who had once frightened me, had so much to share. Through many telepathic sessions, they helped me shift my belief that animals' capacity for understanding was inferior to that of humans. It was mainly the horses that taught me about the complexity involved in being a partnership, a team, that experience of being two beings who must collaborate instantly in a training program. I also learned how important it is to examine the owner's and rider's own responsibility and role in making a behavioral change possible.

I still had tremendous respect for horses, mainly when I sensed they carried a lot of energy, were unpredictable, or exhibited explosive behavior in general or toward me, and I'm glad I did. Because today, I understand the importance of respecting their size.

Over time, however, I learned that once I had established a connection, a kind of *meeting*, I could quickly sense whether I could approach them physically or not. Clients who have followed me over the years also know that, I never entered a horse's stall to greet them. I stood politely outside the closed stall door and spoke to them from there.

As the years have passed, I've become much more experienced and courageous and now gladly step into a horse's stall. I even treat them physically today, when I work as a craniosacral therapist or healer.

Once, I visited a stable and I felt that the horse was aggressive as soon as I stepped onto the stable aisle. I slowly approached its stall and sensed that it began to cry inside. The horse was skeptical of me, but when I said, *You need to feel my heart,* I could see and feel it calmed down. The horse sensed that I had no agenda, no goals, no stress or panic. I was present, without any expectations, that builds trust. I walked up to it and reached my hand into the stall. It placed its large head in my hand and closed its eyes. The owner burst into tears in front of me. She told me that the reason she had called me was that the horse lashed out at everyone who approached its stall, and it was stall-aggressive and outright hostile toward people. It was profoundly moving for her to see that even before we began the actual session, the horse and I had already had a peaceful encounter, without aggression.

Gradually, I came to trust my abilities increasingly. I was constantly being validated that I could help animals and people, every single time. It gave me the strength and belief I needed to throw myself more fully into this work with animals. At the time, I had only heard of a school called *The Animal University* in Denmark. Aside from that, there were no educational programs except for clairvoyance or mediumship training. There weren't many animal telepaths in Denmark at the time, and I felt a strong urge to be one of those who would help spread this knowledge more widely in the country. One way I could share my knowledge was by creating an Animal Telepathy Training program. To me, the techniques were so simple, yet it was hard to comprehend when trying to apply rational explanations to how this could even be possible.

I started my first course group in Copenhagen, and later held training sessions in cities all over Denmark, from the cities: Aalborg to Horsens, across Funen, and most of Zealand. Today, I also teach abroad. As I helped more animal owners, especially those with horses, which became my primary niche, more riders gradually began to open up to alternative methods, such as telepathy with animals, when it came to behavioral problems.

I was always the *last resort*, the one people turned to when everything else had failed. Many horse owners and riders would call me and ask, *"Can you help me for free? I've spent over $15,000. on all kinds of other treatments."* Most emails or phone calls usually begin with the sentence: *"I don't believe animals can talk at all, but can you help me..."* And the contact always ended with them needing my help in one way or another.

Later, various horse magazines and journals began to feature my work. I was asked if I wanted to participate in various TV programs that dealt with spiritual abilities. Every time, I said no. I knew deep inside that if I were ever to appear on something broadcast to households across Denmark, it would have to be with a very serious and respectful angle. Later, those opportunities came, and I suddenly became more visible within the horse world, and among dog owners who were also watching. I got busy, literally swamped, and I ran as fast as I could to help as many animals as possible, without realizing that I first needed to help myself to stay somewhat balanced in such an energy-demanding line of work.

I had never truly believed that Gjertrud's visions would one day come true, but they did. It was a long and arduous journey marked by skepticism, ridicule, and mockery. There I stood, in my early twenties, somewhat naive and idealistic. I believed that most horse owners knew far more about horses than I did. I wanted everyone to have the opportunity to receive the amazing insights that I received through the animals. I had this hope that deep down, animal owners knew that their animals have thoughts and emotions. Why else would anyone get an animal? But I also had to learn the hard way that new thinking and alternative perspectives trigger resistance in some people.

The Resistance

I often experienced that people who were a bit skeptical of alternative practices, especially clairvoyance and telepathy, would look at me and quite bluntly say, *"Well, you don't look like one of those."* That always made me smile. Because what does *one of those* even look like? What does a clairvoyant look like? A telepath? Is it supposed to be a witch? Or maybe someone wearing beads around their neck, sitting in a circle with a guitar, singing folk songs?

Is the therapist supposed to be an older man or woman in a woolen sweater with big glasses on their forehead, maybe someone who smokes a pipe? The prejudices and preconceptions are numerous and remain so in some areas amongst people who don't know better. I came to think that you don't have to look a certain way to *be* a certain way. It's just the packaging. Whether you're Jesus, the Virgin Mary, Gandhi, the Dalai Lama, yourself, Mother Teresa, or even the American actor Jim Carrey, for that matter, the messages are essentially the same. A message, broadly speaking, of: *"We are here to help others, and there is something greater than us."* Something we don't fully understand, but that we can choose to accept. The animals kept choosing me as their voice to their owners. And those owners continued to book me, across the country and abroad. That made me rise again, every time, and tirelessly speak on behalf of the animals.

Of course, animal owners ridiculed me in the early years. At first, it seemed entirely wild for people that *animals could talk.* Then, as I became more open about the fact that I believed animals had personalities and independent thought processes, there were many violent and adverse reactions. These came from skeptics, academics of all sorts, veterinarians, breeders, and riders of the *old school educational system,* who saw the animal as a *means to an end.* There were several harassment cases, and people who wrote threatening letters to me. Some of these letters included death threats. Many of these letters came from the public, who had attended or followed me when I gave lectures or clinics around the country. They had observed me, some had even followed me without my knowing. I was so focused on being in my world with the animals I worked with, whether in arenas or on riding grounds. Although I felt skepticism around me, and still do when I hold a clinic, it has become good training for me to stay detached and ignore the outside world and negative energies surrounding me. I even had the police and PET (Denmark's Security and Intelligence Service) involved in some of the most serious threats against me. I also had a protected address. When doubt overwhelmed me, I thought to myself: *"Were animal owners so desperate that they would be willing to listen to anything? Would they accept what was being said if it was wrong? Would they speak highly of me if all my work turned out to be a scam?"*

I always concluded that people will only pay for something they feel has value, and they would only refer me to other people if they believed in my abilities and telepathy was a possibility even though they never understood how I did it. The horse industry is significant, yet it is also a small, tightly knit family. If you do well, word spreads quickly. If you do poorly, the word spreads even faster. Therefore, I wouldn't have a three-month constant waiting list if the effect of my work were so poor. I knew deep down that the information I received wasn't something I could Google my way to. I had to trust what I felt and saw, no matter the level of resistance I encountered. I gathered myself and rose again. I've had that internal dialogue many times over the years, and still experience resistance today, but not to the same extent. I spent many years trying to prove that *horses can communicate*! The simple communication that, for me, had become a natural part of who I was, and always had been. The simple technique, where the animals could have a voice, which I believed in, even though there was little under-standing of the method, made me continue, pushing forward as if I were a steamroller, wanting to wake up horse owners. Deep inside me, there was also a faint wish just to be good enough and be taken seriously: In my existence, in my work with animals, and a desire for legitimacy, to be allowed to exist here on Earth, where I could just be myself. The people who were curious enough to book me didn't openly talk about it at first. There were many places where I wasn't welcome—at riding schools, riding clubs, or stud farms. And I had to either stand out in the paddock and talk to the horses along with their owners, even in winter, or I was sneaked into the stable aisle in the evening when there was no one else there except for the horses, all of whom were calm when I entered the aisle. They looked at me and asked, *"Would I talk to them?"* Initially, I felt divided. I wanted to, and I was also curious. But I also knew that I shouldn't and couldn't talk to all animals just because I could. First of all, I knew I couldn't use that much telepathic energy, as it is very exhausting to practice telepathy. And secondly, I hadn't gotten permission from the animals' owners. Over time, I've learned that I must work and focus on the horse whose owner has booked me. And accept that I can't talk to them all, even though they all *speak* to me or have something on their minds. When skeptical animal owners said to me, *"It's absurd that you talk to animals,"* I would always ask them, *"Don't you talk to your animals?"* Could it be an egotistical way of thinking to believe that animals are not capable of communicating back? Are we, humans, the only creatures on Earth and in the entire universe that can speak? The first step in believing that nonverbal communication is possible is to stop and ask yourself, why do you talk to your animal if you don't think it understands what is being said?

Other skeptics found it highly unusual that I knew so much about horses when I had never ridden or owned any animals myself. It was also quite strange, but I also felt that I had the best teachers I could dream of. I got my knowledge from the animals themselves. I didn't just explore what it was like for me to be a horse when I felt them; I investigated what it was like for the horse to be a horse. Over the years, through further education and techniques gained from both my therapeutic training and clairvoyant and spiritual education, I developed my own methods. I learned that the ability as a telepath was effortless! I just had to make myself available as an interpreter and not think that I knew anything at all. It was an enormous relief, because only through this could I interpret clearly, without my thoughts or projections getting in the way.

Some horse owners found it much more credible that I could stand and say all the things I did when I was in the same room with them. Others found it most credible when I wrote the information down in an email. *"If I didn't know anything about horses and couldn't even read one in the stable box, then it must be coming from the horse"*, most people exclaimed.

Some people thought that I should learn more about dressage, jumping, military, hunting, western, Icelandic horses, vaulting, pony games, equipment, saddles, vibration floors, feed, more anatomy, Kinesio taping, bits, Bemer blankets, and so much else, which I didn't intend to do, and it would take me several years. I often considered it, but each time, I came to the big question inside me: *Why? What would I use that knowledge for?* I didn't, and still don't, believe that we need to know everything, but we should become experts in a few areas, excel in them, and delve deeper into specific subjects.

I often think about where the resistance comes from. What is it about, and what happens if there's no recipient for it? Is resistance created in a person to avoid facing the life they live? The truth they know, and what they believe in, or have learned in one way or another, and only this is true for them? Could resistance also be about the fact that one might have been raised to believe that one must have a long academic education to be good enough? Would it feel like an insult if another person, without the same education, could receive the same information? What if there's more between heaven and Earth? Imagine if the world around you could sense the vibrations you emit. Imagine if someone could read your thoughts or feel how you feel, no matter what you tell yourself? That's the part people are most afraid of when it comes to my abilities. I'm often asked, *"Can you read what I'm thinking?"* And I can guarantee them that I won't, because it takes so much psychic energy to do so. When I have time off, I want to be Ditte and have a break. I love sitting and listening to other people's lives and thoughts, without having to deal with them, other than just listening and offering support to those who need it.

There are still days when I feel the resistance, when I am reminded of how some people once believed the Earth was flat. I know that even before the birth of Christ, humans discovered that it wasn't true. But there's a reason why the belief persisted for many years. I think of all the women who were burned at the stake or thrown into rivers with stones tied to their legs to drown because they believed that they could cure people, among other things, with herbs. And I would have been one of them if I had lived back then.

Why is there such massive resistance to things that are not proven or that we cannot create evidence for? Why not be open to the unknown? Why think condemning thoughts like, *"Those who believe in the alternative are unintelligent, or very undereducated, or untrained?"* What if the case was reversed? What if those who need to hold on to resistance are unintelligent and undereducated? What if there is not just one truth? What if everything you've read in textbooks and all your beliefs turn out to be just a fraction of the truth? Thank God, science is increasingly catching up in areas such as telepathy. It makes me happy to read an increased number of articles about research studies that've discovered animals can communicate, understand what's being said, pick up on energies, and create machines that can translate animal body language so that they get a voice, among other findings. Even the U.S. government has been using telepaths for years, including in warfare, to ensure that the enemy didn't intercept signals, something that could be done with Morse codes, for example. Some of you may have heard about one of the CIA's remote viewing programs, also known as *The Psychic Espionage Business*. It became known as *The U.S. Stargate Psychic Spying Program*. This was the code name for a secret U.S. military unit. It was established in 1978 at Fort Meade, Maryland, by the U.S. Defense Intelligence Agency (DIA). It was run by Dr. Ed May and laser physicists Hal Putthoff (Ph.D. as an electrical engineer from Stanford University) and Russell Targ (an American physicist and parapsychologist known for lasers and laser applications). The company was based at the Stanford Research Institute. Their primary work focused on remote viewing. It was a job where you, as a telepath or medium, had to see what was happening from a distance or in the future.

In 1975, the CIA asked Russell Targ and his team to locate an individual with no prior experience in participating in experiments. The person Targ chose was his friend, Hella Hammid. She was to participate in nine double-anonymized trials to locate distant and outdoor locations. In the first trial, she answered correctly in five out of nine cases. In another trial, she was correct in four out of nine cases. The likelihood of this result was 1 in 500,000. The CIA was interested in utilizing the remote viewing program for espionage purposes. Hal Putthoff and Russell Targ had previously succeeded in describing a secret NSA cryptography facility in Virginia, USA. In the trial, the test subject, Ingo Swann, accurately identified the location and recited code words from archival documents, which the NSA and CIA later confirmed to be accurate. Some projects were more successful than others. Unfortunately, the project was shut down in 1995 due to concerns that the validity of the results in some projects was not always upheld. I can't help but think of all the results that did hold but were, of course, classified and kept secret. Why else would the project have been maintained for so long?

Over the years, I have become better at keeping myself *free* from criticism when I meet people who write nasty things about me and my ability to communicate telepathically. They think it's nonsense and humbug; some even call me a scammer and a fraud. I can't help but smile when I come across it. Imagine that, through my abilities, I can provoke such anger, fear, and resistance in others, simply because the method has not yet been proven and published in enough scientific papers? The most important exercise I do when I encounter resistance is, once again, to view the energy around me neutrally. I focus on ensuring that the resistance doesn't have a recipient in me. And then I feel the heavy energy slip away and float away from me. The beauty of this exercise is to send love to the person who wishes me harm because they are hurting in their soul. And I like to think that my love for them and my energy from my strong magnetic field, of course, finds its way to them.

Evidence

How do we prove energy and spirituality? Several researchers and scientists have already proven it through multiple scientific experiments. The challenge is that every time they arrive at a result that is evidence-building, the skeptics raise the bar, making it almost an impossible process, as long as the resistance does not understand the result and wants to know more. It's some knowledge so vast and complex that most people's brains can't keep up. The second major challenge is that research of this caliber requires money. A lot of money to get the wheels turning. Unfortunately, very little funding is allocated for investigations like these.

Most people's opinions and beliefs are shaped by what they've learned throughout their lives. Either from what they've been raised to believe or to feel accepted in their childhood family. For example, it could be value sets and political beliefs: *"In this house, we only vote RED or BLUE, and we are strongly opposed to anyone who votes differently than us!"* If a child overhears phrases like these, it is almost logical that they would never consider voting for anything other than what their parents do.

Opinions, and thus what becomes the truth for an individual, can also be acquired through what one reads in books and what feels right for the person. For some people, the truth is also found when they realize that others have researched and investigated various aspects, so their conclusions must be considered valid. The scientific studies and verbal or written descriptions thus become the truth for most people. Some accept it uncritically, without questioning it, because they believe what they hear or read. *"If it's written there, it must be true!"* And other people ask about these studies and delve deeper until they find a thesis or result that makes sense to them. Or one that is so convincing that there is no doubt. For example, this could be a pier group that is so large that the researchers are convinced that regardless of whether they took 300 people from the study or 300 others from a different study, the result would be the same. One would thereby have proven significant and valid evidence.

Perception

When I think about creating evidence for the paranormal, which telepathy is still considered to be, I always think of the question: *"How long is a piece of string?"* or a similar question might be: *"How blue is the sky?"* Relative to what? For me, the answer to both questions, or similar questions, would be: *"That the truth depends on how this is sensed and thus experienced by the individual, both in the present moment and in a given situation."*

Imagine that you see a white light inside the stable on a gray day, as if you saw a soul moving inside your horse's stall. But you saw it as a fleeting glimpse. You know it wasn't sunlight shining into your eye. You understand that the fluorescent light on the stable corridor has just been replaced, and it doesn't typically flicker. Your rational mind has thus examined all the factors that could explain why you saw the flash of light. Or why it might not be possible that you saw a light flash. Would you trust that what you saw was real? Or would you only have seen it if your friend, or mother, who was standing right next to you, saw the same thing at precisely the exact moment that you saw it? Would you trust your senses? Would you trust what you have experienced yourself? And if your friend or mother didn't see the light flash, would you then doubt your ability to see what you saw with your naked eye? Human perception of reality is subjective, and according to many scientists, we have never had access to any objective reality. This leads me to think that if we are to investigate the paranormal and create evidence for this field, it requires that we study perception to a much greater extent.

Perception is the process by which we become aware of the world through our senses. It is, therefore, our understanding and interpretation of what we sense. Perception is influenced by, among other things, our background, expectations, and the principles of Gestalt psychology. The Gestalt laws are the principles that Gestalt psychology believed were fundamental to human immediate perception (the way we perceive phenomena in the world around us). To perceive is to see, hear, feel, taste, or smell. Moderate rationalists, such as Aristotle and René Descartes, as well as all empiricists from John Locke to Bertrand Russell, claim that perception is a source of knowledge, and for empiricists, the only source. It is therefore necessary to have a philosophical theory of perception that explains both how and what is perceived.

In modern leadership development programs and courses such as *Leadership in Practice,* theories like *The Inner Map* are used. This theory focuses on the sender and receiver and how, through this model, one can create transformative or strategic communication. *The Inner Map* is a managerial communication model that illustrates the elements of leadership communication that contribute to a shared understanding of communication. *The Inner Map* primarily consists of a message from one person to another. The external landscape refers to the outer world and/or an event. How this is perceived is influenced by the senses and how it is processed. The brain then filters the information received based on values, beliefs, memories, thoughts, personal traits, heritage, and environment—essentially, projection. The art lies in avoiding distortion and generalization. After reflecting on this, an inner map is created. This generates a feeling and an internal state. From this, we can develop a form of communication and behavior.

If evidence is considered the truth for most of the population, what interests me is that we ask ourselves: Is there a truth if it hasn't been read, or if others haven't witnessed it, or if it hasn't been documented? Is there a truth if you only feel it—completely alone? Is there a truth if it's experience-oriented and sensed within you?

If, as a human being, you do not gain personal experience from an event, then your knowledge of experiences in general, and thus a part of the world, remains incomplete. Perhaps you can relate to a situation where you go through a divorce. A farewell that may be good for you or necessary for you to feel better. Suddenly, everything you knew is turned upside down. What you learned until now is now forever changed, and you play a role in breaking up a whole family. Your children are hurt; they react, and now they must be shared between two homes. Your spouse, who may disagree that divorce is the only way out, must also be *faced.* And every time you see the twisted face of someone you've just ended a relationship with, you inevitably feel that you've hurt another person. You are responsible for the fact that many others have been hurt, either because you are so deeply hurt that you can no longer stay in this marriage, or because you've grown apart and want to find happiness elsewhere. Maybe with someone else? By yourself. All your friends are still happily married, and the *club* you used to be part of now makes you feel like an outsider because none of your mutual friends understand your inner world. *"Why do you need to realize yourself at such a late age? Why do you need to follow selfish dreams? Are you going through a midlife crisis? Can't you fight a little longer? Maybe until the kids are grown, or just a little older? Maybe you can give your spouse just one more chance,"* even though you know deep down that the last chance was used a long time ago. You may feel that none of your friends understand what you're going through, and you feel entirely alone, starting to doubt whether what you're doing is the right thing. Even though you feel the truth and power within yourself, it's hard to stand entirely alone with it.

A few years later, one of your friends calls you and tells you that they are now getting divorced too, and *NOW* they understand you. NOW they know what you went through. And NOW they wish they could rewind time and have been there for you when you went through the crisis of your life. This is just one example out of many where I sense and see that, as humans, we can only perceive something as *right* or *true* if we experience it ourselves, on our own bodies and in our inner world. Therefore, can it be true that an experience only becomes true if multiple people support it? What I can conclude and live by, at least, is that I know a lot, and yet I know nothing at all. But what I sense, and experience is the truth for me. I hope that one day, in my lifetime, I will have the opportunity to experience proof that energy exchange can occur non-verbally, not just outside Denmark's borders, but in Europe as well. But how we will get there, I don't know yet. Having the privilege of being part of the big podcast show *The Telepathy Tapes* is a major steppingstone in the right direction. However, there is still a long way to go. How can we ever prove emotions and how we individually perceive the world? How would you prove that you love your child or children more than anything on earth? Or the amount and power of the energy of love for your horse, your partner, your spouse, a friend? How would you measure it? How would you weigh it? And how would you create proof that it exists and is therefore true? You can't. There are still no scientists, neurologists, or doctors who have succeeded in measuring the *paranormal* with the known and standard measuring tools like CT scans, MRIs, and so on. Maybe we don't have the right tools yet? Until then, we cannot prove love as a form of energy. You can prove it in actions and words. Some people do services for others as a declaration of love. Some people buy gifts as a way to show how much they value the person. Others spend time, presence, and their physical presence to show, *I like you, so I spend time with you.* If we remove the actions as proof, what remains?

What makes you and me human, besides a physical body? The proof lives inside you. Your memories, your thoughts, your goals, your desires, your emotions. The fact that you have a soul! Your way of sensing the world makes you unique, and no one else on this entire planet can be exactly like you. I have a deep wish that everyone trusts that an individual's world and feelings *are* the truth for that person. Love, attraction, and emotions are energy exchanges between two people. Just because we can't measure them doesn't mean the experiences and feelings are any less true, right? Wouldn't you be frustrated if you had to prove that you love your spouse or your child or children?

A very specific, everyday example is jealousy between partners. One partner loves the other more than anything in the world. But because the other partner doesn't love themselves enough and is insecure, there's resistance in believing, *I am truly loved. What my partner says doesn't ring true.* The partner can buy flowers, bend over backwards, and repeatedly tell their partner throughout the day, to the point of exhaustion, that they love them. Yet, it still doesn't help. As long as the resistance is there, and the other person cannot accept the love, they convince themselves that the love they receive isn't real.

Can you imagine a greater frustration? Imagine what it would be like if you weren't allowed to express your love through actions or physical contact? That's the proof I feel is missing, and right now, it seems impossible to provide. Proof that many scientists are diligently working on cracking the code. I know that you, as someone with an animal, love it more than anything else on earth. Maybe you love it as your loyal partner and friend? Maybe you even love it more than your partner, though you might not fully admit it for fear of hurting their feelings. But I know that with your animal, you feel some form of connection that is indescribable if you could only describe that meeting in one word. For me, that word is love. For others, it could be freedom. For some, it could be mirroring, and so on.

Other people in the stable, where you might be standing with your horse, may not see your horse in the same way that you see them. It can be hurtful if others misunderstand your horse's behavior or actions. And it can be comforting and liberating to know that only you and your horse can exist in a symbiosis together, in your own shared space and your herd. You tell each other things that you don't share with others. And here, you can feel that your horse listens, that it comforts you, that it understands you. It receives the words and feelings you share without you being able to explain what you are feeling. But just because others cannot validate what you think, does that make your feelings untrue? Because you don't have proof that your horse comforts you and that you feel it responds to what you're telling it through your emotions and, thus, energy, does that mean it's not real?

Regardless of the feeling you share with your horse, the evidence of this meeting and exchange, which only you and your horse can experience, is the recognition of the information that comes when someone else articulates it or observes you together. When you don't feel that you are alone in your experience, THEN it must be true! For me, the proof can also be seen in a changed behavior in the animal that I've had a nonverbal interaction with. It can also be found with a veterinarian who discovers the injuries that I or another animal telepath has seen, felt, or sensed, either through blood tests, scans, X-rays, or other examinations.

The evidence for the respective pet owners, I often hear, is experience-oriented, based on the animal's changed behavior. I have found that most animals change their behavior simply by being *communicated with*. Not because I've wished to change something or made a targeted effort to alter anything, but merely because they've been seen at that moment and understood. Right there, I have repeatedly witnessed that it has set them free. And in that moment of freedom, love, and care, it has become their new reality and self-image. Can you imagine? When it comes to finding proof that you and I can communicate non-verbally with animals, what if we are using the wrong tools to find the method?

The Meaning

As the years went by, the animals inspired me. They helped teach and refine my skills. Most importantly, amidst all my stress and rush out in the *real world*, I discovered that with them, I could be present in the moment. It almost felt as though they required it. Maybe because their brains are the size of a walnut? Perhaps because they don't reflect on the future or the past due to the lack of a neocortex in their brains? And maybe because they've a grasp of the *bigger picture* and know how to trust their instincts and inner peace when they feel safe. This was necessary for me to be a *pure* interpreter between them and their humans. I knew that all the knowledge I gained, and continue to achieve every day, was helping me develop both personally and spiritually. That's why I had a desire to pass it on and inspire people to go a layer deeper into themselves. A journey that begins with their animals, but with all the tools they gain, can also be applied to other areas of life.

My niche today is addressing behavioral problems in animals, with a primary focus on working with dogs and horses. I prefer working with these animals because they are so dependent on their humans, and only in this way is it possible for both the animals and humans to experience personal growth. The tools I use to achieve these incredible results are telepathy, combined with a psychological understanding of what happens between, for example, the horse and rider, and vice versa. I find it inspiring every time I communicate with a horse. It can *stand in its light*, exactly as it is. It describes how it is and what it feels, senses, hears, and perceives. It doesn't question its behavior. It questions our behavior. It can be questions like: *"Why is she hitting me? Why does she want to get rid of me? Why does he think I'm not listening when I do this?"* and so on.

In a way, I feel an innocence and purity, as if I were talking to a small child. I am overwhelmed, happy, and touched every single time I sense that purity. Because in that energy, I feel pure love and a desire to exist as I am. And in all the years I've communicated with animals, none of them have ever questioned why I am the way I am. What a relief. What a release. I can breathe. I can just be. And it is precisely for this reason that most people love to interact with animals and be connected to them. Because we humans pick up that energy from them, so that we are accepted as we are.

What can make it very difficult for a horse to be in the world is that it often happens in the relationship with its human, whether they handle it, own it, or ride it. Time and time again, I feel and experience that this conflict arises because the human has a wish, a need, or a goal, for both. Because the horse does not simply rebel against the human's desires, it will always make itself available. It will be grateful for the good things in its life. This can range from being allowed to roam the pasture to running free in an arena. I always think, when I see conflicts between a horse and a rider, *"You shouldn't just think. You should feel!"* I believe more riders should be aware not to assume they hold the truth just because they have the *power* to decide. Most riders can sense what their horses like and dislike. It's beneficial information if you want a partnership based on equality, where there is space for both YOU and THE HORSE.

The horse collaborates with its rider, no matter the conditions. In many ways, horses can be interpreted as being demanding, loyal, cooperative, loving, insightful, and much more. But you could also view that relationship from the perspective that, as humans, we will always have the *trump card* in hand if we choose to misuse the *power* we have over our animals.

Because, as humans, we are technologically superior to animals and, in many ways, more intelligent than they, does that make them less valuable than us? Should they bow to our honor? Is there a right way to be in the world? Are the measurements we have from various IQ tests the ultimate truth? Since we know that people from Asia score highest in IQ, followed by Westerners, and people from third-world countries are at the bottom, could it be because the way we define intelligence is solely based on mathematics or technology? Does this mean that people from Asia or the West should have more power in the world than the rest of the global population, based on the assumption that they are smarter, as measured by IQ tests? We must find some tolerance and space for diversity. Otherwise, the world will become a very gray and dull place to be. It is precisely diversity, differences, and cultures that make the world a wonderful place to live in. People enrich themselves by traveling abroad, savoring French wines, indulging in tapas in Spain, relaxing by Lake Como, savoring pasta in Italy, scaling Mount Kilimanjaro, embarking on a yoga retreat in Bali, and immersing themselves in the spiritual energies of the East. Can we walk together, humans and animals, in this world, which none of us owns, but which we all share, and look at what we give each other and what develops us individually and together, without turning it into a discussion of religion or one opinion over another? Or should the perception of the worldview of each individual be debated endlessly?

With all these thoughts, all my knowledge, and a continuous pursuit of spiritual enlightenment, I wanted to share this with you. I also knew that I had to, and still must, deliver many of these pieces of information in doses. I, too, must find room and patience to be the best communicator within my own beliefs and field, without losing people. Over the many years I've worked as an animal telepath, I've often been on the verge of giving up when the criticism became too harsh. I've felt like giving up and stopping my work with animals. Because how on earth could I build a bridge between heaven and earth when I thought that the planet was *too heavy to dance with?*

I had a feeling of wanting to lighten the energy and play with the information, much like the soft, silk-like energy I felt I was experiencing and passing on. Only to meet an energy of running into a massive wall, a massive resistance, which was unshakable and cold. A wall the size of the Great Wall of China, where I lost my breath just thinking about ever having to dance down its length completely alone. Maybe because I'm stubborn? Perhaps because I'm persistent? And maybe because helping animals is also my *calling*, I kept going, despite the hard resistance I met at the beginning.

Today, I love being in a world where I see, feel, sense, laugh, and go to work in these energies every day. Today, I understand that being different also has its strength. Today, being different has become a source of my strength. And all the beautiful experiences, all the beauty I see, feel, and hear from either the animals or from the spiritual side, make sense to me and enrich my life.

Chapter 2

What Is Telepathy

Telepathy is the transmission of information: thoughts, images, or feelings, between individuals by means other than the five senses. The term *telepathy* was coined in 1882 by the classical philosopher Frederic W.H. Myers. He was one of the founders of the Society for Psychical Research, established in England in 1882. The American Society for Psychical Research *was founded in 1885.*

The Danish *Selskabet for Psykisk Forskning* (Society for Psychical Research) was founded in Copenhagen on November 25, 1905. This Danish society became the third oldest of its kind in the world. Since its inception in 1905, the Danish Society has been an interdisciplinary association comprising scientists, doctors, engineers, psychologists, and laypeople.

Over the years, the association has had prominent figures as chairmen and board members, including the director of the Copenhagen Zoo Julius Schøtt (1856–1910), the director of Magasin du Nord Carl Vett (1871–1956), the engineer and founder of the company Kemp & Lauritzen in 1882, Severin Lauritzen (1850–1924), and the military historian Karl von Kohl (1869–1958). The society's purpose, then and now, is to investigate phenomena that seem inexplicable within the realm of parapsychology. This includes telepathy, clairvoyance, telekinesis, psychometry, precognition, and more. I had the privilege of being invited to give a lecture at the society a few years ago. I conducted a two-hour talk on telepathy between animals and humans, which occurred without spoken language (including conditions such as aphasia, selective mutism, dementia, and autism), and it was met with great interest by the participants.

I like to refer to telepathy as *non-verbal communication*, as it somehow seems easier for most people to grasp and accept. I also refer to it as spiritual consciousness, a state of awareness in which one is open and receptive to both sending and receiving messages non-verbally, on levels beyond what we perceive here on Earth.

Increasingly, people are beginning to sense that something is happening around us, something that can't be fully explained. We experience telepathy all the time, without necessarily realizing that's what it is. The man who thinks about how much he would like meatballs for dinner comes home from work to find a freshly cooked pan full of them, complete with potatoes and gravy, despite not having spoken to his wife at all during the day.

Soldiers in war who sense they are walking into an ambush and manage to avoid an attack from that direction, possibly because someone in the group has an especially sharp *antenna*? Or perhaps because all senses are heightened automatically in life-or-death situations.

A new mother, in deep symbiosis with her baby, intuitively knows whether the child is hungry, upset, needs to burp, or is in pain, even though the baby cannot yet express its needs verbally. A celebrity who senses that a photographer or paparazzo is taking pictures of her from 300 yards away with a long lens, despite not being able to see them. And yet, when the photo appears in a magazine, she's looking straight into the camera, as if she saw the photographer, without ever having laid eyes on them.

Despite the ridicule and mockery this ability often receives from skeptics, it is an innate characteristic in all living beings that enables them to survive. I am convinced that this ability is hardwired into every one of us, without exception. Some people are more trained, have a stronger sensitivity, or are more naturally attuned to using it. We also see this ability at its sharpest when we find ourselves in hostile territory or in situations where we feel unsafe. Whether it's a war zone, a dark alley at night, or a crowded space with heavy, unpleasant energy. In dangerous situations, this ability tends to operate on a subconscious level. The response can't be rationalized or explained, it's just a gut feeling that something is wrong.

The American biologist and author Dr. Rupert Sheldrake conducted a series of interviews with professionals whose jobs involved observing others, including police officers, surveillance staff, and others. Many of those interviewed reported that specific individuals seemed to *know* they were being watched, even when the observer was hidden entirely.

You might even have felt it yourself. Or you could test it. Try focusing your attention on a specific person in traffic, even if you're standing far away from them. I'm convinced that the person will sense your gaze and suddenly turn their head in your direction, looking for whoever is watching them.

You can also explore this idea while sitting in a car. Keep your head facing forward in the direction of travel but shift your gaze to the driver in the car next to you. I'm sure that they'll sense your stare and turn their head to look at you.

Twins (of which I am one) are also known for being able to sense one another, regardless of whether they are physically close or even in different countries. They can finish each other's sentences and think alike. This is often the case even when they haven't grown up together.

Extensive research has been conducted into what is inherited, what is shaped by environment or genetics, and what may be explained by a complex interplay between them. Could this be because they are born with a shared *we-connection?* Could it be that twins more clearly demonstrate an ability to share some form of mutual consciousness, where they can sense, feel, and intuit each other's state? Many researchers have explored these kinds of questions, both abroad and within Denmark. My twin sister and I have personally participated in several studies, and I'm pleased that research into this area continues to grow and develop.

I see it in romantic couples as well, those who can finish each other's sentences and are continually surprised by their deep, intuitive connection, even when the relationship is no longer new. It also shows itself in the moments when we feel a sense of love, familiarity, or recognition with someone that can't be explained. Some people meet for the first time and immediately feel as if they've known each other their entire lives. The same happens to people who fall in love; there's a connection they can't put into words, a feeling of either finding *home* in the other person or of being reunited.

Perhaps it's because we've been together in a past life. And maybe the people we are drawn to, whether friends, partners, spouses, colleagues, or others, are precisely the ones we are meant to be with and grow with—life after life, in different roles, within our shared connections.

The Brain And The Illusion

The brain and our waking consciousness are resources that we, as human beings, possess. That same resource can also become our greatest challenge, as we often complicate situations more than necessary. This may happen because our environment, culture, heredity, projections, past experiences, future concerns, worries, and many other factors influence us. Many researchers have sought to establish a connection between spiritual consciousness and the brain. What they have proven is that if the brain is damaged for any reason, there is a weakening of thought processes. Damage can be caused by malnutrition, brain tumors, cerebral hemorrhages, or inflammation, among other things. In such studies, it makes sense that people believed consciousness and the brain were the same.

However, none of these studies or observations have produced evidence that spiritual consciousness is limited solely to the brain. This has sparked primary debates, particularly in cases involving coma patients who display brain activity and later wake up with memories they should not be able to recall while unconscious. Memories of things their relatives whispered to them during the coma, or near-death experiences they remember upon waking.

The American physician Larry Dorsey describes it beautifully in his book *One Mind: "Think of your television. Although you can physically damage it and destroy the picture on the screen, this does not prove that the television creates the picture. On the contrary, we know that the image results from electromagnetic signals that originate outside the set itself, and that the television receives, amplifies, and displays the signals but does not produce them."*

The English author Aldous Huxley (1894–1963), known for his 1932 novel *Brave New World,* developed a deep interest in parapsychology later in life. He was one of the figures who helped usher in an era of experimentation with psychedelic substances. He described one such experience in an essay titled *The Doors of Perception,* which is said to have inspired the name of the band *The Doors.* Huxley believed that since we descend from animals, our inner primate and survival instinct require a brain to stay alive. In situations of potential danger, he suggested, the all-encompassing consciousness must be channeled through the brain and nervous system's reducing valve. He said: *"What comes out at the other end is a measly trickle of the kind of consciousness that will help us stay alive on this particular planet."*

So, is it possible to make telepathic contact? And how do you do it? Behind the left-brain ventricle lies the pineal gland (Corpus Pineale). Some people believe that the pineal gland is the part of the brain that allows us to connect with our spiritual consciousness. We can *open the gates* and allow telepathic information to flow through to us. That's why all people can practice telepathy.

I once read that many thousands of years ago, it was measured that the pineal gland was about the size of a golf ball. Back when we lived in hunter-gatherer societies and had to activate all our senses to survive and bring our prey down within range. Today, the pineal gland is measured to be the size of a pea, which suggests that we have always had this potential, but stopped utilizing the part of our brain that allows us to connect to a spiritual consciousness, where we can sense on all planes.

As the years have passed an increasing amount of people seek to develop themselves on both personal and spiritual levels, we are once again activating the pineal gland in the brain, allowing it to regain its original function. A gland that enables us to use all our senses and receive messages and energies in a way other than solely through our sense of hearing and sight. Especially in recent years, there has been a massive awakening to the spiritual, holistic, religious, and metaphysical realms, and I know that more of us are developing our brains, which is why we also experience other physical symptoms that we cannot explain. Perhaps we chalk it up to coincidence, but for those who are working on developing their senses and *retraining* the pineal gland, it will not be unusual to experience headaches, migraines, tinnitus, ringing in the ears, jaw and joint pain, dental issues, tingling in the forehead or at the top of the head. Because we know so little about the pineal gland, we often associate it with the brain, but it is an independent entity that most of us rarely utilize. We activate it when we meditate, when we work spiritually, or when we are, for example, healed.

The pineal gland resembles a pinecone. Like a pinecone, it starts from the bottom with a thick base, and as you move upwards toward its top, it becomes more pointed. The corpus pineal, also known as the *pineal gland*, is located in the center of the brain. It is positioned above a significant pathway for cerebrospinal fluid, which is worked with, for instance, in craniosacral therapy. The brain's ventricles produce a fluid that is rich in salt and protein. In humans, the pineal gland is not technically part of the brain, although it is located within it. It is formed from specialized cells during fetal development, specifically in the fetus's palate. It is placed very close to important emotional and sensory centers in the brain, such as the visual and auditory colliculi. These centers serve as a relay station for the transmission of sensory data to other parts of the brain, which are involved in abilities such as perception and interpretation. This means that the electrical and chemical impulses we receive through our eyes and ears must pass through the colliculi before we can experience them as visual and auditory stimuli.

The pineal gland is also surrounded by the limbic system, also known as the emotional brain. This is where we feel. Therefore, the pineal gland has direct access to the emotional centers of our brain. For many years, researchers believed the pineal gland was like an appendix, much like the appendix was once thought to be. However, in 1958, dermatologist Aaron Lerner discovered the hormone melatonin, which plays a crucial role in our sleep cycle and circadian rhythm. It is the only organ that is not divided into two, and it remains a mystery for many researchers today.

Herophilus, a Greek physician of the Hellenistic period, living in the third century, was the first to describe the pineal gland. Later in the 1700s, René Descartes also explained it. The man who famously said, *"I think, therefore I am."* His studies of our mental nature led him to search for a *seat* for these thoughts. He concluded that this seat could be the pineal gland because he believed that the brain can only think one thought at a time. And since the gland is unpaired in the brain, it might be the place where thoughts reside.

Today, most research focuses on melatonin production, and scientists still debate the exact function of melatonin and the pineal gland in humans. This includes questions such as the significance of melatonin about Seasonal Affective Disorder (SAD), jet lag, sleep, cancer, and many other topics. It has been demonstrated that melatonin is also a potent antioxidant, playing a crucial role in the immune system. Since melatonin has shown an impressive range of anti-cancer benefits, much research is dedicated to understanding how it can reduce chemotherapy side effects and increase the treatment's ability to destroy cancer cells.

Treatment with melatonin, in addition to standard chemotherapy, increases the survival rate of certain cancer patients from 28.4% to 52.2% over one year.

When we, as humans, begin practicing telepathy, we also start with a foundation of exercises that will gradually sharpen the ability and unfold within the pineal gland. Slowly, these abilities become more refined and sharper, and over time, as a telepath, you will become more precise in your exercises and telepathic abilities.

We use 8-10% of our brain capacity for conscious actions. The brain is such a sophisticated control system that we don't fully comprehend, sending messages to the body's cells and organs that we are never aware of. Most of our body is controlled by our thought processes. Everything starts with an unconscious thought or the soul's awareness. This is then transformed into a conscious thought in the brain. What we think about ourselves, our standards of living, our values, going to work, being with others, our view of the world. And it can be daunting to consider how small a part of our thoughts truly originates from our core self. The vast majority are influenced by society, upbringing, and other factors—things that lie outside our true selves. Our core.

A thought creates a connection to a specific part of the brain or an organ, such as the adrenal glands, which produce hormones or substances like adrenaline. This is then sent throughout the body and gives us a feeling. Therefore, we are in control of whether we live a good life or a bad one. Whether we are happy and content or unhappy and dissatisfied. Whether we are hopeful or anxious, and so much more. I also know that what we send out from our thoughts and thus our bodies is an impulse and an energy that affects other people and even animals, much like magnetic fields influence each other. In this way, we attract the things we send out from our thought processes and control system because like attracts like.

For example, if you expect that you will always find difficult relationships, you will continue to attract difficult relationships. Suppose you always wish to attract horses that need saving and are in danger of being euthanized. In that case, you will continue to attract horses that need to be rescued in one way or another, and unfortunately, often they will end up being put down. If you view yourself as a magnet, which is also controlled by your thoughts, imagine that you non-verbally emit some magnetic fields. These magnetic fields cannot be measured, and therefore, it cannot be proven that non-verbal communication and telepathy occur. This would require 8-10% of our brain capacity to develop a measuring device capable of detecting the remaining 90-92% of our brain's capacity.

In many ways, the brain is our best friend, but in other ways, it can be our worst enemy. The brain can create an illusion.

Imagine a situation where you are looking at the clearest starry sky. You see a shooting star, and you take a deep breath, exhaling in awe, overwhelmed by the fact that you've just witnessed one of our solar system's wonders with your naked eye. You tell yourself or the person you're with, *"Right now, I saw a shooting star."*

But if you think carefully about it, your experience in this moment is authentic in your present, but untrue if you were to ask quantum physicists. What you're witnessing in this moment is a star that burned out thousands of light-years ago.

To become a skilled telepath, it is therefore essential that you become capable of discerning between telepathic information, illusions, projections, and filtering out conscious thoughts.

For me, and for all those who wish to be inspired to connect with themselves and, as a result, become able to communicate with animals, plants, practice clairvoyance, and more, the art lies in learning to switch off the *thinking brain* and activate the *pineal gland*. It sounds so simple, and yet it is a very challenging exercise that most people aren't accustomed to. It may seem absurd that it is hard not to think. When we, as humans, stop thinking, we also remove prejudices, projections, and experiences, as previously described in *The Inner Map*. One could call it becoming neutral. When you remove yourself from the equation and become an observer, you inevitably gain a larger and, importantly, broader perspective. In that space, there is room for empathy and compassion to grow.

A very everyday example of this is if you think of a situation where you've had a falling out with someone close to you. Some truly hurtful things were said, making you feel hurt. And you've also said things in return, which you know have hurt the other person. Emotions got the better of both of you and boiled over. You may need to take a walk or step away from the situation for a couple of hours to reflect on what happened. In your thoughts, you replayed the scenario from one person's perspective and then the other's, perhaps drawing a conclusion. This conclusion could be that you're firm in your feelings. Or you came to understand what happened with the other person. Regardless, your perspective grew when your emotions weren't in a frenzy. That means you looked at your argument and disagreement more neutrally, and through that, understanding emerged.

The difficulty in the exercise of becoming an observer lies in the intention to remain neutral and no longer hold an opinion. You, as a person, must not impose yourself on the situation in which you should be helping. As a human, you must put your ego aside and make yourself available. As I write these words, I think to myself that this is such a beautiful thought. Most people want to possess this ability and probably already believe they have it. Simply being aware of this mindset can bring about a significant change for you and those around you. When you are conscious and practice trying to be more neutral, thereby becoming more compassionate, the world undeniably becomes a better place to be.

Conscious Awareness And Spiritual Awareness

When I practice telepathy, I begin with a thought, an intention that will gradually clear my mind. The art of it is to *turn off the brain* – the conscious part of the brain, the waking consciousness. To connect with the spiritual consciousness requires shutting down the waking mind, the *thinking brain* as I described earlier. This is a challenging exercise that requires extreme concentration and endurance to complete. At first, even the smallest sounds can be incredibly distracting and throw you *off course*. But the more you practice, the easier it becomes to tune into the spiritual consciousness and access information that lies beyond the daily, mundane thoughts.

I work in a meditative state when I practice telepathy. This state allows me to set aside my own needs and avoid projecting my thoughts, feelings, or experiences into the information I receive. Remaining neutral is essential, so that my perceptions do not color the information I receive. In relation to the stages of sleep, we can be in a similar state of consciousness during telepathy, as we are in specific sleep stages.

Sleep consists of four phases:

1. **Stage One:** The transition phase between wakefulness and sleep. In this stage, brainwaves change from 8 to 12 Hz.
2. **Stage Two:** Light sleep, where brainwaves slow down and larger fluctuations in brain activity occur, helping to keep us asleep.
3. **Stage Three:** Deep sleep, where it becomes harder to wake up. Brain function can be reduced by up to 50% if woken during this phase, causing a feeling of grogginess.
4. **Stage Four:** REM sleep, where dreams occur. In this phase, brain activity is almost identical to wakefulness, with an increase in both pulse and blood pressure. This phase represents the highest level of brain activity, comparable to a state of clear consciousness without physical wakefulness.

This understanding of brain phases can be relevant when practicing telepathy, as it requires entering a kind of *consciousness state* where the brain is capable of receiving information without the daily thoughts and emotions interfering with the reception of that information. It's like becoming a kind of channel—a neutral observer, where everything that doesn't originate from the *unconscious mind* gets filtered out.

The state I enter when practicing telepathy is similar to the one we experience during meditation or the first stage of sleep. It can be compared to a hypnagogic state. Being in a hypnagogic state is also called *sleep paralysis*. However, this state is typically characterized by a disruption of REM sleep, where the body appears paralyzed and the muscles are completely relaxed. You wake up and can see, but you can't move. When I practice telepathy, it feels as though I am both awake and asleep at the same time, but I can still move and verbalize the things that come to me in the form of images, thoughts, or feelings. The main difference between the hypnagogic state and telepathy, for me, is that it requires my brain to be still active and thinking to convey the messages I receive. I do this by speaking to the animal I am communicating with, as well as to its owners, if we are together. It also happens when I write down the telepathy on my computer so that the animal's owners later receive a report of the entire communication.

The practice requires me to be in a meditative state while also having my brain *awake enough* to form a thought that can lead to an action, all while maintaining a trance-like feeling in my body. All of this happens without me falling asleep. My conscious brain's purpose during a telepathic session is to act as a symbol for the analyst. My main task is first to feel and be spiritually aware, then analyze the *data* I receive from the animal so that the output speaks to the conscious brain of the person who is the observer. The information at that moment becomes the truth. This can be seen, for example, when I filter out certain parts of the information I receive if I sense that the animal's owner or rider is unable to absorb it. If I were to say it out loud, resistance would immediately arise, and that person wouldn't be able to listen to the rest of what I had to say.

For me, we cannot separate our stem cells from the body. Just as we cannot separate our consciousness from the spiritual world, we are all a part of it. For me, being a telepath is also an exercise in creating balance between consciousness and spiritual awareness. To put it in everyday terms, it is about creating a balance between being grounded and being able to *lift into the clouds* to connect with my intuition and spirituality. For some people who are too grounded, I also see skepticism, and the resistance is greater. For others who are completely *up in the clouds* with no grounding, I often see tendencies where they are on the verge of mental illness, or they cannot tolerate being on *the higher level* anymore because they can no longer distinguish between reality and the many pieces of information they can access elsewhere.

I am utterly convinced that some people among those who have had a mental illness in the past, especially those hospitalized in psychiatric institutions, may have had abilities. They may have sensed presences, seen a *ghost*, or perhaps had clairaudience, hearing voices. But if they had no grounding, they might appear schizophrenic to others, or they might be diagnosed with other conditions such as psychosis or personality disorders.

Even today, I have seen psychiatric questionnaires where some of the following questions are asked during diagnostic assessments. I respect that these tools help psychiatry in managing and diagnosing many patients who are suffering from mental health issues of various kinds. The test contains several hundred questions, of which I will highlight only five.

The Test is called SCID-II and is a semi-structured interview that allows for a precise diagnostic evaluation of personality disorders, as defined in the American DSM-5 diagnostic system.

- **Have you had personal experiences with the supernatural?**
- **Have you felt that you can make things happen just by wishing or thinking about them?**
- **Do you believe you have a sixth sense that allows you to know and predict things that others cannot?**
- **Have you ever had the feeling that there is a person or force around you, even though you can't see anyone?**
- **Do you often feel nervous when you're around other people?**

When I first read them, I was deeply shocked, and then I began to smile. A laugh sank into my body and down to my stomach, and I burst into a huge laugh. I thought about how much money, along with many of you who understand this book, I am saving the state in hospitalization bills and staff costs within psychiatry. I thought about the grotesqueness of it: *If we are going to use these questions to assess people, then psychiatry must also investigate the paranormal more, if I am to find it worthwhile to have such questions in such an essential process like an assessment.*

However, if we are to keep our feet on the ground and maintain a sense of grounding in the work of being a telepath, then that work begins with an intention, which can slightly shift our daily consciousness so that our senses can fully awaken.

In intention, there exists only one energy, which is a feeling. I intend to help, love, embrace, and heal. And through that power, I witness miracles every day.

Being Visual, Listening, And Empathetic

Telepathy is the transfer of images, thoughts, and feelings from one soul to another, directly to the inner eye. To explain the pictures I see, they are not as clear as if a movie were playing right in front of me on a screen. These are images for the inner eye. Images that are formed in this way. Imagine that I ask you to open your refrigerator in your mind. Describe to me how many shelves there are and what is on each one. Are there drawers in the fridge, and what have you put in them? If you are visual, you will now see an image in your mind's eye, just like when you fantasize or think about situations or memories from your life. My primary task is to interpret the images as detailed as possible, and this requires practice and skill to create a good and credible telepathy. The pictures do not appear as a long movie for an hour, but rather as fragments that I need to interpret and make sense of through telepathy with a horse and communicate that meaning to the owner. It's like reading a book through a keyhole. I can see the book in front of me. I can see the open page, but I am not allowed to read the book from start to finish in one go.

When I work telepathically with image transfer, I expect of myself—and of the many students I train across the country—to carefully observe the countless details that emerge in the images conveyed to me from the horse. When I work telepathically with image transfer, I demand of myself, as well as from all the many students I have around the country when we train this, that I observe the countless details that appear in the images transferred to me from the horse. The horse may reveal its health issues to me. In that case, I must know whether it has a *kissing spine* or if it shows me a sore muscle over its back.

The thought transfer comes to me as if I suddenly think of something. Words or sentences will come into my head, which I am now experienced enough to know are not my own. It is crucial that I do not project my emotions. That is, I must not unconsciously interpret based on previous experiences, prejudices, or personal interpretations of the animal I am working with. It requires that I remain as pure as possible, like an interpreter between the animal and the owner. That I give the animal the voice it does not have, to make itself understood by us humans, so that it can get through to us. We often determine their fates. And what a power and responsibility that is to have, I think.

Emotional transfers are an extension of empathetic abilities. Do you know the feeling when you watch a movie that moves you, or when a friend shares some thoughts or concerns with you that touch you so deeply that you get tears in your eyes? Children cry sympathy tears. We all possess this quality to some extent. Feeling the emotional transfer requires an extraordinary degree of empathy. It is demonstrated, among other things, by the ability to transfer physical sensations, such as pain, from one soul to another. Or an emotional transfer, which is felt through empathy, whether it is sorrow, stress, love, or anxiety, among others. The feeling, as previously described, is that I take on how it feels to be the animal I stand in front of. I think it, I sense it, I become it, and through this, I can put words to it and *humanize* the horse because I feel it so intensely while I am engaged in it. I sense what it wants, what makes it scared, how it thinks about itself, about the people around it, or on its back. I feel every fiber, muscle, and cell in the horse's body as if it were my own. And that's why I can articulate it and interpret it. This also requires that I, as the practitioner, am in contact with my own body.

When I feel a sensation, I need to understand what it's about to articulate it, and what I feel physically, whether it's a feeling, a tension, an irritation, a pain, or something else.

My primary task is to gather all three elements and interpret them for the animal's owner, ensuring that the information is cohesive and logical, and providing a professional and detailed insight into the horse that the owners can use and potentially act upon based on the guidelines and tools they are given.

It is an interpretive task, nothing else. I have been given a special ability to perceive it extremely clearly on a detailed level, besides the fact that I have spent many years practicing and refining my skills within this field. Not all animals are equally communicative, and thanks to my therapeutic background, I can always extract information from the animals I help. There is no animal I cannot establish a dialogue with, meaning I can exchange energies with, which I can then relay to the owner. Suppose some horses are skeptical of a stranger like me or are not particularly communicative for one reason or another. In that case, I always inquire about it and always receive an answer. This way, we are in a dialogue, and then it is my job to maintain the connection, so it becomes a more fulfilling conversation. It is crucial to *break the ice* or break down any possible defense mechanisms or habits in the horse I am communicating with. There is always a reason why some horses will not speak. They may be anxious, passive, shut down, skeptical, or something else, either due to something innate, a coding, or experiences and memories they carry with them, just like we humans do.

It would be much more *palatable* for many if I referred to my work as facts: *"This type of horse is like this and this. This type of horse will typically suffer from this and that."* Instead, it feels entirely natural for me to say, *"Your horse feels, or says, that it has this kind of personality, and it shows me that it is suffering from these issues."*

If I were to describe it in a much more fact-based way, I would have to generalize. And over the years, my experiences have shown me that I cannot do that. The horses are as individual as we are. The only things I have been able to observe and generalize are the horses' personalities and the ways they interact with one another in relationships.

These personalities and the explanations for the behavioral problems that accompany them are described in my first book, *Understand Your Horse.* For me, telepathy has become a part of my truth. It is so integrated into my daily life and work that I no longer need further confirmation or proof that it is possible. For what is truth? Is it the thoughts I've shared with you earlier, either based on factual evidence or through stories from people, that make these stories true? One animal owner after another tells me every day that what I tell them is true, even though it's the first time I've met them and their animals. It ranges from the struggles they face to the challenges they encounter in training or their general interactions. It is all those many hours I have spent with people and their animals, where we laugh and cry together because both the humans and the horses and animals I help are seen for what they are and as they are. I don't judge, I don't criticize, I mirror the situation and their relationships as they are. And through that, a new meeting occurs, a release, and a strengthening of the bond between the human and their best friend.

Those who are advanced in their spiritual development, striving towards the goal of becoming complete in their love for others, will be more open to all that cannot be proven. For most of us, there is still a long way to go, but a high spiritual level means that you feel and sense more than many others. Furthermore, we also carry karma from one life to the next, which is created from birth and strengthened through our childhood, upbringing, and life experiences. A highly developed person, who is an old soul in a human body, with great insights and a deep knowledge and flair, especially for the alternative, may never utilize these abilities in this life. The reason could be that this person's karma is to learn something about *being acknowledged.* This will be the person's theme and title in life.

No matter which direction the person looks, which jobs they take, which relationships the person enters, or which people the person meets along the way, they will constantly have a feeling of not being acknowledged for themselves, for their job, for the way they are, for the way they love, or for the way they interact with others. This person may be highly skeptical of the alternative and all that cannot be proven, because they might choose to follow *the acknowledged path,* which often is the academic route in today's Denmark, and completely shut down all other possibilities for acquiring knowledge within the same field or about life in general. What I always find interesting is that it is often those individuals who are most skeptical and afraid of the nonverbal and everything that cannot be proven, who are the most talented once they unfold their abilities.

Some people are given the life mission and purpose of passing on knowledge to others, and therefore, they are born with a natural talent in the field they later choose to pursue. This, of course, makes them more available to possess abilities. Within telepathy and the alternative world, I often experience that many practitioners who choose to enter this field have had a difficult life or have been physically or mentally ill. I do not train people with major mental illnesses, as they need as much grounding as possible in this life. They should not work in a profession or on topics where they risk losing their grounding completely. When we, as humans, have lived a life in pain in one way or another, many often find it liberating to be in an energy where they don't need to prove anything but only experience pure love, pure speech, pure communication, and pure relationships. Therefore, many practitioners have faced difficulties. It is part of their karma, and perhaps some are even atoning for a past life. In other words, they are paying the price for their actions in a previous life and must atone for them by helping others. Hence, they are open and predisposed to developing strong abilities, which will enable them to do so.

To become a highly developed spiritual being, one must be able to embrace and be loving towards others. This can be achieved, first and foremost, by loving all aspects of oneself. This development and learning can be achieved by fully understanding all aspects of human abilities, both positive and negative. It may also mean that a person must experience both being the executioner and the victim to gain a complete understanding of all, and thus create and feel love for everything, and therefore, for oneself.

Being Sensing

We know that we have the five senses: hearing, smell, sight, touch, and taste. We've heard about the sixth sense—the sense through which we perceive something around us. It might be when someone is looking at us (whether living or dead), or animals sensing magnetic fields or radiation.

Telepathy is also referred to as the seventh sense; the ability to exchange some form of communication over long distances without being able to explain or measure it.

For many, understanding it's crucial. It was for me as well. However, over time, I've come to realize that I, too, cannot fully comprehend, explain, or prove the state of the mind, the subconscious, or consciousness. That doesn't mean it doesn't exist. Just as I don't fully grasp the technical details that enable me to use FaceTime to call my friends in New York, it's still a communication tool I utilize, much like the telepathy I use with animals. I have no idea how either one works.

Turning on your senses is something everyone can do. But it requires a conscious choice on your part to do so. When I activate all my senses, I make myself available to receive and to be, as previously described, *neutral*. This means I may feel completely exposed. I feel like my soul is fluttering around without a physical body to inhabit, one that could protect me. No shield, no defense mechanisms ready to raise my guard in an instant. Just a state of being willing and open to whatever may come—no fear of verbal or physical attacks. Just standing there, completely uncovered, and receiving whatever is being sent in my direction.

It's a highly vulnerable feeling, but it makes sense to me. Because only in the honest now can I meet the animals where they are. In a world made only of the present moment, where we can sense and feel each other. Without judgment, backstories, interpretations, or knowledge. Just a meeting where we see and where we feel, where we hear and where we sense each other exactly as we are. And that makes the meeting immediate and straightforward. It turns the meeting into a liberating experience filled with laughter, smiles, love, and respect for one another, both as sender and receiver. And that's what makes nonverbal communication so easy for me to engage in, even though it also requires a lot of effort to keep the rational, thinking part of the brain from taking over. To shut down the part of me that is accustomed to planning, structuring, and being solution oriented. In the meeting, in the present, there is only a need to be—and be together.

The concept of being *highly sensitive* has become more recognized globally, and it explains a great deal for many people. I am one of those who sense more than most and therefore become overstimulated and saturated with impressions much faster than those who are not highly sensitive. In my experience, those who possess strong abilities in this area are all highly sensitive. That means they already sense more than others and are thus more receptive to the impressions and impulses around them.

Often, this makes it challenging to be in a room full of people, and if one does manage to be, it is only for a short time to avoid an *overload*, which can be deeply exhausting afterward. It can also feel very lonely and isolating, especially when managing very little activity during a single day. Every student I've had in my courses or training programs has described feeling this way, and they often find it easier to be around animals than people, because animals don't demand anything of them beyond their presence and attention.

I've asked several horses how they perceive telepathy. Did they know what we were doing when I spoke with them? And how could they communicate when their brain is only the size of a walnut?

The horses all answered me: *"It's completely natural to communicate nonverbally, that's what we already do in the pasture with other horses. And yes, we know you're a human, but you mean well. It's humans who don't always mean well toward us, so we don't understand why you're surprised that this kind of communication is second nature to us."*

They told me: *"We don't understand what you mean when you say our brain is the size of a walnut. We use the abilities we have, and we don't question size. We focus on being.* A few horses ask me how it's possible that I can send them images, simply because they are not used to receiving that kind of communication from a human. In those cases, I always explain it to them through thoughts. I think of the sentences in my head or speak to them out loud, telling them that I am one of those humans who find this natural, and I ask if they understand what I'm sending. Not a single horse has ever answered *"No"* when I've asked that question. They find it natural and part of a world they already live in. They're just not used to humans doing it. And think how much we humans are missing out on. Our senses are available to us. Nature is available to us. Our feelings are available to us. All of these can give us a sense of freedom and love; two things I know most of us are chasing in our fast-paced lives.

As a therapist, when I ask the people I help at my clinic in the city center what lies at the root of their stress and why they work so hard, their answers are usually either that they are seeking external recognition or that they want to earn enough to provide for their family and create a sense of security. But when I ask what they expect will happen once they've achieved those things, they say that then they will work as much as possible and make money to feel free. Financial freedom, so they can do what they want, travel where they want, eat where they want, be with the people they enjoy, and pursue the interests that bring them joy.

But first, space must be cleared from their busy work life before there's room for that feeling of freedom. And that's quite a paradox, working so hard to achieve a feeling that is created in the brain and felt in the body, a feeling that is already available to us. Freedom is an inherent part of existence and already resides within all of us. Freedom is a feeling you can access if you remove the pressure you place on yourself in the pursuit of that very feeling. We humans often make things more complicated than they are. What lives inside us is precisely what we spend our lives chasing: love, freedom, safety, and a mirror. And with horses, a mirror is right in front of us, if we're willing to see it. Horses reflect us as humans: our thoughts, our emotions, and our actions. I'll dive deeper into this in the chapter called *The Mirror* later in the book.

In the autumn of 2007, I visited a stable in north Copenhagen. It was a small, private stable where six horses lived. I was immediately drawn to one of the mares. She seemed calm, and I felt so pulled toward her, though I didn't know why. When I looked into her eyes, she lowered her head, walked over to me, and sniffed me. Then she said to me, *"Hello Ditte, I would like to speak with you. I want to tell you that I am a queen here—the kind who rules over the others. And I have great insight,"* she said to me. By *queen*, I understood through the energy she sent me that she meant she was the lead mare in the herd. I asked her what kind of insight she had. And she answered, *"Well, I can tell you that you and I have something in common. I'm in foal, and you're pregnant. I know you don't realize it yet, but you are, and you'll give birth to a boy who is very special. He will help you teach other people."*

I started to cry. I was moved, standing there in my oversized coat in that little stable, feeling the warmth of the mare's body and muzzle as the mare breathed into my hand, smacking her lips and sending all of these thoughts into my mind. I remembered that Gjertrud Berlon had told me the same thing a few years earlier. I was both overwhelmed and curious. I asked her why he was special and what I would be teaching people.

She smiled, and I felt her warmth and care as she sent it into my body and replied, *"You don't need to know everything right now—just wait and see, you'll find out in time. But remember, he is touched by God, Ditte."*

I wondered how she could possibly know that. And I had a feeling that she could sense another heart beating there in the stable, even though I couldn't see it or was aware of it myself at the time.

In the summer of 2008, I had my son, who was born blind. It later turned out that he is also an infantile autistic with mild cognitive impairment and hypotonia. Over the years, I've had a great teacher, and his name is Philip. He has taught me to sense, listen, and perceive on an even deeper level, and he has shown me that the structure animals need is not so different from what most autistic individuals need.

Today, he can see, despite being visually impaired. We have trained intensively to help him develop his vision, and it has paid off. He has learned to manage with the resources he has, and he doesn't question the things he lacks, because he doesn't know anything else. He is *himself,* and through him, I've learned that it is not he who should adapt to the system, because he can't. It is the system that must adapt to him. The system encompasses various elements, including the structure of society, the educational system, social norms, and others.

We live in a time where increasing amounts of children are born highly sensitive. I call them *Indigo children,* and the later generation I call *Star children* because many of them have very special abilities. These are also known as the *Crystal children.* An increasing number of parents call me to ask whether it's normal that their children see dead people, or if it's just their child's imagination. I always *tune in* to sense whether it's true that the child has clairvoyant abilities and can see spirits, or whether they are simply making it up. In 99 percent of the cases, the children do have clairvoyance, either it is still developing or already very advanced. Far more advanced than my own is today. As children become increasingly sensitive, they are also born with a greater spirituality and a deeper understanding and acceptance that there are things in this world, and in the universe—that we cannot see. Philip is one of them.

The downside of being so sensitive, for many of these children, is that they struggle to fit into our current school systems. Many children get diagnoses like ADHD, ADD, Autism, and so on, and we see an increased number of neurodivergent children all over the world these days. They don't have the same kind of filter that previous generations did. They express what they want and don't want, what they like and don't like. And in a slightly outdated system, this kind of behavior is often interpreted as *rude* or *badly raised*. Many parents reach out to me for help with their children. The children go into therapy, and I often end up working with the whole family through family therapy, because parents need to learn how to handle and accept their child as they are. At the same time, of course, the child needs help through parenting, structure, and boundaries—things that create a sense of security.

When people laugh at the fact that I don't even have a horse myself, I smile to myself and think that I have Philip to teach me so many things. I would love to ride more, but I have no desire to own a horse at the moment. I don't have the necessary time to care for one right now, and with the knowledge I have about what they need, what they want, what makes them happy, and how they feel loved, I couldn't justify it. I've chosen to focus on Philip, on my development, and on learning even more so I can pass it on, either by helping people directly or by assisting them to understand their animals better. And through that, give animals better lives, regardless of their intended use. Because isn't that what we all want? To be seen, heard, and understood just as we are?

In the years leading up to having Philip, I had been working with animal telepathy alongside my job at our country's biggest National TV station, where I worked as a production planner for the TV News Department. I had also trained as an organic and body therapist. That means working without a fixed goal as a therapist, being present with the client exactly where they are, and flowing with the moment they are in.

A concrete example might be when a client says, *"I feel good, and I also feel bad."* Many practitioners would prefer to focus on the part that feels bad. But it's just as important to follow and strengthen the parts of a person's life where things are going well. Being a body therapist means I work with how the body stores stories, because cells, the nervous system, and muscles all remember. And in those places, there can be hidden shocks, traumas, stories, and more. Things that block energy, cause pain in the body, or show up as other symptoms of stuck energy.

My therapy training has been an enormous help in creating behavioral changes in the animals and humans I assist, primarily when we work together to make everyday interactions easier and improve communication, both on the ground and during training, particularly when behavioral issues are involved.

When I had Philip, returning to a traditional job with rigid structures and long workdays was no longer an option. I decided to become self-employed. It was during the financial crisis, and I was scared. There was no stable paycheck, no paid sick leave, no vacation pay , no pension. There was no guarantee I could make a living from the clients I already had, whether in therapy, clairvoyance, or telepathy with their animals. But deep down, I knew I had to face my greatest fear and go for it, trusting the process. To this day, it's the best decision I've ever made for myself. I've always wanted to be a kind of messenger. I have a strong desire to discuss spirituality and animal intelligence in a grounded, down-to-earth manner that everyone can understand.

There have been days when I've looked back and wondered why I was the one given birth to Philip. I felt that carrying the responsibility of being the mother of a disabled child was a heavy burden. But as the years passed and acceptance fully settled in me, I also came to understand that through him and his way of being in the world, I have become even more sensitive than I already was. I now live a life where I am constantly sensing, both at work and when I'm off, spending time with my little teacher, Philip.

Chapter 3

How I Practice Telepathy

I practice telepathy in two different ways. One method is being physically present with the horse and its owner. I prefer the horse to be standing in its stall or tied up in the stable aisle. This is because, as mentioned earlier, I enter a meditative state or light trance when working as a telepath, and I quickly lose concentration if I must stay aware of where the horse is physically located, especially if it's moving around me.

The other way I work is by looking at a picture of the animal I'm helping. It can be sent to my email address so I can view the animal electronically, or the animal's owner may bring a printed photo, show it on their phone, or display it on a tablet when they visit me at my practice.

When I channel—that is, connect with *helpers* who vibrate at an even higher frequency than ordinary spiritual guides, I feel a tingling sensation on my forehead, and it's as if someone is lifting me from the ground. I gain a sense of overview and a deeper understanding of the person I'm helping. There are many paths to support and healing, and I never tire of learning something new or exploring different methods and techniques to help and communicate. I believe that clairvoyance, channeling, and healing are just a few of the ways to connect with the universal.

When I work clairvoyantly, I experience the vibration around me changing. In the energy that arises between me and the person I'm helping, the air becomes heavier—so heavy that we both become a bit tired yet also grounded. The air changes for me because there are others in the room besides just the client and me. These are the spiritual guides, often referred to as *the guides* or *the guardian team*. Some of them you are born with, while others change over time as you are meant to learn new things throughout life. You can compare it to your time in school. As you advanced through the grades, your teachers would sometimes change when you began new subjects.

Over time, I've discovered that when I work telepathically, there is no change in the vibration of the air around me. However, both the animal I'm helping, and I experience a strong sense of grounding, to the point where we feel heavy and earthy at the same time, in our legs and heads as we exchange energy. It's a demanding and even draining process for both parties. A few horse owners have become physically unwell when standing too close to my magnetic field and energy during telepathy sessions in the stable. They've become dizzy, developed headaches, and one person nearly fainted. That's why I always tell owners or riders to step slightly aside, to ensure they aren't too affected by the energy flowing between the horse and me.

Cats tend to fall asleep or leave the room to avoid becoming too exhausted from the energy we're working in. But I still maintain telepathic contact with them, even if they're not physically present in the space. That's precisely why borders don't limit telepathy—energy will always find its way. Dogs become so relaxed that they lie down and sleep. Horses blink slowly, some fall asleep, and others yawn, as a way of releasing the stored energy they've simply been waiting for someone to receive from them—energies that carry their stories and reveal what is on their mind.

Do all people have this ability? I'm often asked that question. And yes, everyone has it because it's something we are born with the capacity to do. But that doesn't necessarily mean that everyone is meant to use that ability. I train people domestically and internationally, and I teach everyone how to telepath within just a few minutes. Of course, refining your skills in the world of telepathy and learning how to support behavior change takes time and requires serious training. My only requirement for new students is that they are open to what unfolds. Naturally, some people are more gifted than others. That's no different from any other skill or interest. Some want to learn football, and some end up on the national team. Others want to learn piano—a few might become the next Mozart or Bach.

There are simply some people who possess natural talents, are more empathetic than others, and therefore can master telepathic skills more easily, if they learn how to control them. That's part of what I teach them when they choose to deepen their knowledge and skill in this field.

Being Physically Present

When I'm physically present, I position myself in front of the horse and explain who I am, telling it that I've come to speak with it. I do this because I respect that I'm facing an independent being, a soul with feelings and intelligence. When I sense that it has given me permission for this, which also tells me something about its personality, depending on how quickly it happens, we begin a longer and more in-depth conversation. This conversation typically covers a few key points that I always discuss with the owner to gather detailed information, which often shocks them. It's also a way for me to get to know the horse quickly. I continuously use therapeutic and coaching questions in the conversation to elaborate and refine the information I receive, allowing me to see the images sent to me as clearly and in as much detail as possible. This way, the information becomes tangible, concrete, and valuable for the owner or rider.

I travel extensively throughout the world, but due to the long waiting times I've experienced for many years, I've discovered that it's easier for me to help the vast majority of animal owners online with a picture in front of me and the animal owner on Zoom. The advantage of working with this method is that the owner can continuously ask questions about the things I convey from the animals. Suppose the owner thinks of other questions along the way, which often happens when they realize what their animals are capable of communicating. In that case, they have the opportunity to ask questions.

Helping Through Distant Healing / Image Telepathy

The second method I use is called image telepathy. The correct term for this is *Photometry*. In this case, the horse owner sends me a picture of their horse. The owner can do this via regular mail, but I prefer to receive it via email. I then place the image on my screen in front of me and write down the entire conversation as I communicate with the animal I'm looking at. It typically amounts to anywhere from 6 to 12 pages in *Microsoft Word*, with detailed descriptions and specifics about the horse and its thoughts.

The advantage of this method is definitely that the owner receives all the information via email. There are so many details that it's hard to remember them all, and with image telepathy, as a rider or animal owner, you can review them repeatedly. Additionally, this serves as a form of journal, which can be shared with other professional practitioners, veterinarians, and alternative colleagues who may need to collaborate on the horse's well-being, especially when it comes to health-related issues.

The advantage for me of doing it this way is that the conversation is exclusively about the horse and me in an uninterrupted dialogue in a calm and quiet environment, where I enjoy delving deeply into each question I ask the horse. I always delve into the details with the questions I ask the horses, but there can be sessions where the rider or owner has a specific question they want to know about, something that matters most to them. In those cases, they don't want me to go deeply into each point I discuss when it's just the horse and me communicating. This way, I can, without interruptions (which is, of course, completely fine), immerse myself in the horse's world, while remaining in a meditative or trance-like state, letting my fingers glide over the keyboard. When I finish writing the last words, I have forgotten every single word I just wrote. And that's when I know for sure that it has come from another place, and I have switched off the conscious part of my brain, since I cannot remember it.

I enjoy being a channel, nothing more, for the horse I am communicating with, and I am also convinced that this is a form of protection for me, so that I cannot remember what I've written afterward. I have spoken with so many horses that I wouldn't be able to hold each one of them in my memory in minute detail. And even the images that have made a strong impression on me, or the complex emotions I have experienced during the treatments, I'm glad I can release them when I let go of one horse to help the next. In this way, I also free myself from past experiences with horses and take each one as it is, with what it brings in that moment when I meet it.

Many people have difficulty accepting that it is possible to communicate via photometry. The reason it's a possibility is that energy is present in everything. Since there are no physical laws or boundaries within the more spiritual or alternative work, it's not a problem to work in this way. I usually say to those who ask me how it is possible: *"You should think of clairvoyance and telepathy as energy work. Energy will always find a way, exactly like electricity always finds its way, no matter what boundaries you set."*

We humans need borders. No other beings on Earth need to set up a boundary, a fence, or a sign to know who owns what. Animals have territories, partly to mark their presence to other animals. It may be to make themselves known, or it may serve as a defense mechanism to tell other animals, *"I rule here, and this is my territory,"* but they also know that no one owns the planet Earth.

It is said that dolphins are some of the most intelligent creatures on Earth. I have personally communicated with them and with whales in the Maldives some years ago, and that is when I understood what that meant. My experience was that they had a shared understanding and answered as a *WE.* They are emotionally intelligent. I realized that they are capable of communicating through sonar, which they have developed in their brains. A sonar that sends waves of sound, and thus energy among them, which they pick up from each other. They always knew where all their friends were, even if they were several kilometers apart. My experience is that all animals have this ability, whether it is developed or not. However, not all animals have the same sense of community that I encountered with the dolphins and whales.

Telepathy is a job that can be draining. It's demanding to constantly see things with your inner eye, absorb others' emotions, and transfer pain to the body to convey it to the horse's core, which includes the rider, owner, part-owner, stable staff, trainer, practitioners, and family members. Therefore, I also prefer to work no more than 4 hours at a time telepathically, and then my brain is *completely shut down.* If I work more than 4 hours telepathically in one stretch, I get extreme headaches and can't think for the rest of the day and evening. I can barely find words in my mind or make decisions about anything. So, it's not worth the price for me if I can't function in my personal life after work. There are some stories I remember better than others. I especially remember the horses that have been a form of teacher for me, where I either had a big *aha moment* or those that have deeply moved me, particularly through their great insights or before a euthanasia.

One of the telepathies I remember is the pony *Alex* from Jutland, mainland Denmark. I don't remember exactly which town. The mother called me and told me that she needed my help because Alex, as we decided, could get the quickest help if they sent me a picture. So, the mother sent me a picture of Alex. I received the image of Alex by email and sat down in front of my computer, which I always do when I help animals via email telepathy. I closed my eyes and saw pony Alex's head in front of me. It came closer, and then I knew we had made contact. He told me that he was a *Playful Child* and a *Prince*. So, he was very active and wanted to show himself. When I asked what the reason was for him throwing the poor girl off, whom he loved very much, he replied: *"I don't think she functions very well socially in her class. She only cares about me, and everything she thinks about and talks about revolves around me. So, I feel like I'm doing her a favor. A favor that she will thank me for later. If I throw her off, maybe she'll like me less. And then maybe she'll start caring more about her classmates."*

I, of course, informed him about the consequences of his misunderstood kindness and deed, and I also helped him change his behavior so that he stopped throwing her off. But it was a somewhat shaken and moved mother I spoke to when I had to pass on the messages, he had given me as a declaration of love to her daughter.

During a photo-telepathy session, I have my own *rituals*, where I listen to music before I start. Then I meditate and feel that I am completely clear inside, allowing all everyday thoughts and my conscious mind to fade away. Then I am ready, as the neutral interpreter, which I see myself as, between the horse and their humans. I always keep a glass of water on my left side so that I can drink, as I tend to dehydrate quickly during work, and it also helps me cleanse myself. If I don't get water, I get headaches more quickly from telepathic sessions.

It's physically demanding work because I must constantly visualize images in my mind and sense the impulses that are transferred to me, such as sounds, smells, phrases, pain, and more. Therefore, it is rarely something I *do* if people say: *"Can you just talk to my cat, now that you're here?"* I am very proud of my work and always want to deliver the best and most detailed work, so that *quick look* is something I don't want to do, because I feel like I'm compromising the quality of my own work. I want to be mentally prepared to dedicate myself to helping fully, and that requires that I am balanced and have peace within myself. The few times I have tried to help horses via telepathy when I was emotionally out of balance have also been the few times I have made a couple of mistakes during a telepathy session.

A couple of mistakes could be that I misinterpreted the rider's weight distribution or confused the right and left sides of the horse. As a perfectionist, I find this unacceptable, which is why I have learned from that lesson. I therefore also encourage all the students I teach across the country to be mindful of having humility when it comes to *looking into* others' thoughts, and that it requires that they are emotionally well. Therefore, not many people can live off this work every day because it requires both abilities and maintaining a constant balance.

I am also *only human* and am not emotionally balanced all the time. However, I have learned over time to set aside everything that may fill me up and fully dedicate myself to another soul, whether animal or human. This also requires that I allocate time to stay in balance, and I do that continuously through supervision, healing, craniosacral therapy, massage, and many other forms of treatment.

Chapter 4

What Horses Hold In Their Hearts

"The human being is the only creature that refuses to be what he is."
— **Albert Camus**

I have always believed that everyone is capable of communicating with animals through telepathy. Yes, you read that correctly. YOU are capable of communicating with your animal, too. The art lies in learning to trust what the horse sends back to you. Of course, there are a few individuals who possess a particularly special ability and are more predisposed to telepathic connection than others. However, all living beings are capable of utilizing the five senses with which we are born. From there, we can develop the sixth and seventh senses. We all have that potential within us, in our brains (both the conscious and the subconscious parts) and in our hearts. But we have chosen to stop utilizing that potential in the brain and soul because we live in a society where sensory perception is not as engaged as it was in hunter-gatherer times.

That's why I started teaching courses throughout the country and internationally and still do. I wanted *telepathy with animals* to become more widespread, and I could only achieve this by passing on the techniques so more animal owners could spread their light, their abilities, and help more animals out there. I alone could not help everyone, even though more practitioners were working with animal communication. And it brings me the greatest joy to see group after group, filled with people who, in the beginning, feel wrong, lonely, and strange. To see them develop their abilities and begin to trust in what they've always been able to do but never had support for from the outside world, whether that be from spouses, partners, family, friends, or even from a lack of internal trust.

I don't know many animal owners who haven't had a sense that something was wrong with their horses before it was confirmed, for example, by a vet. And as I always say, it's essential to trust your feelings. It's precisely like with parents and children. Parents know best. Hopefully, they have a sense of what their children need. The same applies to their animals as well. Trust that, and disregard what others say. Most people with an opinion tend to project their own experiences onto others. What worked for them may not necessarily work for you or your horse.

Horses respond to your thoughts and emotions, reflecting to you a mirror of your nature. Therefore, it is imperative that you are in balance when you are with your horse. If you are not in physical or mental balance, it will affect your horse. Some horse owners are lucky enough to have experienced their horses comforting them when they have been in a bad mood or feeling down. The horses have placed their heads on the owner's shoulder or even *hugged* them, healing them as they stood together. The owner may not have necessarily told the horse that they were feeling sad or upset, but the horse could sense it, as they can feel energies and the magnetic field around us.

If you know that horses react to feelings of sorrow or sadness, you must also understand that horses react to the entire emotional spectrum. This means they also respond to a range of emotions, including joy, stress, frustration, anger, despair, and more. Horses absorb our energies and reflect them back to us, which is why they are such a gift, if we are willing to accept it. Horses can mirror our energies and emotions by absorbing the same energy in their nervous system and responding similarly to how we behave with them. For example, if you are stressed when you arrive at the stable, your horse will quickly become stressed when you enter their stall. That is why it is an excellent idea to take 10 deep breaths before entering the stable, to release any residual emotions or thoughts that don't belong to the interaction with your horse.

They can also respond to our energies and feelings by wanting to care for us or by setting boundaries with us. Alternatively, they may choose to withdraw from us if they do not like the energy we are bringing. Remember that many horses bond with their humans, and from the moment you acquire a horse, you are connected, and thus your herd is created. You will see certain behaviors from your horse depending on its personality. The horse will find its place in your relationship and the hierarchy you share, acting based on who you are, how it perceives your energy, and your mental strength. It will instinctively assess whether you are a leader type, whether it can trust you, and whether you are dominant, insecure, or passive, and it will respond accordingly.

To understand this automatic mechanism, you, as a horse owner, must be receptive to what they show you and keep this in mind during your interactions with them. It's a good idea to check in with yourself to see if you are frustrated on the day you plan to ride your horse. You might, in your frustration, *accuse* the horse of being frustrated during the ride. It's also possible that you felt insecure that day, and there could be many reasons for this. Perhaps you're feeling sad, maybe you didn't feel seen or acknowledged that day, or possibly your self-esteem is low. If that is the case, watch for signs that your horse begins to seem insecure during training or while riding. For example, it might suddenly behave as if it's *scared of something*. You could also watch for it becoming overly dominant and taking over. This doesn't mean that the horse *doesn't trust you*, which is an expression I often hear, but instead that the horse feels there is no leader, and every herd needs one. Unconsciously, the horse will step up and take charge, even if you haven't asked it to.

Your horse is directly influenced by the energy and mindset you bring with you. Depending on its personality type, as I have described in my book *Understand Your Horse*, it will either reject your energy if it feels threatening, stressful, hectic, overly ambitious, and so on, or it will meet you in your happy and loving energy because you resonate on the same frequency. In such moments, you may feel as though you become one with your horse, blending through your breath and pulse.

I have mentioned this before, and I will repeat it because I never get tired of repeating it. It's extremely valuable information for understanding the horse's mind. I love the fact that no horse I've communicated with can lie or manipulate. They can't, because they haven't developed the part of the brain (neocortex) that enables such behavior. This means they only relate to their state in the present moment. They will always be honest. Being able to manipulate and lie is not a trait we humans should be particularly proud of. Unfortunately, I observe that it's only humans who possess such unfortunate qualities, and the same applies to *female wiles*.

As I often share in the workshops and lectures, I hold, you, as a rider or horse owner, should look at your horse as a brilliant little child or as a man. And I always say this with a smile, especially to the men out there. However, if you're a woman reading this book, you most likely understand what I mean when I say that men's brains aren't as calculating as women's brains, and I hope you do forgive me. Men rarely ask trick *questions*. These are questions where a woman might *test* a man instead of expressing her feelings or what she wants to hear. Most men can't guess the correct answer, and even fewer get it right. Horses also *say* what they mean and do what they mean. They have no filter and are always brutally honest. They do what is either in their nature or what they feel in their hearts.

As a communicator between the horse and its human, my most important task is to convey the horse's messages in the most motivating and diplomatic way possible. My work as a therapist and clairvoyant often supports me in this task.

I've often been asked if there are messages that I don't pass on from the horses to their owners. For example, it may be that the horses don't want to work for their humans because the training method or approach is demotivating for them.

It's always a judgment call on my part; how receptive the rider is to the messages I can pass on from their horse, and how resistant they are to hearing what they are being told. I always have to consider the consequences for both the horse and its human before passing on difficult messages. If I can see that the horse has a message that could elevate its human by ten levels in their personal growth process, I need to feel into the situation and ask the horse if it's realistic for the owner to receive those messages.

If I can help their horse move the human just one level in their awareness, or even zero levels, I will always settle for that one level, even if the horse tells me things that could potentially move their owner four levels forward in their self-awareness and personal growth. But if I sense that the resistance is too strong, the owner or rider will shut down to the messages as a defense mechanism, and then we're back to square one.

For example, a horse might sense that its rider has low self-esteem. The horse will know this because it picks up on the rider's energy and can feel how grounded, or ungrounded, the rider is, how centered they are, and how confident they are in their self-love and authority as the leader between the two of them. This also extends to how the rider engages with other people, which the horse perceives as part of its larger herd. When I sense and see this, I always ask the horse if it has any advice for its human—for its rider. Advice from the horses might be: *"I wish for him or her to learn how to set boundaries lovingly."* Or: *"I hope he or she soon understands how skilled they are as a rider and stops seeking validation from the outside."*

If the rider is open and receptive to such advice, then I pass it on without holding anything back. However, if I sense that the rider doesn't even grasp that the horse can communicate about itself, then I also know there might be resistance to the idea that the horse can understand what's going on inside the rider. In these cases, I might choose to deliver the advice more gently, for example by saying: *"Have you considered that you ARE a skilled rider, and others tell you this all the time? Have you thought about how you might finally connect with that feeling yourself, so that you don't need to seek it from others anymore?"*

However, if in that same situation I stood with a rider who was open to the messages the horse conveyed, both from its inner world and its perception of its human, and who understood that everything the rider holds and thinks flows directly into the horse, then I would deliver the messages and advice without any form of censorship and say things as they came.

Naturally, I have challenged the horses on whether they are entirely free of irony, cheekiness, or humor. I have found that some horses can be cheeky and, for example, tell me they want more food. But when I ask whether it is out of desire or necessity, they always answer honestly. Even here, I witness repeatedly that horses cannot lie. The word *"not"* seems distant to their consciousness and almost does not exist as part of their world. They constantly seek what they *may* do or *should* do. They can appear manipulative to us humans, but I have learned that this often happens simply because they can, such as when there is a lack of leadership from the rider, or because they are playing and having fun, for instance, by biting at clothing, opening a gate themselves, and so on.

In a few cases, I have met horses that have withheld something from me. These were health-related challenges, where the consequences of what the owners might do with the information would be too severe for the horse; for example, a broken leg, kissing spine, or head-shaking that would never improve or heal, or a concussion, and more. In such cases, the horse may fear being euthanized or sold due to problematic behavior. Situations where they knew their owners did not intend to change anything within themselves but expected the horse to change because I asked it to.

In some cases, the horse knew that their human would not give them the necessary time to heal or recover. There can be many reasons for this. For example, financial constraints or goals of competing at a high level do not allow for months of waiting to see whether a horse might recover, especially without any guarantees that the effort will succeed.

As a result, I have learned to clearly explain to owners what they can realistically expect when inquiring about health-related issues. I've also realized that animals only share what makes an impression on them in the present moment, or what I specifically ask about, which is why I always guide the conversation. Therefore, they might not tell me they've recently lost a paddock companion if it no longer impacts them emotionally when I speak with them some months later.

Horses inspire me deeply because they are always present in the moment, both mentally and physically. This also means that, regarding health, they cannot always speak about future health conditions, which would be ambitious to expect, even from humans with far more complex brains, who also don't know what illnesses or events might await them in the future. Horses can answer questions about things from the past, but only if those things are still relevant to their current state of being when I communicate with them.

I've found that the most essential thing for horses is whether they are in balance, both with and without a rider. To shed light on those aspects, I've broken it down into several subtopics. These topics and the way I approach them are, to me, what makes working with horses so exciting. It is complex because there is both a rider and a horse who must learn to cooperate. It is almost a form of couples therapy for me as a practitioner, where I get the opportunity to use every tool in my toolbox. I aim to highlight the areas that together form a picture of whether there is balance between the horse and rider, and within the horse itself, even without the rider.

Personality

Horses are just as individual as we humans are, and yet over the years, I've noticed certain personality traits that tend to recur. Horse owners often describe their horses' personalities based on what they've felt from them, observed in their behavior, or intuitively sensed. I've grouped these personalities into six different horse types, all of which are described in detail in the book *Understand Your Horse*.

These types are:

- **The Playful One**
- **The Sensitive One**
- **Princes and Princesses**
- **Kings and Queens**
- **The Rigid or Lazy One**
- **Shock or Trauma**

When I communicate with horses, the first thing they typically tell me is about their personality and how they see themselves. They'll describe how they perceive themselves, how others see them, including the people around them and the animals they spend time with in the paddock.

If there's a mismatch between how humans see the horse and how other animals see it, it often indicates a conflict between the horse and its person. This can stem from a misinterpretation, a misunderstanding, past negative experiences, projection, or even a power struggle. For example, a misinterpretation might occur when a rider insists on seeing the horse in one way, perhaps they've decided the horse is a *Prince* and fail to recognize the mischievous, playful side that I refer to as the *Inner Street Kid*, or *The Playful One*, which the horse also embodies. A misunderstanding might arise when a horse displays a specific behavior and the rider assumes this is simply part of its personality, when in fact, the behavior may be situational rather than a reflection of who the horse truly is. And this is also where past negative experiences come into play.

A rider might interpret a horse as being *"naughty"* or *"wild"* simply because the horse displays behavior that reminds the rider of something they fear, either from past experiences or from another horse they've known. Then there are projections, which happen when the rider is unable to recognize certain traits in the horse because they're not in touch with those same traits within themselves.This is often the case with the Sensitive horse type. These horses are typically alert and highly aware of their surroundings, and many of them are easily overstimulated physically—something that can be misinterpreted as being moody or challenging to handle. For instance, they may not tolerate touch for long periods, or they might clearly express discomfort if a blanket doesn't sit properly.In situations of power struggle, what I often see is a fight for dominance, which has nothing to do with authentic leadership. In these dynamics, where the horse feels misunderstood, it usually exhibits behaviors that essentially convey a *"no, thank you."* Depending on its personality type, this may be interpreted by the rider as resistance or defiance. The horse might try to bolt out of the arena, ignore the rider's signals, or even rear up if the pressure becomes too much. Understanding your horse's behavior requires, first and foremost, an understanding of its personality.I always ask the horses directly: *"Who are you?"* or *"How do you see yourself?"* From there, they show me images in my mind's eye that reflect their posture and energy, which allows me to interpret whether they feel proud, sensitive, nervous, cautious, fearful, depressed, and so on. They also convey feelings to me, which I experience in my own body, and by combining these impressions, I can form an understanding of their personality and how they interact with the world and their herd. Some horses behave one way in the pasture and very differently during training. But there is always something at the core that reveals who they were born to be. As with all personality profiles, some qualities feel *"most like me"* and others that are *"least like me."*

To give a concrete example: I may stand with a horse who shows me that it has a playful, childlike mind. It loves speed, needs a lot of stimulation, and struggles to focus when things get too serious. I interpret this as the *Playful One*. But when I show the horse a mental image of a competition setting, its energy suddenly shifts. It grows taller, holds its neck high, and sends me a proud energy full of a desire for recognition from its rider. I now feel a focused horse. I interpret this side as the *Prince*.

My task is to distinguish between these two aspects of the horse and help the rider understand that the horse contains both, but in different situations. Which brings me to the following topic: how well the two partners understand each other as a team?

Their Relationships With Owner, Rider, Part-Lease, Trainer, etc.

"Do horses even want to be used?" That's a question many people ask me. And my answer is: YES—absolutely! It may go against the nature of some horses to carry a rider, but in my experience, most horses are naturally inclined and historically shaped to engage with humans. They sense our presence, feel our energy, and often recognize that we have something to offer them. In other words, animals and humans rely on one another, and they mutually develop.

Whether it's been to carry people, such as the Native Americans, help retrieve sheep in the Icelandic mountains, escort royalty in carriages, or perform in parades, horses have worked alongside humans for thousands of years. And not only out of force.

I'm convinced that many horses, if they genuinely wanted to, could escape their paddocks, outdoor stables, enclosures, and pastures, and never come back. But just like us, horses are herd animals. They seek safety, food, and a sense of belonging. And safety also means love, connection, and knowing where you fit in. That's why they show up for *work* just as we do—so they can later relax and enjoy time with their closest companions, much like we enjoy time with friends or family. Horses do the same with each other in the pasture.

All the horses I've communicated with over the years have expressed deep gratitude for the positive relationships they've had with their owners. They would never want to be without them. Not one horse has ever questioned *why* they were being trained. What they *have* asked is the misuse of power or the exploitation of their abilities, especially in high-performance settings, such as when they're not allowed any turnout time at all, yet are still expected to perform—day in and day out. Often, for riders who don't build a genuine emotional connection with them, it's because they are driven by something else. That *something else* can be ambition, or ego—a mindset where it's more about the *"I"* than the *"we."*

These are often the kinds of situations I describe in the chapter *"How Are You in Partnership With Your Horse?"* in the book *"Understand Your Horse"*, under the relationship called *"The Star and the Striver."*

Horses can sometimes wonder why their owners don't have more time for them. Why do they get a part-time rider if the horse doesn't feel that this person truly cares—body and soul? It's rarely for the horse's sake when the leading rider no longer has the time to train or spend time with them and instead brings in someone else.

Many riders may believe otherwise, or perhaps they carry a sense of guilt because their lives have become busy. They may want to keep their horse fit and active but lack the time or resources to manage it themselves. There are many reasons why a rider might need help from others. But the horse wants its *primary person*. That could be the owner, the part-time rider, or a regular trainer. What matters most is that the horse bonds with the one who is most present.

I often hear horses speak kindly about the other people in their lives, but in my conversations with them, the message is clear: they want a genuine connection with their rider.

I've met riders who throw their arms around their horses, full of affection, and have no reservations about showing their emotions, whether others approve or not.

Some horses don't enjoy that and see the rider as overly clingy or smothering. Especially if the horse has what I call a *Royal* personality, and the rider is inexperienced. The rider may mean well and want to learn, but the horse might find the enthusiasm a bit much. That said, many horses thrive on this connection. They *want* to feel their rider's emotional presence on every level. But I also meet riders who don't express their emotions so openly. They love and care deeply, but they hold back their affection.

This might be because they're afraid of losing the horse, or because they once lost a horse and now hesitate to bond too strongly again. Others may find it hard to express big emotions—they keep themselves *in check.* Horses always accept this as it is. Still, some may wonder why their rider doesn't let go more.

Some question why the rider expects the horse to fully surrender and trust when the rider doesn't do the same. When I tell the rider that I don't sense strong feelings like deep affection or emotional intensity, some take it very personally. They worry I'm saying they don't love their horse. They get upset. However, I often explain that this is just the current reality, and there's nothing wrong with it. Still, deep down, the rider usually *knows.* Some decide to do nothing. Others choose to make a change. The horse gives them the chance to practice — to express love in small, awkward, vulnerable ways, even when it feels hard. Isn't that precisely what makes the horse a teacher? A teacher who helps the rider grow, learn to open, let go, surrender control, and do so in the safest space possible on earth? I genuinely believe so.

When I work to support horses and riders, I always look at the relationship between them. That means I assess the horse based on its personality and whether the rider truly understands it. Next, I explore whether the rider can embrace the horse exactly as it is, both its light and shadow sides. Because every personality comes with both strengths and challenges. Challenges, however, are not a problem for the horse. It simply exists as it is.

The challenges arise when the rider fails to understand the horse's behavior or refuses to accept that the horse acts in a certain way. Take, for example, a horse with what I call *The Playful One* personality. This is a horse bursting with energy, needing an immense amount of stimulation to feel balanced. If you are a sensitive and calm person, this can be a real challenge. You might interpret the horse as being naughty, disobedient, or trying to test you. But as I described in my first book, a horse *can't* deliberately manipulate or deceive you. It simply *is.* And if you must see it that way, then it's only doing what it's allowed to do, because it *can.*

This means it's also essential to examine your leadership skills in your relationship with your horse. Are you being a guiding presence, a dominating one, or are you passive, perhaps even intimidated by your horse's behavior? Horses reveal to me the people in their lives. This includes almost anyone who's made an impression on them—former owners, current owners, sales barns, part-time riders, trainers, professional riders. But the most important relationship I focus on is the one they have with their current rider.

I always ask horses: *"What kind of relationship do you feel you have with your human?"* Their answers vary. They might say, *"I see my rider as a mother, an older sister, a younger sister, a soulmate, or as an equal and a friend."*

Then I ask more detailed questions about *why* the horse places their rider in that role.

This tells me a lot about the dynamics of the partnership—something I describe in detail in my book, *Understand Your Horse.* It also gives me insight into how the horse sees itself and its rider within the hierarchy.

Horses care deeply about how their humans are doing, both mentally and physically. They absorb the energy around them, so it matters to them whether their person is in emotional balance. If the rider is not mentally well, some horses may try to compensate for their rider's mental well-being. Driven by a strong instinct to care, they may naturally attempt to help their rider regain balance. In these moments, healing can occur within the relationship.

Most riders I've spoken to are familiar with this feeling. They describe being with their horse as a kind of therapy—a sacred space, where they feel recharged and find peace away from the world.

Horses become a mirror of their riders when they absorb their energy and emotions. It's the same phenomenon we see in highly sensitive people. They pick up on the atmosphere around them and absorb the emotions as if they were their own. It takes time for them to decompress and shed the energy that doesn't belong to them. Horses are herd animals. If they've bonded with their humans and see them as part of their herd, they will, in most cases, take on the energy their humans' project. This also means that the horse, by nature, wants to cooperate. It needs something to mirror itself in, to feel safe. If it were completely alone in the world, it would likely feel a deep sense of vulnerability, perhaps even fear, that it couldn't survive on its own for long. That's its nature and instinct.

Being left alone would signal danger—like the threat of a lion. And in this way, horses are not that different from humans. We have more complex psychological defenses that can mask the fear of being alone. But the fear itself; that deep existential anxiety lives in all of us. That's why we owe it to animals to care for them deeply and consciously, especially with this knowledge in mind. Once we've socialized them, they become dependent on us. For a partnership to be healthy and balanced, I need to examine the dynamic between horse and rider. The most important part of my work is always to highlight whether the rider truly understands their horse. Because I know this for sure: The horse has always understood its human.

Resources and Challenges

Horses reveal to me their resources in general, as well as during training. I can't always tell if a horse is a dressage horse, a western horse, a military horse, a show jumping horse, or a trail horse just by looking at it or its breed. I don't find it relevant to know, because that would be a form of bias or generalization, something I'm very cautious about. Especially in a world where increasingly many riders are tuning into what the individual horse needs and building their training, play, and daily interaction based on that.

What matters to me is what I sense from the horse. I do this to ensure I'm staying true to what motivates the horse, and through that motivation, joy, freedom, and play come into the relationship. From there, the rider gets the most balanced horse, one that enjoys working repeatedly for its person. I might encounter a horse that's motivated by jumping, even though its rider plans to use it for dressage. In most cases, the rider also picks up on this, sensing when the horse gets a high and good energy from doing something it maybe shouldn't be doing in its *professional* role as a riding horse.

Will the horse enjoy working in dressage? Yes, it will, because horses want to cooperate and be loyal to their humans. But not at any cost. If such a horse is not allowed to jump at all or experience play and freedom, it can potentially *shut down* internally, becoming rigid, lazy, or even depressed in its behavior. The same applies to all types of horses, depending on what motivates them. Dressage horses may express whether they prefer speed or collected movements, whether they feel like elegant ballerinas dancing ballet, or bodybuilders with large muscular bodies that love to be used and demand the rider's help in that regard.

Since I'm not a *horse girl* myself, I sometimes feel a bit out of my depth when I try to demonstrate the exercises the horses show me that they want to work on. But over the years, I have learned most of the exercises. If not, I simply show the owners, and we all have a good laugh, with them nodding in recognition as I stand there in the barn aisle, bouncing around like a clown trying to convey their horse's messages in a jumping *piaffe*.

Show jumping horses also tell me about the types of jumps that motivate them and what they are anxious about when it comes to the jumps. It could be over water ditches, how they feel about oxers, triple bars, cavalettis, crossbars, and so on. They might have difficulty jumping at an angle or feel nervous about a corner in the arena, among other things. In detail, they can send me images, which I then pass on to their riders. These riders follow the precise instructions their horses give them through me, along with explanations of what different obstacles and exercises do to both their horses and themselves, both mentally and physically. They tell me how they feel about the place where they stay. This could be the pasture, the box, the stable aisle, the staff, the other horses, the overall atmosphere, and more. They can share what they like about the place and what they don't like. Most horses prefer peace in the areas they live, and depending on their character and personality, some can get stressed in large spaces with too much traffic of people coming and going in the barn aisles.

Some horses don't thrive in small boxes. Most people prefer a box that allows for a clear view. They need to be able to stick their head out of a window to feel that freedom, and the connection to nature is close. Sensitive horses don't want to be in an outer box where they must deal with the traffic on the stable aisle. Horses that are more dominant and want to be seen and heard thrive best in an outer box, where they are seen first and, not least, fed first.

All of this helps the horse to stay motivated. Since horses, for the most part, are willing to cooperate and work for their rider once they are socialized, it's a crucial point for me to address. If they are allowed to use their resources and *engage in what they do best* such as jumping, even if they are dressage horses, there is nothing they wouldn't do for their rider. Depending on their personality types, I unfortunately also see that if they are not allowed to do some of the things they feel they have resources for, or what gives them a sense of play or freedom, they must resort to their primal instincts and defense mechanisms, which are either:

- **Fight**
- **Flee**
- **Freeze**

In the fight response, there is conflict riding or a rider who may eventually become afraid of their horse. When a horse flees, it runs, and often I see that the horse is labeled as *naughty* or *it doesn't trust the rider* when it seizes the opportunity to escape the arena as soon as the gate opens. And finally, the horse may freeze by shutting down its energy. It could either be by coming to a standstill with no forward movement, no matter how much you try to *spur it on*, or it may show no spark in its eyes, and no one understands whether the horse is in pain, has an issue with its food, or why it suddenly is not thriving.

Horses can also show me what is difficult for them, which are their challenges. This can range from situations that make them scared or insecure, as I described in my book *Understand Your Horse* in the chapter on behavioral issues. Or it can be exercises in training that are challenging for them. Riders can always recognize this when I describe it to them, because it is usually for the same reason, they asked me to come in the first place. In most cases, a horse's challenges arise from misunderstandings between the horse and rider in how they relate to each other, memories from previous owners, or incidents that are locked in the horse's nervous system, causing it to react based on what it used to do, even though it is now in a new stable with a new rider. Or it could be because the horse is experiencing pain somewhere or discomfort in its body.

Health Issues

One of the topics that also concerns the horses (because they are fight-or-flight animals and need good health to escape any potential danger), and not least the riders, is their state of health. At the same time, it is also one of the most challenging topics to address. Very few animal communicators can perceive health issues in detail. The animal communicators I train are coached repeatedly in this area because I know how complex it is. It is complicated because the horse exists in the present moment. And then it becomes even more complex because one must distinguish between the past, the present, and possibly the future.

Finally, there is also the matter of the rider's responsibility, mainly when the horse is used for riding. The rider naturally affects the horse, either from the saddle or through the bit, the saddle itself, the spurs, the bridle, the cavesson, and the equipment in general.

As mentioned, horses typically show me the things that make a particular impression on them in the present moment when I communicate with them. If injuries occurred in the past, they may not always be disclosed to me, and that's because those experiences no longer leave a lasting impression at the time of our communication. In their minds, those events are *done*, and no longer part of their current memory.

They also don't always disclose injuries they may currently be experiencing. That could be because those issues don't make an impression on them, which also means they are not in pain. But in rare cases, it can be because they are afraid of the consequences of telling their rider or owner that they are injured. The result could be that the rider decides to part with the horse if they discover it has an injury that means it cannot be used as a riding horse, whether temporarily or permanently.

I don't experience that horses manipulate or lie, but when it comes to fear and consequences, they may avoid telling the truth. This surprised me a lot the first time I encountered it in a horse. If I ask directly about a health issue, it's also been my experience that the horse will tell me. This has taught me that if a rider urgently needs to know whether something is wrong with the horse, then I also need to know what specifically to ask about. Usually, I let the horse tell me first what stands out most to them. If they don't bring up the issue the rider is concerned about, then I ask the rider to tell me exactly what they want to know regarding the horse's health.

The horses show me where they are in pain, either directly on their own body or by transferring the pain, blockages, or irritations into my body. This means I need to be in very close contact with my own body and physical issues, so I can distinguish between what belongs to me and what belongs to them. When I'm shown their health problems, I see it as specific areas of their body suddenly becoming highlighted in front of me. I then tune into what the horse is trying to show me, whether it relates to muscles, joints, blood vessels, bones, organs, neurological issues, or something else. I always ask how these symptoms manifest so that the rider can recognize the physical challenges they face. I ask whether the issue is affecting the horse's performance in their work under saddle and whether the problem they exhibit is located where I see it, or if it stems from another area of the body.

I need to know whether I'm being shown the cause or merely the symptom. I also want to know if the pain radiates throughout the body, whether it crosses diagonally, stays on one side, or is limited to, for example, just one leg. They can show me anything from discomfort caused by a bit, which bit they prefer, dental or jaw joint issues, neck and spinal vertebrae, shoulder injuries, leg and back problems, spinal column, dorsal processes, sacrum, lower back, saddle issues, hooves, girth, feed, allergies, the cranial edge, internal organs, stomach, tissue, joints, muscles, bones, and much more.

They also show me what they need. These can be practitioners such as chiropractors, osteopaths, massage therapists, acupuncturists, physiotherapists, veterinarians, and others. And they show when they are lacking minerals, vitamins, nutrition, homeopathy, and so on. I am not a veterinarian and will never diagnose a horse or judge whether an animal should be euthanized. I collaborate with an increasing number of veterinarians and consult with them when I notice or suspect health issues that may contradict what another practitioner or veterinarian has told the horse's owner or rider. In recent years, I have begun working more intentionally toward sharing knowledge between veterinarians and myself. In this way, I aim to pave the way for a bridge between alternative practitioners and traditional veterinary medicine.

Alternative treatments are here to stay, so my wish is to create a shared platform that makes sense for all of us, rather than fighting each other or holding prejudices about each other's work, simply because there is still so much, we don't know about one another. Building that bridge and exchanging knowledge about the horses' history and overall well-being will, in my view, allow you as a rider to feel more secure when entering any treatment system with your horse. Just as medical records are shared between hospitals or healthcare institutions, so too should animal treatments and medical cases be shared. It must be frustrating for many veterinarians to be involved in a treatment process, only to be told that an alternative practitioner has recommended a product or treatment that perhaps doesn't align with what the vet has advised, without any prior discussion or dialogue.

At the same time, I know how frustrating it can be to hear from an animal owner: *"You're our last hope, because the vet has given up, so now I need your help urgently, preferably for free because we've already spent so much on expensive vet bills."* In these moments, I feel a tremendous weight of responsibility on my shoulders, a responsibility I don't wish to carry. I am simply a translator, and I can only speak to what is happening in the present moment, together with the horse that is being communicated with or treated by me.

When it comes to euthanasia, that responsibility lies heavily with the veterinarians. In the end, it is up to the horse's owner to feel into and decide when the time is right to let their horse go. Some owners are apparent and quick to sense when that moment has come. Others find it extremely difficult to accept the reality of the situation, and they may *drag things out* before the horse is finally put to rest.

Case: The Prix St. George Horse Park Avenue and His Health Issues. In Collaboration with Veterinarian Berner Olsen and Chiropractor Mikael Lundstedt

In 2011, the rider Louise Kjær contacted me for the first time. She wanted me to communicate with her gelding, *Park Avenue*; also known as Palle. I drove to her place, where Palle was stabled. It was a beautiful place with old barns in a lovely area, just north of Copenhagen.

At that time, a dressage rider Nicklas Von Eckendorff was riding Palle, and I quickly discovered that Palle was truly a star. Palle *told me* that he was a rather sensitive prince. *"He bonded deeply with his humans, believed in the good in everyone, and just wanted to be with us as his herd. He thought very highly of himself."* That was evident both in his personality and in his work as a dressage horse. His balance and movement were harmonious and light as a feather. Palle was so refined that he almost seemed too fine to be standing in those old stables. Palle pictured himself in the future, living in a grand and elegant place, in a beautiful stable with white fences.

Louise and I laughed a lot about that—a young boy with sophisticated tastes. But over time, it turned out that Palle had reason to think that way. In mid-May that same year, he won both the MA1-A-Horses dressage class at The Danish Sports Riding Club, Algestrup, and the Prix St. George at Glostrup Riding Club with the elite rider Nicklas Von Eckendorff. Palle was a seasoned Prix St. George horse, and he was talented and knew it.

Louise had previously been a show jumper, and now she was preparing to start dressage riding with her lovely *Palle boy*. But she quickly discovered that he was incredibly stiff to ride. She had expected that a horse who had been in training his whole life would be as soft as butter, but he wasn't. Louise took Palle to their regular vet in North Zealand, who diagnosed him with a locked neck. Palle received chiropractic treatments at the vet clinic, but unfortunately, it didn't help.

After that, Louise took Palle to a man who worked with him from the ground. They had to do all sorts of groundwork exercises; bending, lateral movements like traversals to loosen the hindquarters.

They practiced rein-backs for 3–4 months and did lots of trotting and running from the ground. They followed these prescribed exercises consistently for four months. The vet believed the problem was a locked sacrum. And then the time came. Louise was finally going to get back on Palle, only to discover that he still wasn't okay to ride. A new problem had now emerged: Palle was 12 years old at this point. He had been in the game for many years, was starting to age, and was now out of shape. Suddenly, he began going lame on different legs.

Louise thought this must be typical for older horses. When they no longer have the muscles and tendons to hold everything together, it begins to fall apart. They decided to call in another vet, this time from one of the larger clinics in Denmark. He believed that Palle had spavin in his hind legs and began treatment on them immediately. Louise was instructed only to walk Palle—nothing more. She was starting to get a bit worn down after six months of on-and-off issues and still not being able to ride him seriously. Louise was also pregnant and had a baby on the way. She decided to put Palle on a water treadmill. She left him in the care of the wellness center *Healthy Horse* in the city of Skibby. Sandie, my friend and colleague, who owns the place, noticed that Palle was very inconsistent on the treadmill. Some days he would move energetically, and other days it was as if someone had switched him off. He became a shut-down boy on the inside. Sandie tried letting him out in the paddock first as an experiment, but nothing worked. No one could figure out what was going on inside Palle's head.

Sandie decided to consult several colleagues about Palle's case. Among them were my friend and horse physiotherapist Claus Toftgaard and chiropractor Mikael Lundstedt from Sweden. Louise was at a loss. Her beloved horse wasn't functioning, and no one could pinpoint the problem.

Mikael Lundstedt came out and gave him chiropractic treatment. He said there was an issue with Palle's right hip and right shoulder. He treated Palle for that on the spot. But since no vet confirmed Mikael's findings, Louise ended up forgetting about it and didn't mention it again. Then Louise asked Sandie to have me come out. I didn't know anything about what had been going on. Louise didn't need me to come urgently. She wanted to know how Palle was feeling and what was going on with his health.

Sandie called me, frustrated and at a loss. It was the day before Christmas Eve in 2016, and because I vaguely remembered Palle, and because Sandie is a dear friend and colleague, I drove out there right away. I arrived at the cold stables on a late December afternoon. I hadn't been told anything about the medical history from the past six months, or the many challenges Louise had faced with Palle. When Sandie led him out into the stable aisle, I smiled. I recognized his energy. A sensitive and princely boy, and I could feel that he was happy to see me, too. The first thing he sent to me was: *"Ditte – they're treating the wrong legs!"*

I told Sandie everything I saw and felt. I saw that Palle was putting a lot of weight on his front end. I saw that he was right-sided, and he compensated by putting a lot of pressure on his right shoulder and front leg, which contributed to locking up his hip joint. Palle showed me that the joints the vet had been treating weren't the ones causing problems. And he couldn't understand why. I said a vet should treat his right shoulder and right hip instead of both hind legs. Palle seemed relieved and happy that I had passed that on.

Sandie was surprised because she remembered that chiropractor Mikael Lundstedt had said the same thing, but no vet had confirmed it at that point. Sandie called Louise and told her what I had gotten from Palle. Louise also now remembered that Mikael had said the same thing as I had. Sandie immediately called the vet who was treating Palle at the time. And it was true—he had been treating Palle's hind legs for spavin.

Sandie later told us that the vet didn't believe Mikael's and my statements, and of course, Louise confronted him about it. He acknowledged that there could be stiffness in the hip and said he would consider placing a block in the lower back before any work resumed so that the area could relax. But he wasn't willing to treat the two specific areas. Joint treatments, he said, were something to be taken seriously and not just performed lightly. I was puzzled. If joint treatments were so serious, how could anyone justify treating the *wrong* joints? I took a deep breath and left it up to Louise to decide what she wanted to do next. Louise decided to get a second opinion from another vet. Sandie suggested contacting vet Berner Olsen. He was open to take a look at the horse first, and he wanted to help. He watched Palle being trotted and lunged at Sandie's place and said that what Mikael and I had pointed out made sense. Palle wasn't bringing his right front leg forward the same way as the left.

About my work, Berner said to Sandie: *"There's a lot I don't understand about women, but Ditte, she can do something. She's right!"*

Later, when I spoke with Berner myself, he said: *"You've managed, much to my frustration, to figure out what was wrong. And it's not that* you're *frustrating. It's just that I get annoyed with myself for not understanding* how *you do it. Because I can't explain it in professional terms. But I do believe there's more between heaven and earth than we humans can explain. I've had other practitioners like you turn out to be right, too. So yeah, there's something to it."*

Chiropractor Mikael Lundstedt from Sweden made this statement about his treatment of Palle: *"First of all, I asked that a dentist treat Palle. What I often see is that if a horse has an issue on the same side at the front and back, it usually stems from something up front, such as the neck, jaw function, teeth, or even the neck's range of motion. What I observed with Palle was that the forward motion was blocked due to restrictions in the jaw and neck. He had an indirect weight-bearing issue in his right hind leg as a result. As a result, his ability to shift his weight evenly to the back became compromised. That's why I understand how a vet might assume it starts in the sacroiliac joint or lumbar area, but that wasn't the root of the problem, even though there were clear issues there. Palle had a slower motion in his right front leg, but he wasn't lame. The vets didn't feel there was anything to treat. But the scapula wasn't moving freely. There were multiple restrictions in the neck, which created a compensatory issue in the lower neck that's directly connected to the shoulder and forehand during forward motion."*

Mikael refers to this as the *forehand syndrome,* a term he uses to describe a complex of issues involving the neck, shoulder, spine, and ribcage. *"Typically, you'll see that the horse isn't lame but has an inefficient, shortened stride in the front legs. You can't block the pain from the knee down, because the problem doesn't originate in the legs. The legs aren't initially involved but often become part of the problem over time. It's the scapula and shoulder joint that may require treatment, depending on the findings. Sometimes these issues are identified through ultrasound rather than X-rays or flexion tests. It's comparable to a 'frozen shoulder' in humans, where the nerve signals to the rest of the body are weakened or dulled. Many horses will also trip more because they can't lift their hooves fast enough. The shoulder doesn't move properly when turning to the same side. In Palle's case, that was to the right. This kind of reaction does not always follow a straight line. Once the issue in his neck was addressed and the movement in his jaw was restored through dental treatment, I was able to proceed with further treatments. That also helped prevent the passive, compensatory posture from the hind end that reduced the efficiency of the right hind legs forward drive."*

Regarding the way we both work, Mikael says: *"I also very quickly see and sense what the horse is 'telling' us—in its communication with us and other horses. I then confirm what I feel with my hands, through testing, biomechanical analysis, stress provocations, balance testing in motion and at rest. Often, it's necessary to lunge the horse or do a ridden assessment with the rider or a 'test pilot'. The sensation that Ditte and I get, without even knowing each other, feels to me like we have an internal scanner. I believe it stems from having observed many horses over the years.*

I also work in cooperation with vets and follow diagnoses through their testing, scans, and X-rays. I very quickly see muscle tone and posture—also in people. I believe both Ditte and I can spot imbalances and compensations almost instantly, and we combine that with an understanding of how the animals feel and whether they're thriving. We can both see how an animal should *move, and we can tell when it has mentally 'shut down, often to protect itself. A high stress level is usually a warning sign of underlying physical issues. I think we observe in much the same way. Like Ditte, I tune into the animal. I focus intensely on the individual, and then the information comes to me—paired with testing of the horse's movement, muscular development, and pain points. That combination gives a clear direction. So, while we use different methods and skills, we often identify the same problems."*

Palle had spent three months at Sandie's and was now strong enough to begin his rehabilitation at home. Louise decided to move Palle back to Hillerød Sports Riding Club, where he had been stabled before. The veterinarian; Berner treated Palle's joints twice—his hip and right shoulder—after he returned home.

Louise rode Palle and worked on his rehab. Sara and Ulrik, who own the sports riding club, were very focused on riding him deep. He didn't need to do all kinds of challenging exercises, even though he was capable of doing so. They went back to the basics; getting him to relax and loosen his topline. Now, the focus was on getting the riding right. Palle carried all the weight on his neck and had developed an enormous stallion neck. In hindsight, Louise could see that this hadn't been very healthy for him.

Sara helped her reshape Palle. Louise just rode him in the forest a couple of times a week, while Sara took care of the training sessions to get him to let go and relax. He leaned heavily on the reins, as if you had an entire horse in your hands. Palle wanted to put everything on the reins. If you rode him in a competition frame, everyone was happy. But as soon as you asked him to flex or go deeper, he couldn't manage it. They sought a horse that was soft and supple. During this period, Mikael continued to come and adjust Palle with chiropractic treatments. His right hind leg could move a bit more freely, and then veterinarian Berner Olsen treated him again. And since then, there have been no issues with Palle. He trained for half a year and was in good shape—back to his previous level. After that, Louise decided to sell him as a fun and friendly leisure horse. She knew how deeply Palle bonded with people, and since she had just had her baby and only had time for a couple of forest rides a week, she constantly felt guilty. She believed he needed a rider who would be there for him every day. Palle needed stability in his life.

Today, Palle lives in the beautiful city of Sommersted with a woman named Emilie. She wanted a horse that was fun to ride and could teach her new things. Palle is the perfect prince for that. He now enjoys life in beautiful surroundings; with the lovely stables and nice paddocks he always deserved.

Behavioral Problems

Most of the inquiries I receive from horse owners are generally about riders interpreting their horse's behavior as either a behavioral problem or being unsure whether the horse is in pain, or if *it's all in its head.* As I explain in my book *Understand Your Horse,* there are several reasons why horses behave the way they do. Their behavior is typically the result of a combination of their personality type, their relationship with their humans, their health, stored experiences in their nervous system from past adverse events, and, finally, their innate way of being in the world shaped by instinct.

I have divided the six personality types into passive, dominant, or lead horses. When assessing a behavioral issue in a horse, I examine each of these categories. First, I analyze what the horse would naturally do— what it was born to be and how its instinct would lead it to respond. A Sensitive horse will react very differently from a King type. Imagine, for instance, that you're riding in the arena and you have a Sensitive horse that shows behavioral issues related to disliking or fearing other horses. The typical reaction of a *sensitive* horse in that case would be to flee when it sees other horses. It might jump to the side or try to bolt out of the arena without paying attention to the rider.

You may also have a horse that's a mix of personality types, such as *The Sensitive Prince.* Here, it's essential to understand your horse to determine in which situations one personality type becomes more dominant than the other. In a fear-inducing situation, you must recognize whether the horse is reacting from its *Sensitive* side or its more *Princely* side.

A horse that fits the *King* profile—a herd leader—will typically pin its ears at other horses or send out such intense energy that the other horses move out of its way in the arena. You might interpret this behavior from your gelding as aggression and not understand why. But in a *King* type, this reaction is usually a way of hiding vulnerability. He doesn't want the other horses to sense any weakness in him, so for him, attack becomes the best form of defense. This often leads me to investigate potential health issues.

Next, I investigate whether there could be a physical or medical explanation for the horse's behavior—what the rider sees as a behavioral problem might, from the horse's perspective, not be a problem at all. The horse might be sore or in pain and trying to get the rider off as a response to discomfort, which could easily explain its problematic behavior.

I often meet riders who tell me that their vet couldn't find anything wrong with the horse. Upon closer inspection, however, tensions and soreness may stem from other factors, such as the rider's balance in the saddle, rein handling during training, tack that restricts the poll, stress, incorrect feeding, and other things that wouldn't necessarily show up during a standard veterinary check without a rider on the horse.

Next, I look at how safe or unsafe the horse feels with its rider or owner. Again, based on the horse's personality type, I assess whether the horse feels insecure, mirrors the rider, feels understood, enters conflict, or feels safe with its partner. These different ways of being in partnership with a horse vary widely. That's precisely why I love working with horses and riders, because it's complex, yet always solvable when you understand the horse's mind and personality.

Finally, I always examine the horse's autonomic nervous system. The body contains several types of nervous systems. The nervous system is divided into the central nervous system and the peripheral nervous system. The body contains an intricate internal world, comprising various systems and mechanisms, including the central nervous system, the peripheral nervous system, the somatic nervous system, the autonomic nervous system, the sympathetic nervous system, and the parasympathetic nervous system.

What interests me when working with behavioral issues is evaluating how balanced the horse is, both mentally and physically, and whether there's a shock or trauma buried in the system that might be contributing to unwanted behavior for both the horse and the rider.

The nervous system is almost a world of its own—it doesn't reason. It has no sense of time. It cannot distinguish between past, present, or imagined future scenarios you create in your mind's eye. In that sense, the autonomic nervous system isn't intelligent in the way we usually understand intelligence. In some ways, it functions much like the horse's thinking in its most basic form. At its core, it's all about survival —just as it was for the animals we evolved from, and in that context, the autonomic nervous system is our greatest ally.

It consists of nerve cells located outside the central nervous system.

It's divided into:

- **The sympathetic nervous system**
- **The parasympathetic nervous system**
- **The enteric nervous system**

The sympathetic nervous system also known as the SNS, activates when we perceive danger. It triggers what's called the *fight or flight* response. What we experience as danger, whether we're humans or animals, is highly individual. It can be anything from people, sounds, smells, darkness, and so on. When we encounter something that requires us to fight or flee, adrenaline is released into the body. This enables us to run faster, perceive more quickly, and become hyper-alert. The SNS causes our blood vessels to constrict, our bronchi to dilate, reduces activity in the large intestine, increases our heart rate, dilates our pupils, and can lead to sweating, among other responses. When the body has had enough of releasing adrenaline and enters a state of full alert, it instead begins to release cortisol—the body's long-term stress hormone. If cortisol continues to be released over an extended period, and the body doesn't return to a resting state, it will eventually result in stress, and possibly chronic stress. Cortisol breaks down muscle tissue and impairs short-term memory, among other things.

The function of the parasympathetic nervous system is to bring the body back to a state of balance once the danger has passed. It creates a deep state of relaxation after high-energy activity or a stressful situation.

The enteric nervous system, also known as the ENS, regulates digestion. It's simpler in structure than the brain, yet it contains between 200 and 600 million nerve cells in the human body. This system is primarily located in the stomach and intestines, where it helps the body convert food into energy through chemical processes. The walls of the intestines contain cells that can detect the chemical composition of what we eat. The ENS triggers the production of digestive enzymes that break down food into molecules the body can absorb. It also helps measure the acidity of the food we ingest. Essentially, the brain *hands over responsibility* for digestion to the ENS.

The ENS also plays a protective role. For example, it can trigger strong contractions that cause vomiting or diarrhea if the body detects harmful substances, such as during poisoning. There is a strong connection between the gut and the brain. You may have noticed that certain foods can improve your mood.

Research suggests this is because the ENS triggers a chain reaction in the brain that makes you feel happier. This explains why some people turn to comfort food when they're feeling down. Scientists are even exploring whether artificial stimulation of the ENS could be used to treat depression. Another example of gut-brain communication is the sensation of *butterflies in the stomach.*

This feeling may occur because the ENS redirects blood away from the digestive system when the brain senses stress or anxiety. When we feel pressured, the brain can also cause the ENS to change the gut's regular rhythmic contractions, leading to nausea. According to experts, the communication between brain and gut is closely tied to what we call *gut feelings.*

The enteric nervous system can produce emotions, but it can't think for you or help you make decisions. In other words, you only have one actual brain. The ENS won't help you write songs, manage your finances, or do your homework. But its complexity continues to fascinate researchers.

The next time you enjoy a meal, take a moment to appreciate the incredible amount of measuring, processing, coordination, and communication that happens inside your digestive system. If, at this point, I haven't found a clear explanation from the previous areas I've examined,

I show the horse a mental image of what the rider perceives as a problem. I do this by creating a mental image of the situation in my mind's eye. In my experience, what the rider sees as one problem is often, for the horse, three separate challenges. For example, a rider might tell me, *"My horse gets stressed in the stable aisle."*

But for the horse, this could mean:

1. **Stress when alone in the aisle**
2. **Stress when other horses or people walk past**
3. **Stress caused by specific horses in nearby stalls**

For the horse, we're dealing with three very different explanations and scenarios, even though the rider sees it as one single issue. That's why I always train my students to approach behavioral problems from multiple angles and ask a variety of questions about the same behavior. It also means that I, myself, must constantly cross-check the horse until I feel calmness and balance in all the situations and scenarios I present to it.

Another example is when someone says, *"My horse gets stressed on hacks."*

However, going on a hack can mean many things, it could be walking away from the stable, leaving the pasture, being on the road, entering the forest, or feeling stressed because it wants to rush back home. For years, I experienced some horse owners trying to *test* me by asking, *Can you tell me what my horse is afraid of?*

What they didn't know was that to answer that question, I had to mentally present the horse with a wide range of objects, scenarios, and images, and then gauge its reaction to each one I projected. I would show it things like loud sounds, buckets, benches, paper bags, umbrellas, the arena, other horses, men, the vet, the whip, the farrier, the bridle, the blanket, shadows, water, and all kinds of vehicles. Eventually, I would feel a wave of fear in my own body, as an energy the horse was transferring to me, when I pictured a set of clippers.

Sometimes this process would take a few minutes, all in silence. Then I'd look up at the rider and say, *I sense your horse is afraid of clippers,* and they would seem convinced, because how could I have known? But today, I no longer answer questions like that.It takes too much energy, and the horses just end up staring at me blankly as I ask them a thousand questions, simply to prove to the rider that we're communicating nonverbally.

For me, this also means that if I want to ensure real behavioral change after my visit, I must be able to sense calmness and balance in the horse across all the scenarios I present, even the ones that previously triggered fear.

Unfortunately, I cannot guarantee with 100% certainty that I can change a horse's behavior. That's because what the horse needs often also depends on the rider—on whether they're willing to help or change something themselves. The horses also sense if the rider is too stressed in their daily life and carry that energy into the stable.

If your horse is a *Sensitive* type, it will respond negatively to that kind of energy and politely say, *"No, thank you."* This work can never be a *quick fix,* because it requires you to be aware of the energy you bring with you, and most importantly, to take responsibility by pausing and breathing calmly before you even approach your horse.

Another example could be a horse displaying behavior that makes the rider feel like, *It doesn't trust my cues,* or *it's not listening during training.* In those cases, I analyze why the horse isn't responding, how it feels about you as a rider, how you sit in the saddle, how motivated it is to be a riding horse, and not least, how it feels about the discipline you've chosen for the two of you to pursue together.

Their "We"-understanding and "We"-connections

If only all riders truly understood what horses can give us as humans, we would be the wisest and most enriched living beings on earth.

At times, I feel as though the gods touch horses, because I see a simplicity, and at the same time, a complexity in them that I can hardly put into words. But to make it as simple as possible, I'll try to say it in one sentence:

"Horses help us humans find balance—both physically and mentally."

I'll go into much more detail on this in the chapter *Personal and Spiritual Development for Horse and Rider*. But to start from a simple place—one that most riders can relate to—you can usually recognize the *we-understanding* when you feel that you genuinely understand your horse, and your horse understands you. When you are connected, you'll also notice that your horse is more *with* you. It will likely be less hyper-alert, less watchful, and less fearful. For example, it won't overreact when it sees a lady in a red raincoat. It won't respond as intensely to outside stimuli as it might if you hadn't established a connection with it. When a horse connects with you as its friend, leader, companion, mother, father, or sister, it's because it desires to be a *we*.

Just like many dogs don't fully relax until all family members are home, or children want everyone to be at their birthday party, it's part of the horse's instinct and natural desire to be together. They do this because they are herd animals, born with a herd mentality. Most horses are aware of where the other horses are. That means they *know* if the others are in the paddock, in the stall, in the arena, or out on a trail with another rider.

Dominant or lead horses are often concerned with being first or leading the way when you're walking together or riding out in the woods. If they didn't care about their position in the group, based on their personality or their place in the social hierarchy, they wouldn't care whether they were at the front or back of the line. Typically, you'll see that more *passive* horses don't take the lead, because they know their place in the hierarchy and accept that a more dominant horse takes charge. This also gives them a sense of security.

You can also observe this *we-understanding* among horses when the herd dynamic changes. This might happen when new horses are introduced, others are removed, or when one passes away. It takes time for them to reposition themselves and shift the hierarchy, and you'll often see that this causes stress. Most horses feel safest with what they know, once a sense of calm and balance has been established in their daily life.

In my experience, horses are in balance because they live in the *now*.

They spend most of their waking hours eating.

They require contact, from other horses or humans, and need some form of stimulation.

If they don't get it from their humans, they'll create it themselves, often by playing with each other out in the paddock. When we, as their owners, and therefore also as their *masters*, change their balance, the horse must find a way to restore that balance on its own. As humans, we can disrupt their balance on both physical and psychological levels.

You can physically affect your horse through training, and this will typically show up as your horse having to compensate for your imbalances, which often results in it developing a stronger and weaker side. That's why I always feel it's essential for the rider to look at themselves, their posture in the saddle, and how they carry their weight, and take responsibility before they start wondering, becoming frustrated, or even blaming the horse for what are often seen as flaws in the horse's performance. Unfortunately, this is something I encounter all too often in my work.

You'll also affect your horse mentally, in the sense that it will always absorb the energies you emit. I believe that most emotions are controlled from the brain and sent downward to the center of the abdomen—a place that, in more alternative circles, is known as the *solar plexus center*. This is the energy center in the body that generates power and represents the body's largest magnetic field, both outward to the world and inward to our internal systems. In this way, the solar plexus functions like a battery, sending energy to the rest of the body and to the chakras that are connected to our aura. In addition to this, the *heart center*, which exists in its energetic realm, also affects the horse. Together, these two centers radiate energy into the human magnetic field, and this is what the horse picks up on.

Another area where a person may carry an imbalance is the physical body. Horses are affected by how the rider bears their weight in the saddle. And because the horse wants to cooperate and perform for its person, it will attempt to do what the rider is asking—using its body to interpret what we call *signals*.

If the rider collapses slightly to the right in the saddle, the horse may either find it easier to work on that side or it might feel blocked and unable to access space, freedom, or forward motion on that side.

I often see horses overcompensating on the opposite side, in this case, the left, to maintain balance for both them and the rider.

In both a physical and psychological sense, horses are constantly compensating for the rider's *flaws and limitations*. This is one of the reasons I consider them to be among the most caring and generous animals I've ever worked with. They are so thoughtful and cooperative —always trying to stay in sync with us, day after day in training—until, eventually, they either can't do it anymore physically and are forced to stop, or they end up with a rider who doesn't understand them, and they finally feel compelled to protest. Sometimes, this may even result in them bucking the rider off.

It is in the horse's nature to maintain balance, both physically and mentally, as part of a team. To give a concrete example: if you lean too far back in the saddle and sit heavily on your seat bones, you may end up locking your horse's hindquarters, preventing it from producing the impulse you're asking for. In response, your horse might shift more weight onto its forehand and drop its head to balance against the pressure coming from behind, which, over time, can cause strain in the front legs and shoulders. My hope in sharing this is that you, as the reader, will choose to work even more collaboratively with your horse moving forward, and remember this simple truth:

Whatever you don't do, your horse will try to do for both of you.

Changes in the Horse's Physical Balance

My experience has shown me that most horses are naturally either right-handed or left-handed in their approach. That means they will always have a dominant, stronger side, and a weaker, less coordinated side. You can usually see this clearly when lunging the horse or riding in circles.

Very few horses distribute their weight evenly, with a 25% load on each of their four legs, allowing them to carry themselves in perfect balance. Because horses are so focused on maintaining equilibrium, they instantly go into *overdrive* the moment a rider gets on their back.

And to this day, I have never seen a rider who sits in perfect balance. To achieve this would mean sitting entirely centered, with weight equally distributed to both sides—in every part of the body: the head, shoulders, arms, and the contact through the reins to the horse's mouth. It includes the position of the upper body, whether the rider hunches or rounds their back, and whether the pelvis tilts forward, backward, or rotates to one side.

It involves whether the hips twist, whether both legs are the same length, and whether the rider carries equal weight in both feet. Because we—as babies—must rotate through the birth canal or are pulled quickly out of the womb via C-section, it's almost impossible to avoid some form of rotation or imbalance in our bodies. If these issues are not addressed early in life, they can become ingrained over the years and lead to more pronounced physical misalignments.

That's why I love treating newborns with craniosacral therapy and deeply admire the mothers who take their babies to a chiropractor right away, because they already understand this connection. If the neck or pelvis is blocked in an infant, it can affect the digestive system, and I often see babies who are suffering from *colic*. The medical world still doesn't fully know what to do about it, but fortunately, I see more parents recognizing the link between physical imbalances and stomach issues. I can't scientifically prove that the same applies to horses. But I *have* seen and treated enough horses to say this: when their neck is blocked, there's often a related restriction in the lower back or sacrum. And when that happens, there is no *flow*—no energetic connection—in either direction.

The moment you sit on your horse, it will try to hold the balance for *both* of you. In addition to focusing on the exercises you're asking for in training, it now also must concentrate on keeping you both upright. And the only way it can do that is by compensating.

We humans do the same thing. If you broke your right foot, for example, you would automatically start relying more on your left side. Over time, your left leg may become stronger and develop into your dominant side, but your spine might begin to shift out of alignment. You may start to feel tension in your lower back on the left, or even in your shoulder and neck. This is why, when I'm told a horse has a behavior problem, the very first thing I do is investigate the rider's role. Are they helping their horse stay balanced—both from the saddle and the ground, mentally as well as physically?

Another situation where it becomes clear to me just how focused the horse is on its physical balance is when a horse is interpreted as being *afraid of the farrier*. Of course, if a horse has experienced a traumatic or forceful event in the past, its nervous system will remember that moment as highly unpleasant. Since the nervous system stores anything it registers as a shock or trauma, the horse will become re-traumatized every time it encounters a similar situation, which, in this case, will happen every time the farrier comes. Most horses have shown me that what truly provokes anxiety is the sensation of *having the legs taken from underneath me. What if I fall?*

They send me this feeling in images, and I receive a wave of fear from them. Sometimes I hold my breath or feel a sudden jolt of alarm. And I understand them. I would feel the same fear if someone suddenly tipped me over without giving me any say in the matter. My best advice to you, if you know your horse tends to fall onto the forehand during training, is this: if it's scared of the farrier or doesn't want to lift its legs, you'll often find that the legs it's most reluctant to give up are the front legs. That makes perfect sense to me. If the horse carries most of its weight on the forehand, lifting a front leg will make it feel like it's about to fall forward, face-first.

Similarly, if your horse tends to carry more weight in the hindquarters, it will likely be more anxious about giving up a hind leg. That's why I encourage you to become more aware of how your horse rests when standing still. Notice where it carries its weight and try to help it shift that weight before lifting a leg. Avoid starting with the leg it's resting on. Instead, begin with a leg that the horse can more easily *spare*, so it can maintain its balance without fear or struggle.

In every situation, if you start to focus on your horse's need to be physically balanced, you may begin to sense more deeply with it. You might start to *feel* what it's like to walk on just two or three legs out of four. This awareness may help you better understand your horse's behavior on different surfaces, when walking uphill or downhill, being loaded into a trailer, standing on a wash rack, jumping, or carrying a rider. I hope that this brings you to a deeper understanding: in 99% of the cases where you might believe your horse has a behavioral problem, what it's trying to do... is stay physically balanced.

Changes in the Horse's Emotional Balance

As I mentioned earlier, most horses want peace and order. In their daily life in the paddock, in their work as riding horses, and in their place within the social hierarchy. You should know that your horse has a sense of hierarchy, even if it lives alone in its paddock. Horses don't need to stand side by side to communicate. They are entirely aware of who is who and can sense the energies others emit from several meters away from their physical body.

In my experience, most horses prefer consistency. It creates calm, balance, and a sense of safety. It's no different from children who like having a school schedule. Or perhaps you prefer knowing exactly what to do when you arrive at work every day. There's nothing more stressful, or for some, unsettling, than not knowing the plan, the framework, or the structure. And the same goes for most horse personalities.

This also means that your horse may experience stress when there are changes in its daily routine. One of the most significant stressors for a horse is moving to a new place. First, it has to say goodbye to its herd and everything familiar. Then it must adjust to new smells, sounds, stalls, paddocks, and more. Additionally, it must relate to the new horses at the facility and establish its place in the hierarchy. And then there are the latest people in the stable, whose energy it also needs to process.

Some horses, for one reason or another, are moved many times during their lifetime. And sometimes it just becomes too much for them. One way they try to find balance and cope with the stress building up in their system is by sleeping, eating, or developing stereotypical behaviors. This could include crib-biting, running their teeth along the bars repeatedly, chewing on the edges of the stall, or kicking the walls—simply because they don't know what to do with the over-stimulation they're experiencing. In the worst cases, this kind of stress can even result in stomach ulcers, as I've seen in some of the horses I've worked with.

Another factor that can disrupt a horse's emotional balance is having to relate to multiple riders. This may happen, for instance, when a horse is sold and must adjust to a new rider. Or when you, as an owner, choose to have more than one person ride your horse. Fortunately, most horses enjoy having a part-time rider. They know that the part-time rider can do things with them that their owner may not be able to. They understand they might get to go out into the forest more often because they have someone else riding them.

But in some cases, I meet horses that become extremely confused when they have to deal with more than one person. This is especially true for Sensitive horses, who in many ways act like *co-dependencies* and tend to bond deeply with one single person. These horses don't want to relate to multiple energies, moods, riding styles, and so on. They feel that the task is already big enough with their current rider.

Based on this knowledge, I would like to emphasize that horses exhibit different temperaments throughout their lives. This becomes apparent depending on their personality type. Some horses can tolerate more than others—just like people. Some horses can handle moving three times in a year. Others become stressed or unsettled and may start showing stereotypical behaviors as a result. Some horses become anxious when they arrive at a competition venue, simply because there's so much going on and everything might feel unfamiliar. Other horses don't react at all and behave completely *cool* both in the warm-up arena and in the competition ring.

All the horses I've communicated with are, of course, deeply connected to their sense of *self*. This is reflected in their basic needs, including food, touch, training, or stimulation, as well as their need to release tension, such as through relaxation, treatments, or letting go of overstimulation.

Horses are also aware that there is a *you*. Meaning, they're very attuned to you as their friend and partner—one way or another. They know everything you're thinking, even if you don't say it out loud. They sense energy and vibrations. They know whether you're stressed, happy, worried, or angry. You don't even need to say a word. They feel the energy you bring. And they do this with everyone they meet. I see this especially in horses who dislike, for instance, the farrier or the vet.

You can try to fool them as many times as you like, but they've figured it out long before you think they have. I have a theory that they not only pick up on our intentions, but also on the vibration and energy we carry with us. For example, if I think to myself, *"Right now we're just standing here with this man,"* I still know deep down that he's the farrier, and I also know that in five minutes, he's planning to shoe the horse standing in front of us.

And suddenly, out of nowhere, I see the horse lunge toward the farrier, even though none of us have said anything. The horse has picked up on what we were planning.I've also seen this when a horse knows the vet is coming and starts getting restless in the stall, even though no one has told it verbally. They read our thoughts and emotions. And in that way, they sense our true intentions.

And finally, it is part of the horse's very nature that there must be a *we* for them to feel connected to a herd, because that's how they are wired. When part of a group or herd, it's less threatening to face a large predator, such as a dangerous lion. They can either distract it by running in different directions and solving the challenge together, or they can stand their ground as a group and appear stronger that way.It's not so different for us humans. Most people who are afraid of standing alone with their opinions tend to say things like *people also think* or form *we-statements*. For example, in a situation where you need to set a boundary, you might be more inclined to say: *"I'd like you to remember to clean up after yourself in the aisle... and actually, others have mentioned they'd like that too."*

In that way, it becomes less frightening to speak up and stand by your own opinion. But if you flip the situation around, the message can quickly become more threatening to the receiver, because within that sentence lies an unspoken *us versus you*. Based on all of this, I see horses as individuals with uniquely beautiful minds and souls. Through their way of being in the world, I hope you are someone who aims to understand them truly, so that there's room for you, me, and *we* out there. And maybe, just maybe, let that thought and energy ripple outward like waves in water—from your energy field and mine—to be picked up by everyone around us, whether they realize it or not.

Case Study: The Mare Nád – Showing Us Her Way of Reacting to Imbalances on Both a Physical and Mental Level, *In collaboration with veterinarian Anette Munch and chiropractor Jacob Schrøder Anderse*

Veterinarian Anette Munch once had a long-term patient at her clinic. The dog's owner had brought a friend along, who said she sensed that the dog had a tumor in one of its legs. Anette thought the friend was *crazy* and dismissed it as nonsense. But despite her strong skepticism, she decided to take an X-ray. There, she found a bone tumor, exactly where the friend had said it would be. The only options were to amputate the leg or take a biopsy. The friend offered to heal the dog, and she managed to suppress the tumor for several years. At one point, the cancer even disappeared through healing. Eventually, however, the tumor became too aggressive, began to grow again, and sadly, the dog had to be euthanized. However, the alternative treatment had significantly extended the dog's life and provided a good quality of life for both the animal and its owner.

This experience deeply challenged Anette's skepticism and marked the beginning of her path in working with animal telepathy. It also sparked her interest in the spiritual world. The first time Anette contacted me was in the fall of 2015. She waited five months for me to come. Although she was somewhat skeptical of my work, she was curious enough to want my help. She had read an article about me in an Icelandic horse magazine, and something resonated in her heart and soul while reading about *The woman who could talk to horses.* I offered to send one of my skilled consultants to help her sooner, but Anette refused. It had to be me.

Eventually, the day came, and I traveled to Jutland, mainland Denmark, where Anette and her husband, chiropractor Jacob Schrøder Andersen, live on their lovely farm. I communicated with all eight of their beautiful horses. And it was spot on for everyone. I described their gaits, strengths, and weaknesses, as well as their personalities; exactly as Anette knew them. I spoke about their health, where they were tight or locked, what they had struggled with in the past, and where they would benefit from future treatment. Anette was genuinely impressed. She thought, *This works.*

The telepathic sessions moved Anette to the point where she realized that if she could learn even a fraction of what I had done with her horses, it could greatly support her daily work as a veterinarian. She later enrolled in my animal telepathy education program in the city of Aarhus. Even there, Anette remained skeptical, wondering how all of us could do this, especially herself. But as the months went on, I watched her let go, *switch off the brain,* and instead feel and sense. She began delivering one beautiful telepathic session after another, together with her fellow students and the animals. One of the horses closest to Anette's heart—her heart horse and her heartache—is the Icelandic mare Nád.

Nád arrived in Denmark still in her mother's womb. Anette purchased her from the person who had imported the pregnant mare. At the time, Nád was just six months old. She wasn't trained under saddle until later. She first served as a broodmare and had two foals before Anette bought her at age six. Nád was named when she was six weeks old. *Nád* means *The One Who Leads*. Later, Anette would discover that the name was incredibly fitting. She was a born leader, a true queen. Anette has had her for seven years. She brought her home immediately, at the time living on a farm in the city of Lystrup, near Denmark's second-largest city, Aarhus.

Anette soon had the opportunity to place a rider on Nád. One month into training, just as Anette thought everything was going well, Nád suddenly began refusing to move. It started with the rider, but quickly escalated. She also refused to lift her legs. It soon became a stalemate—Nád didn't want to do anything in the stable or with the riders. The farrier checked her and said everything looked fine. Anette's husband, chiropractor Jacob Schrøder Andersen, found some tension in the shoulder area. That's when Anette called me again, needing help to uncover the root of the issue.

First, I explained to her that the tension extended up into the neck area, locking the front legs and affecting Nád's balance. It was as if she were wearing a sweater that was too tight—everything felt constricted. I also saw tension in the jaw region. The reason she refused to move was partly because she felt heavy on the forehand, and that imbalance had always been a tendency of hers. But what I found even more interesting was that Nád felt betrayed by Anette. As Nád told me: *"It was supposed to be just the two of us, and then she just put another rider on me, without asking!"*

In our first session together, Nád said: *"I want to go out 2–3 times a week. If I can't, then I'll stand still. I only want to be ridden by Anette."* At the time, Anette hadn't listened. She had assigned another rider, thinking it would be the best solution for Nád. In protest, Nád walked to the corner of the arena, stood still, and just stared into the corner.

And she stayed there. The physical side of things is one thing, but for Nád, the emotional and mental side is just as important. Anette was too busy. With a bustling veterinary clinic, her farm, and life as a wife and mother, she had her hands full. Nád wanted her to learn how to slow down and be present in the moment. Nád became a mirror for Anette, reflecting what she needed most: to pause.

If Anette wasn't fully present, and if her thoughts were elsewhere, then Nád didn't want to be around her. Then it didn't matter. Nád is a *Queen*. The kind who leads the others in the field, who, with a mere flick of an ear, can split the herd or guide them all to follow her. She is a dignified matriarch—a mare whose energetic presence is immense. Truly immense. And when you meet her, you instantly feel the urge to lower your head in humility, because her energy can quite literally take your breath away. No wonder that if I, as a human, can feel it so strongly, then other horses feel it too. They sense her full energy: her strength, her will, her power, and her love, as well as her unwavering resolve.

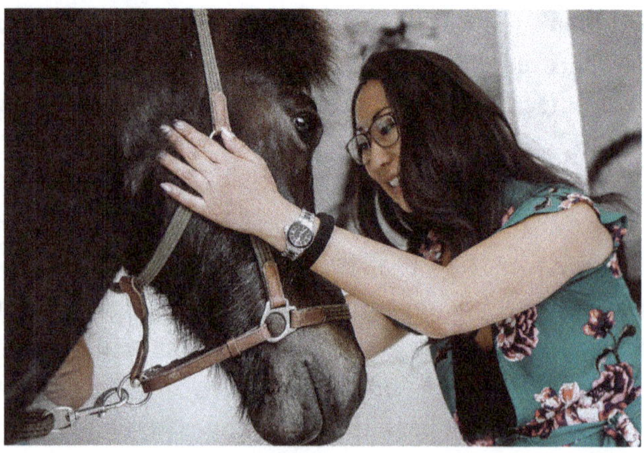

During my second visit with Nád and Anette, one of the significant challenges was that Nád refused to lift her legs. We had a long and meaningful conversation about Nád's balance, and why she couldn't shift her weight back onto her hindquarters when her SI joint was locked. I gave her a series of craniosacral therapy treatments, and immediately afterward, we were able to lift all four legs without resistance.

To me, it made perfect sense: when a prey animal's only real means of escape is to run, then of course a Queen like Nád would fiercely protect her ability to do just that. Naturally, you mustn't *take her legs away from her.* And to her, lifting them felt like exactly that, like taking them away. When Anette lifted one of her legs and Nád felt pain in her lower back, her instinct was to run away from the pain. But she couldn't, not with her leg lifted. So, refusing to lift her legs was the safest option. I showed Anette how to shift Nád's weight back and forth using nothing but her energy—no force—so that Nád could feel safe and in control of her own body again.

That day, Nád also showed me a pain in her left jawbone, and told me: *"I have an intense headache, and the pain is coming from my jaw."* She showed me—on her own body—that she felt locked in her atlas and first and second cervical vertebrae on the left side. She also felt locked in her shoulders and said she was tired of feeling tension and restriction both in her forehand and hindquarters. It explained clearly why she didn't want her legs touched or lifted. Nád, the herd leader, who had always been so emotionally balanced and generous, suddenly began displaying aggressive behavior in the paddock, biting and kicking at the others. Anette had never seen her act this way before. She was on the verge of giving up. There were numerous issues, and she struggled to make sense of them all.

Chiropractor Jacob Schrøder Andersen stepped in and treated the exact areas I had described, particularly the atlas, axis, and shoulders. He found the same blockages I had mentioned, which aligned with what he had previously observed in her body. He performed some adjustments. What I had sensed matched perfectly with what he found.

Anette recalled she had suspected Nád had headaches, and when I mentioned the jaw tension, it confirmed her intuition. Gradually, Nád became calmer, more cooperative, and began lifting her legs again without resistance. But there was no shift on the emotional or mental level—so Anette removed the rider.

One day, Anette tried to take her for a walk. But Nád refused to move at all. Anette became frustrated and turned back, intending to return her to the paddock. Out on the walk, Nád wouldn't go forward, and Anette began to wonder whether Nád was *"just messing with her."* Still, she held on to what I had said. She remembered my words about the tension in the jaw, and she knew it had to be addressed. Later, when Anette had to take her other horse, Feikir, to the veterinary hospital, she brought Nád along as moral support. While they had her there, Anette asked the vets to check her as well, since Nád still refused to work under saddle.

The vets quickly noted that she was displaying a constant *pain face*. They pointed out her flared nostrils, something Nád does when she's angry. During a lameness exam, they were able to flex all four legs. Their verdict: Nád would never be a riding horse again.

They believed the cause of her pain was a tooth putting pressure on her neck, and that it needed to come out. So, they decided to extract it. But during surgery, the tooth wouldn't come out. They had to drill a hole through the jawbone and hammer it out. This left a direct channel from her oral cavity into the sinus, and an infection developed in her jaw afterward. Nád was set back drastically, and the next six months became a long and difficult fight to manage the infection and the pain it caused. Anette believes the vet made a mistake by removing the tooth in the first place.

Nád was now entirely out of action due to the operation, and time passed. While she was healing, Anette once again reached out to me for help. I had no idea what had happened in detail, but Nád said to me: *"Why did you do this to me? I feel like I've been taken out of the game. Why?"*

Nád was angry and frustrated. Naturally, I had to ask Anette afterward what had happened, because what I felt from Nád was an agitated and indignant horse. I had seen her be firm and commanding before, yes, but never *angry*.

During this period, Anette, of course, couldn't ride her. And out in the paddock, Nád was more aggressive than ever, especially after the surgery. She had zero tolerance. The other horses barely had to *look* at her before she put them in their place.

Anette was heartbroken, and I told her that, in my view, there were three main factors behind Nád's behavior:

1. **Nád's physical imbalances and discomfort**, including tension and misalignment in her shoulders, neck, pelvis, and jaw.
2. **Nád's emotional mirroring of Anette's inner state.** When Anette was stressed and overwhelmed, Nád would shut down entirely and refuse to engage.
3. **Nád's recovery from a traumatic jaw surgery and tooth extraction**, which left her fighting to regain her place in the herd hierarchy.

Today, Anette and Nád have come a long way. Anette has done a lot of work with her, and now she can lift all four legs without any trouble. Nád shows no signs of discomfort when her legs are lifted. Anette can now ride her at a walk in the arena at home, and they've been doing lots of groundwork together.

Some days, Nád still flares her nostrils and looks like a bull ready to charge. On others, she's cooperative and connected. She swings between moods, day to day. But Anette feels that mutual respect is returning. She dreams of taking Nád on trail rides in the summertime, and so she's now working on loading her into the trailer to create a new *now*. As the years have passed, Anette is slowly realizing what I've always felt: Nád reflects how Anette is doing, because Anette's stress also fluctuates.

After the infection in her entire jaw cavity following the tooth extraction, a new veterinarian entered the picture, and that's when everything changed. A vet who truly wanted what was best for Nád. And when Nád feels seen and acknowledged, that's when things start moving in the right direction. On her bad days, Nád doesn't want to lift her legs or stand still for the vet. On her good days, she's willing. Anette now has the impression that Nád uses her legs to say: *"If you can't take proper care of yourself, then I can't help you either."*

Anette has discovered that when she thinks: *"Now we need to get going I haven't been down there in four days!"* Nád wants nothing to do with her. She doesn't tolerate dominance or being handled on Anette's terms. Nád seems to *punish* her. She shows up bright and alert, but as soon as Anette starts setting controlling expectations, Nád shuts down. She still wants the connection, but only if it's not forced or willfully imposed. If Anette doesn't show up as a clear leader, firm but fair, then Nád won't engage. Anette has learned that she needs to be consistent and grounded in how she interacts with her.

As she often says during our conversations: *"She'll run circles around me if I don't step up. I must be someone worthy of her. If I get too soft or indecisive, leaving everything up to her, then she gets frustrated again."*

Nád no longer throws her weight around in the paddock. She's returned to her old leadership style; quiet and commanding, where a flick of an ear or a specific look is enough to move the others. She even tolerates others standing next to her while she eats.

The last time I saw Nád was in June 2018. She was physically at ease. A happy horse, eager to do things with Anette. She could feel Anette's joy in everything they did, whether from the ground or in the saddle.

The physical journey and the uncertainty of whether she would live or die have been deeply exhausting for Anette. But in those moments when we used animal communication as a tool, and Anette acted on what Nád expressed, there was real progress.

It was only when Anette truly began to listen to what Nád was saying that things started turning around. Today, Anette uses telepathy in her veterinary practice. She's much more in tune with her intuition now. If she gets a gut feeling about something, she takes it seriously and investigates further.

Sometimes, she even asks pet owners if they're open to trying animal communication. If they say yes, it becomes a full session where Anette works with the animal in a deeper, more energetic way. Mostly, she blends telepathy with her academic knowledge.

For example, when she has an animal hospitalized, she'll sometimes *check in* telepathically to gauge both the diagnostic and emotional state of the patient. She has found this to be incredibly helpful, and it has become an integral part of her workflow.

Anette also reflects on the broader trends in the veterinary field. She notes that it's becoming a female-dominated profession, with approximately 80% of women currently enrolled in veterinary school. She believes this shift may open up more space for telepathy to become accepted. In her experience, women tend to be more open to these intuitive practices than men. And she sees animal communication becoming more mainstream and less taboo over time. As this happens, she believes more veterinarians will begin to integrate it into their work.

One of her colleagues, another veterinarian who ran a clinic in the second-largest city of Denmark, called Aarhus, had to take a leave due to stress. Afterward, she studied Chinese medicine and began integrating spiritual approaches into her practice. Today, she's highly successful and works holistically, drawing many clients who are seeking something more. Anette is also committed to letting this part of her work grow. Of course, it should never compromise scientific integrity, but she firmly believes in honoring both worlds: the clinical and the energetic.

It is important to remember that neither aspect gets forgotten; intuition on the one hand, and evidence on the other. That you might feel something intuitively, and then later confirm it through diagnostics. You undergo an endoscopy or have a blood test performed.

This provides you with data that may help you reach a diagnosis much sooner, whereas previously, you may not have had any idea where the pain was located. You'd be left guessing whether it might be in a particular region of the body.

That uncertainty could lead you to take four different samples when you could have taken just one if the animal had been able to point you in the right direction. Anette believes that skeptical veterinarians need to experience animal communication firsthand to understand it truly. She didn't believe in it at first either. She wasn't particularly spiritual until later in life.

She now believes it's about being open. Not insisting that everything must come from an academic framework. Veterinarians need to witness a moment of communication where, afterwards, it becomes clear: *"There's no logical reason I should have known that, unless something else was at play."* For many, that moment feels unnatural, but also undeniable.

Anette feels that getting to know me has taught her a lot—on many levels. She has no plans to stop working with my abilities.

The last time I visited her, Nád told me: *"In four months, there will be a new now."* That was in January. And that's what we find ourselves in today. Anette is looking forward to building a professional collaboration, both in client consultations and in offering courses and lectures for interested veterinarians in Eastern and Central Jutland, which is the mainland of Denmark. She believes that's what it will take to move things forward.

Ultimately, Anette feels that veterinarians need to be open, but also that this must come from client demand. At the clinic, they have digital X-rays that deliver instant results. They have in-house labs for immediate bloodwork results.

So, the tools are there. It's a collaboration I look forward to, and one that I hope can be expanded nationwide in the years to come. A relationship that can help bridge worlds, showing that academic medicine and animal communication can coexist in a partnership that serves the well-being of both animals and their owners.

Chapter 5

Ride With Your Heart

"Be the change you wish to see in the world."
— **Mahatma Gandhi**

When the relationship between a mother and her newborn is healthy, they enter into a state of symbiosis, where the baby is unaware of a distinct *you* or *me*. For the child, there exists only *US*. The mother has nourished the baby and has, without question, absorbed what the mother has taken in. It has heard her heartbeat, hopefully for nine months, and knows the rhythm of her heart, her scent, her voice, her energy, and her emotions. And most parents in a healthy relationship with their child also know that you don't just trade the child in because it doesn't meet your expectations.

As a parent, you get to see your child exactly as they are. That's also one of the fascinating parts of becoming a parent; meeting your child, your offspring, and discovering, *"Who are you, little soul or being?"*

Over time, the child will exhibit certain behaviors, a distinct personality, and a unique temperament that can elicit different reactions from parents. For example, the child might have a fiery temper, and the parents may wonder where this trait originated. They may be shocked when they encounter such anger. And as parents, they can either meet the child in that anger or attempt to allow it. Unspoken, they may try to teach the child that anger is not allowed in their home. This can happen by sending the child to their room, putting them in the corner, giving them a timeout, and so on. And only when the child behaves correctly again are they allowed to rejoin the family's activities. Quietly and subtly, the message becomes: only then do you get to belong again.

All children cooperate. And in this way, a child's mind is remarkably similar to a horse's. Both are entirely pure, trusting, in some ways naïve, loving, and they seek to be part of a herd—to belong. They will do everything they can to ensure this belonging, because being part of a group brings a sense of safety. And with safety comes the ability to exist in the world and, at its most basic level, to survive.

Most horse owners or riders I've met over the years in my work in the horse world have shown me that when they buy a horse, they're not just buying *a horse*. They are acquiring a friend, a soulmate, a baby, a child, a playmate, or a true teacher. Some even feel that it was the horse who chose them. And for reasons they can't always explain, they sense or feel that the horse has something to say, even if they can't quite put words to what it is they're feeling. The horse becomes their most cherished companion. A friend with whom they spend all their free time. Some are even lucky enough to make a living being around horses every day in the stables. With their horse, they feel free. They feel they can be precisely as they are. They feel loved. They feel understood. There is no judgment, only a sense of being present in the moment, and an experience of pure love. In the rush of everyday life, horses can give us all of this, without even thinking about it. For them, they are simply *being* with us.

Horses offer us the opportunity to feel ourselves through being with them. And precisely because we breathe and, hopefully, are forced to be present in the now that we share with them, the experience becomes deeply calming and, for many, almost addictive. Many horses have shown me that they are puzzled by how their humans sometimes *cut the connection* to them. This typically happens when the rider's mind drifts elsewhere, away from what the horse and rider are doing together in the moment.

A recent research study by Italian scientist Paolo Baragli provides evidence that horses and humans can exchange energy in a way that allows their heart rhythms to synchronize when they are together. This should be physically impossible, as the average resting pulse for a horse is 30–36 beats per minute, whereas a human's are around 50–90 beats per minute. For me, this study is groundbreaking, as it measures energetic exchange in a way we haven't seen before.

For several years, my motto has been *"ride with your heart."* I chose it because I wish to encourage riders to think less and feel more. When you stop thinking, you become more capable of being present in the now. Your brain can only hold one thought at a time. We women like to think we can multitask, but we really can't. What we can do is shift between tasks very quickly, maybe faster than men, but the brain still produces only one set of images at a time while we speak.

In my experience, horses pick up on the images and energies that we emit. They receive everything we think and feel, even if we're not consciously aware that this exchange is happening. When you're in the now, you naturally awaken your senses. You begin to SEE what's in front of you truly. It might be a beautiful sunset, or a clearing in the forest as you ride your horse. You begin to SMELL what surrounds you. The damp forest floor beneath you or the scent of home cooking wafting from nearby houses. You start to HEAR your environment differently, the birds singing or the sound of your breath. You begin to TASTE, even if it's just the taste of your breath, or the scent of your horse's sweat as it trots beneath you. You become aware of what you FEEL. Perhaps it's the seat of the saddle or a tired arm. Maybe it's a stiff neck after a long day at the computer.

All of this, you receive, consciously or unconsciously, while your breathing slows down. And most people associate these moments with a feeling of HAPPINESS. When you think back to a memory where you felt happy, wasn't that also connected to a feeling? And feeling is one of our most vital senses when it comes to sending and receiving energy. As a rider, when you open your senses and connect with yourself, you also connect with your horse, and in that connection, you experience your shared *WE*. Some riders are on an ambitious journey with their horse. They may be competitors, and whether they're aiming for a novice class or Grand Prix, most are in it to win. Few people enter competitions just for fun. Most have some form of hope that they'll perform reasonably well, whether that's to prove something to others or themselves.

My wish is to make space within those ambitions for a greater focus on the horse as an equal partner. If the horse is doing at least half the work, shouldn't it, at the very least, be heard? Maybe I'm ahead of my time in thinking this way. But to me, it feels only natural, because I can listen to, see, and feel what the horses *say* and feel.

When ambition overtakes connection, the energy becomes one of dominance and force. I see a jagged, sharp energy that creates neither safety nor flow for rider or horse. And even if they're not fully aware of it yet, I often see riders lose something of themselves, and their self-confidence, when they try to force the horse into obedience. When you lose the openness and sensitivity toward your horse that I'm passionate about helping riders maintain, you also risk losing something you were born with a natural openness and a love for simply *being*.

About the Perfect Match

In your relationship with your horse, you may find your soulmate: your best friend, your mirror, and your greatest love. When riders ask me if I believe in the perfect match, my answer is always: the perfect match doesn't exist. What does exist is the ideal learning experience, and through that, the match becomes perfect.

With the knowledge I have today, I see everything as a learning process. Even when it hurts or when experiences are painful or disappointing. And of course, also in the good and happy moments—the ones I call the *star moments* in my life. Thankfully, I have many of those. Naturally, by analyzing a horse's personality profile, I can quite quickly assess whether the horse matches the rider's temperament. But deep down, I believe that the rider always chooses the horse, and the horse chooses its rider, and that choice is never random, no matter what the future holds for them.

I'm often asked to help evaluate a horse during the buying process. This gives the rider or prospective owner a chance to get a sense of the horse before it arrives in its new home or stable. I'm happy to help with this, because I believe a horse should come to stay. I don't want the horse to become a *bad purchase* and end up being sold again and relocated. That causes an imbalance in the horse's psyche and unnecessary stress. Often, it's the next buyer who ends up paying the price for a horse that became stressed due to a failed sale. Other times, it's the buyer who feels deceived. A horse can look sweet, gentle, and lovely in a photo. It may behave well during a trial ride. But as soon as you bring it home, you realize the horse has several *bad habits* or is far more alert or reactive than you expected, and you regret your purchase and feel heartbroken.

Sometimes the seller may not have been entirely honest. Maybe the vet checks were flawless, but the horse has had recurring gastric ulcers that weren't disclosed. If you end up with a sensitive horse that's already been moved several times, the stress of another transition might trigger those issues all over again. Unfortunately, this is something the new owner often only realizes too late. This is why it would greatly benefit many horses if riders truly understood what they were purchasing before making a decision.

There are also cases where an *ambitious rider* is reluctant to admit that the dream horse they purchased might not be bred for the kind of performance they were hoping to achieve together. Perhaps the horse doesn't have the physical ability, or maybe it isn't mentally stable enough for the pressures of competitive riding. It's painful when your trainer, vet, or therapist has to tell you: *"I don't think this horse will ever reach the level you're aiming for."* But even here, there's a learning opportunity.

You can choose to lower your ambitions with this horse and pursue your dreams with another. Or you can choose, in sorrow and disappointment, to walk away from your ambition, or your love for the horse. Either way, your choices reflect your responsibility for your feelings, and you will grow through the hard decisions, regardless of the outcome.

Through my work and the many excellent opportunities I'm lucky to have as a speaker and presenter, I try every day to share this message: Horses act only in accordance with their nature. There are no horses that manipulate, misbehave intentionally, or wake up in the morning plotting to make life difficult for their rider. As I've said before, horses haven't developed that part of the brain that allows such thoughts.

If you, as a future owner, take the time to understand your horse's personality, you'll be better equipped to recognize what it needs throughout the sales process. Maybe it needs mental preparation for what's to come. Perhaps it would feel safer being transported with a companion pony when moving to a new stable.

We spend days helping our children adjust to daycare. I still don't understand why it should be any different for our *four-legged children*. I think it would be far more humane if the previous owner brought the horse to its new home, along with one or more herd mates, and stayed with the horse for a few days to ease the transition. Then, when the horse has settled, the previous owner can leave, knowing that it arrived safely and calmly, and a new chapter can begin with the new owner.

Fortunately, in most cases I observe, riders honestly do try to make it work with their horses—both on the ground and in daily interactions, as well as in training. These are, thankfully, the most common cases. Of course, misunderstandings and conflicts can still arise. Because the truth is, your horse also has an opinion. It can say yes, and it can say no. It can communicate gently or with more force and clarity. All of this depends on what the horse was born to be—its personality profile.

If you, as a rider and horse owner, choose to see your horse as a being who can teach you something simply by being itself, then you, too, will grow on a personal level. The first step is to get to know your horse and accept it as it is. If you can fall in love with your horse for who it truly is, then you have the foundation for a perfect match, and a bond of love that can last a lifetime.

Chapter 6

Personal and Spiritual Development for Horse and Rider

"If having a soul means being able to feel love and loyalty and gratitude, then animals are better off than a lot of humans."
– James Herriot

We live in a time where an increasing amount of people are turning inward. They ask themselves whether life makes sense to them or not, and whether they are happy and content. It can involve anything from their job, partner, friends, and much more. We are fortunate to live in an era where we have the luxury of choice in a way that previous generations, just 50 years ago, did not. They were more hardworking, even more loyal in many areas, simply because they didn't have as many options as we do today. They were persistent, and many of them lacked the opportunity or privilege to choose something differently. You didn't just get divorced, move house, or change jobs *just because.*

When I started my therapist training many years ago, it was still taboo to go to therapy or see a psychologist. Today, having a therapist is entirely normal in the U.S., and more people in Europe receive support

131

through the paid healthcare system to talk to someone. That could be a doctor, psychologist, psychiatrist, or other professionals.

We may suffer more in our souls now, or we may become more stressed in a fast-paced world. That's what the Danish statistics suggest when we look at the number of people suffering from stress. But it may also be that we are in the midst of a new kind of movement, where humans want more balance and begin to question aspects of their lives.

As part of this process, I repeatedly see horses unconsciously assisting in that journey. And once one door opens, we quickly realize that many more doors begin to open. I don't know a single person who has shown even a slight interest in what others might call the *alternative*, who hasn't grown hungry for more. It might begin with a first *aha moment*, realizing that acupuncture works, even if they don't understand how. And because the Chinese have been practicing it for over 1,000 years, and our doctors now offer it, it has become more acceptable here too, even though no one can physically see the meridian lines used by acupuncturists and reflexologists.

Many women use acupuncture during childbirth because midwives are trained to give this form of pain relief. The next step might be yoga– to breathe and feel oneself. Some people become interested in meditation, mindfulness, or start consulting clairvoyants or spiritual mediums to find answers they can't yet find within themselves. Some start reading tarot cards, angel cards, seek out healers, or visit a numerologist. The alternative world is vast–and, like all fields, it has its share of good practitioners and less competent ones. What matters most is that it makes sense to the person seeking help, regardless of who they are.

Once we open our sensory awareness, we also become open to more. What *more* is will vary from person to person. Many of my students in my animal telepathy training fear that if they learn to talk with animals, they might also suddenly start seeing dead people. I always reassure them: you only develop the ability of *clairvoyance* when you're truly ready. And the ability to telepathically communicate has more to do with brain function and the senses than with seeing spirits. However, I also know that these two realms, both composed of energy, coexist hand in hand and side by side. When you open the door to one, the other tends to follow.

The key is knowing how to close it, how to discern, and how to feel in your body what is useful and what is not. Everything is good in moderation. I don't believe in an overdose of spirituality either. There's too significant a risk of losing your grounding and connection to reality, and that's not the point of learning to feel yourself or your animals. If we begin with the understanding that horses have a soul, and therefore also a personality, we've already come a long way. To me, this means I view horses with respect and as equals. All souls, in my view, have an equal right to exist in this world.

Personality and Partnership

For each of the personality types I work with, there are both strengths for you and your horse, as well as challenges. These challenges are what I call *the learning*, the lessons you're meant to go through with your horse. Initially, you may not perceive a challenge as a learning experience or a gift. But from my perspective, it is the greatest gift you can receive. If you can solve the challenge together with your horse, you will also solve similar challenges in other areas of your life.

For example, if you have a horse belonging to the royal category, such as *The Prince*, *The Princess*, *The King*, or *The Queen*—you typically have a dominant or lead horse. This means your horse needs you to show leadership. If you're insecure and unclear about what you want for the two of you, your horse will take over the leadership role to create balance between you, because you become a herd when you are together.

In my book *Understand Your Horse,* I go into further detail on how to form a true partnership with your horse and offer practical advice on how to build a resourceful connection with your horse, and thereby also with yourself.

Paolo Baragli has conducted a scientific study demonstrating that horses are individuals with personalities. Based on these different temperaments, the horses solved the same task in various ways. In the study, 26 horses were tested on a task that required them to retrieve food. Some horses took a direct route, while others took a more complicated one.

He observed that dominant horses reached the food reward faster, whereas sensitive and insecure horses took longer. Based on how quickly a horse completed the task, Baragli gained insight into each horse's cognitive approach. He concluded that the horses' personality types were directly linked to how they solved problems. Mental challenges such as spatial division also triggered physical responses due to emotional stimuli. These reactions, he found, were connected to the horse's personality type and behavior. He also noted that behavioral variations were often associated with the autonomic nervous system. For instance, sensitive horses tended to become nervous or anxious more easily. This research greatly supports my experiences with behavioral issues in horses.

The next point I find highly interesting, as part of a rider's personal development, is to examine the type of partnership you have with your horse. In *Understand Your Horse* I've carefully outlined the following relationship dynamics:

- **The Dominant (horse) & The Submissive (rider)**
- **The Teacher (horse) & The Student (rider)**
- **The Child (horse) & The Protector (rider)**
- **The Star (horse) & The Achiever (rider)**
- **The Connected (horse and rider)**

Here, I don't only look at your horse's personality, but also your way of being in the relationship with your horse. As with any relationship, there are constructive ways of being together. Miscommunication, misunderstanding, or projecting your traits onto your horse often leads to friction. For instance, you may see your horse as dominant because it exhibits traits you don't particularly like or feel comfortable with.

Depending on the dynamic you share with your horse, your relationship can become a catalyst for personal development if you choose to see it that way. Your relationship with your horse, regardless of its purpose, will continually evolve. You may find yourself in one partnership type at a certain point, and in another later, as you both grow and develop.

If you have a horse that seems dominant and you feel submissive, then you fall into the category I call *The Dominant (horse) and the Submissive (rider)*. The work lies in your opportunity to grow into a stronger leader for your horse. This means going through a process where your low self-esteem or lack of confidence begins to shift, allowing you to move toward a different kind of relationship once the original dynamic has become more balanced.

When this relationship type becomes healthy, you've become a better leader. You trust yourself, your judgment, and your abilities more. A few years later, you might want to compete with your horse–a horse you're now proud of. Perhaps he even has the personality profile of *The Prince*, and now you've moved into *The Star (horse) and The Achiever (rider)* dynamic. At this stage, your confidence and ambition have grown, and your goals have expanded in tandem with your personal development.

No single relationship type is more right or wrong than another. Being in a relationship is always a movement, like a wave that flows forward and pulls back. This shift depends on which personalities meet and what histories each individual brings. However, regardless of the partnership type you and your horse find yourselves in, there is always room for growth and personal development in your journey together.

Personal Growth

One of the main reasons people love spending time with horses is that, first and foremost, they get to be with a four-legged soul who accepts them precisely as they are. I often hear people, typically those who are also sensitive, say things like: *"Sometimes it's easier to be with animals than with humans. They don't judge."* We as humans enjoy the presence of horses because we are mirrored in them, and not least because horses, in their essence and being, are a gift in themselves. They are a gift because we can grow personally if we are open to the learning that horses offer us, often unconsciously learning how to be.

Personal growth, of course, requires openness and a willingness to look inward. I am entirely convinced that something greater than us. For example, the universe will ensure that this growth will happen for each of us in one way or another, or another example: a rider might repeatedly buy or receive horses that become ill and ultimately have to be put down. After horse number four, the rider might begin to see a pattern, whether they want to or not. The fact that it is the horses who *pay the price* for our learning only strengthens my desire for us to take good care of them while they are with us.

As mentioned earlier, in your relationship with your horse, or horses in general, you might automatically understand them, project onto them, or go into conflict with them when they show traits you find challenging to accept. This is precisely where I utilize my therapeutic background, and this aspect is vital to highlight. It bears many similarities to couple's therapy. Every time you're with other people, this mechanism is automatically activated, unless you're someone with a high degree of awareness or someone who has received a lot of psychological or therapeutic help to avoid projecting. The complexity of this work is both nerdy and exciting. From the six horse personality types I mentioned earlier, each comes with its strengths and challenges. However, it's usually the four *core personalities* that the horse is naturally born with that contain most of the resources.

· · ·

These four core personalities are:

- **The Playful Child**
- **The Sensitive One**
- **Princes and Princesses**
- **Kings and Queens**

I don't include the *Traumatized/Shut-Down Horse* or the *Rigid/Lazy Horse* as core personalities, since a horse isn't born traumatized or shut down. These are states that result from experiences that have affected the horse's nervous system and mind, or from situations that the horse still finds difficult to be in. Just like with people, a frozen trauma or a state of rigidity is a defense mechanism of the system when it freezes or *turns inward.*

If I focus only on the challenges tied to each horse's personality, then the *Playful Child* will typically struggle to concentrate or stand still in the grooming area. It may seem as if the horse is everywhere *but* with you and can appear somewhat intense if they get bored. Your horse might react by suddenly bolting, rearing up, or kicking out – all seemingly without reason.

If, on top of this, you are a sensitive and insecure rider who doesn't fully trust your inner leadership or judgment, it is almost inevitable that you will eventually respond in one of three ways:

1. **You try to *put the horse in its place,* because you won't accept that it behaves this way toward you.** You struggle to tolerate the fact that even your horse challenges you – when so many people already do in your everyday life.
2. **You become even more afraid of your horse and start questioning whether the horse is a good match for you at all.** This may lead you to give up and consider selling the horse.
3. **You become overly worried and protective.** You don't dare *discipline* the horse at all and instead look for external

causes to explain its behavior. For example, you might blame the environment, saying the horse reacted because someone turned on the radio, opened the arena gate, or walked too quickly down the stable aisle.

Depending on which of the three responses you're most likely to lean toward, you may naturally fall into one of the partnership dynamics, simply because your horse has *the Playful Child* personality type. In example number 1, you will typically fit into *the Star and Striver* dynamic. In example number 2, you may resonate more with *the Dominant and the Insecure*. And in example number 3, you will likely lean toward *the Child and the Protector*.

And let me be very clear: I do *not* in any way support the idea that any rider or horse owner should *put the horse in its place* through violence, frustration, or dominance. To me, authentic leadership is something entirely different—it's about showing the horse what you'd like from it in a respectful, balanced way, because horses, too, want to be understood and heard. Therefore, they also deserve to have their polite *"no thank you"* respected.

The complexity arises when your reaction determines what kind of relational dynamic you fit into. Thus, the tools required to transform behavioral issues into something constructive will be entirely different for each.

If your horse happens to be *The Sensitive One* and shows the *same* behavioral pattern as the *Playful Child*, your response may be quite different—perhaps because you more easily identify with this personality type. You'll understand *why* your horse acts the way it does. You'll better recognize that this type of horse needs security and structure, just as you might need that too, as a person. It's often easier to deal with a horse that mirrors your temperament than with one that is your complete opposite and comes across as reactive or intense when you are not. Personal growth emerges when you can explore *why* it's so hard for you to accept your horse's reactions. Why is it difficult to empathize with its behavior? There's a difference between *understanding* a behavior and *agreeing* with it. And perhaps here lies the opportunity to show both understanding and a calm, grounded *"no thank you"* to the way your horse is reacting–with a steady voice, a relaxed body, and a calm heartbeat. Show the horse that you want something different. For instance, you may want it not to jump sideways, not to kick out at you– but instead to be with you in a different way. Show it the alternative. On the other hand, if you're entirely unable to grasp *why* the horse is reacting this way–and deep-down refuse to accept it—then, in my world, it's the same as not accepting the horse itself.

To me, there's an essential difference between:

- **Completely denying and rejecting something**
- **Setting boundaries from a place of love and self-respect**

If you reject your horse's behavior entirely and refuse to allow it to be the way it is, there are many qualities and reflections the horse could have taught you, which you will never get the chance to explore. And with that, you'll miss a personal growth opportunity that's standing right in front of you.

This is also what we call projection, when you cannot tolerate certain traits or behaviors in others, because you haven't come to terms with those same traits in yourself. And yes, this happens even when it's a horse you're projecting onto.

If, instead, you choose to set boundaries because you love yourself enough *not* to fall off when your horse jumps sideways. Suppose you don't want to be kicked because the horse is restless. And if you also don't want to get angry with others simply because someone walks too fast down the aisle, then you're reclaiming your power. In that situation, you stop trying to control everything others do and begin focusing on what *you* can do. Because ultimately, the only thing you truly have control over is yourself–your system, your energy, and your behavior.

Within control lies both our ability to act and our willpower, but also an ego that can easily take over, mainly when driven by anxiety or fear. This fear often stems from worrying about what others think of us or not wanting people to form a wrong impression. And there's always a fine line between a constructive and purposeful kind of determination and a destructive form of control, both for those around you and for yourself.

In my work as a therapist and a clairvoyant, it has become clear to me that both fields focus on the same part of the body: the lower back. In body therapy, this area is often associated with the instinct for self-preservation. In spiritual work, the same point is known as the root chakra. These two approaches work hand in hand. Whether or not there's balance in this part of the body can reveal a great deal. When there are significant imbalances in the lower back, I often see a person who moves through life with full force—no matter the cost, often at the expense of attending to their own needs, such as rest or emotional space. This kind of person may be competent and action-oriented, but also extremely controlling.

The drive for self-preservation is like our inner warrior; the part of us that gets up and fights when needed. Freud described this as the ego drive: a system built to secure survival, both physically and socially. Like so much else in this work, it's all about finding balance. If you're not in contact with your self-preservation instinct, you may find it hard to take action at all. You might fall into rigidity or passivity. Others may even label that as laziness. However, if you're too connected to this drive and it takes over, you risk burning out. You're constantly doing, constantly chasing, and unable to stop.

In spiritual work, a person with an imbalance in the root chakra often feels disconnected from the earth. It's someone who tends to be anxious about survival, focused on their home, career, or basic security. This happens because, on a deeper level, they're seeking a sense of safety and stability. That's why having *enough* money often becomes a core issue. The challenge here is to realize when enough *is* enough. In fear, the person may constantly feel like they're not good enough, or that their dreams will never come true.

When you're open to going on a personal journey with your horse, because the horse is exactly who it is, then hopefully you'll also be able to embrace it fully. And when you can truly embrace your horse with all its quirks, gifts, qualities, and challenges, you also begin to embrace more of yourself.

You'll find it easier to see yourself reflected in your horse. And in that mirror, there's the possibility of meeting—of love—where the two of you become a *we*.

The Mirror

Most people long to be seen and mirrored exactly as they are. We can observe this in your choice of partner, for example. Either you unconsciously choose someone who is very much like yourself, or someone who has traits you wish you had. At work, you will often gravitate toward colleagues who understand your tasks or your way of working. When you choose to spend more time with neighbors, friends, or travel companions, you're usually drawn, often without realizing it, to those who understand the life challenges you're facing at that specific moment.

The same applies when you choose to talk more with specific riders in the stable rather than others. This is often driven by an unconscious desire to be understood and to feel like you belong, like part of a group that accepts you just the way you are. Without even thinking about it, you're drawn to like-minded people who can relate to the advice, mood, training style, or life experience you bring into the space. And just like with the people around you, you will also, often unconsciously, choose a horse that reflects who you are. That horse may have similar qualities, like being sensitive, proud, determined, strong-willed, dominant, playful, childlike, responsible, mature, cheerful, light, or anxious.

When you fall in love with your horse, you're also falling in love with those parts of yourself. When you feel proud of your horse, that pride also belongs to you. But it's often much harder for people to acknowledge these qualities in themselves, to praise themselves, to love themselves, or even to recognize their strengths. Perhaps that has something to do with the *Law of Jante* in Denmark—the cultural idea that you shouldn't think too highly of yourself. Or maybe it's because one of the deeper purposes of life is to develop stronger self-worth.

We are all born lovable, with a natural sense of self-worth. But as time passes and we're raised by well-meaning parents who try to shape and teach us, that original purity can be disrupted. A child might easily interpret correction or discipline as *I'm wrong* or *I'm not good enough.* Some children adapt and behave in a way that makes them feel welcome in the family. In doing so, they may shut down certain parts of themselves to feel like they belong. If they don't behave, they may be scolded, excluded, sent to their room, put in a time-out, or removed from the group. That exclusion may seem minor, but to a child, it signals being cut off from the safety of the group and, therefore, left alone. As primates, just like horses, we instinctively know that being alone makes us vulnerable. In nature, predators can attack.

We humans don't always react like horses do; we don't run out of a room when we feel threatened, freeze in place in the middle of the street, or respond with panic. But some people do experience a form of paralysis in overwhelming situations, and others may snap out of it quickly. Most of us don't fight like wild animals do, especially as mature adults, but some may lash out verbally or emotionally when they feel threatened.

If you recognize that you've had to shut down parts of yourself, you may either carry this quietly, only showing those sides when you feel deeply safe. For instance, you only allow yourself to feel anger when you're in a very secure relationship. This might appear suddenly, surprising your partner who had no idea this side of you even existed. But with them, you feel safe enough to let it out. If you've lost all contact with your anger, perhaps because it wasn't accepted in your family, then you may project it. You might not be able to tolerate being around angry people at all. It could feel deeply uncomfortable.

Other children don't adapt; instead, they push back. They become reactive, defiant, or outwardly expressive by shouting, spitting, kicking, or refusing to comply with instructions. But over time, most children learn that this kind of behavior also doesn't help them feel accepted or understood. Both types of responses often lead to a deep sense of loneliness, and within that, a longing to be truly seen and loved by someone.

Through the mirror your horse holds up to you, they show you not only who you are, but also your current emotional and physical state, if you are willing to see it.

Most people know that if you're stressed, the horse becomes stressed too. Stress is a form of energy, a vibration, that radiates from your solar plexus in your stomach. Your heart rate increases, blood vessels dilate, and your body produces either adrenaline or the longer-lasting stress hormone, cortisol. And suppose you've heard that horses can sense life within a pregnant woman, drawn to the heartbeat and instinctively lowering their muzzle to her belly. In that case, it's natural and logical to me that they also pick up on everything else happening inside us. Especially when it comes to the energy, and thus the emotion, we emit when we're together, because in those moments, we are a herd.

If you, as a person, are very insecure, highly sensitive, emotionally tuned-in, and perhaps struggle to stand firm in your own opinions, your horse will respond to that. If you've chosen a horse that I call *The Sensitive One*, because you're unconsciously drawn to mirror yourself in your horse, then you'll likely notice that the things that make you uneasy or anxious also trigger your horse. If you're terrified of loud noises, your horse will probably also be afraid of loud noises. If you don't feel comfortable around many people, you may have a horse who also doesn't thrive in large stables with lots of horses and people. Stress can, over time, manifest as stereotypical behaviors, such as crib-biting, weaving, becoming aggressive in the stall, or even developing ulcers.

If, on the other hand, you're ambitious and naturally dominant, there's a high chance you'll be unconsciously drawn to a horse that falls under what I call the *Princes and Princesses* category. Through that horse, you might find yourself mirrored and supported in fulfilling your dreams of being seen, of achieving something, of being the most polished, the most skilled, the most admired.

In some cases, I've seen riders hesitate to admit their ambition. They laugh with a crooked smile when I voice the dreams and desires of their horse. But I often sense a quiet pride—a relief, even—when they realize their horse might be the very one to help them achieve those goals. In other cases, riders fully embrace their ambition, either because they work professionally with horses or have clear aspirations of achieving this goal. These riders usually nod knowingly and appreciatively when I describe what their horse is made of, and what they're striving for, both for themselves and together with their rider.

The mirroring happens physically, too. A horse often takes on the rider's physical imbalances. It's genuinely remarkable how this connection is evident. In most cases, I observe a direct correlation between a rider's physical asymmetry and that of the horse. In the few exceptions where they don't match, it's often because the rider has just acquired the horse, the horse is very young or still in early training or has been ridden previously by someone else with different physical patterns. Because I want to protect the horses, I always address this when I see it. I do this to ensure the long-term well-being of both horse and rider, and to help prevent future injuries, both for the horse's sake and for the rider's financial well-being.

The vet bills, treatments, insurance claims, and more can often be avoided if the rider takes responsibility for how their own body affects their horse. In 99% of cases, the horse's physical issues are caused by the rider. That's what's often referred to as *rider faults*.

I don't know a single rider who sits perfectly in the saddle. But the degree of imbalance, how they distribute their weight, how their hips or pelvis are locked, how one knee or shoulder tilts, or if their head leans to one side, varies greatly. The more tension or restrictions I see in a rider, the more I'll see it mirrored in their horse. Conversely, when I see a rider with fewer blockages, their horse often shows fewer signs of physical strain, unless the horse has other issues unrelated to the rider, such as past injuries or trauma that the rider is unaware of.

What I find most interesting is how many riders automatically assume: *"My horse is stiff or tense."* It rarely crosses their mind that it might be *their* tension or stiffness being transferred to the horse. And I often ask myself, *"Why haven't they noticed this?"* My best guess is that most people aren't in touch with their bodies. We naturally compensate, and many of us have learned to *"live with the pain."* Only when someone like me, or a bodyworker, points it out do I see a smile, a sparkle in their eyes. It's that moment of being caught off guard. That I felt something in them; they weren't even aware of themselves.

And this mirroring isn't limited to the negative. Horses also reflect positive feelings and bodily resources. The calmer you are, the more relaxed your horse will be. The more grounded and safer you feel within yourself, the better a leader you become. That presence has a powerful, positive influence on your horse because they feel secure with you. When you can count on yourself, they can count on you too.

The more balanced you are, the more balanced your horse will be. That's why it's so important to examine your own mental and emotional state in the moments when your horse reacts. When you're out on a ride and your horse gets nervous about its surroundings, do you feel safe being alone with your horse? When your horse refuses a jump, are you confident in your ability to judge the distance and approach? When your horse becomes stressed at a show, are *you* completely calm and relaxed, having let go of ambition and performance anxiety? If you can answer yes to these questions, then there's even more learning and development available to you with your horse—something I go deeper into in the chapter called *Spiritual Growth*.

If your answer is no, I hope you'll smile as you read through these small everyday examples and perhaps recognize that many of these behavioral issues may start with you.

Through my work as a translator between horses and their humans, I've found that much of what I do involves coaching the rider. Sometimes this means helping them through shock or trauma therapy, especially if they've had a difficult or frightening experience in the past that still lingers in the nervous system. Naturally, your horse, or even a new horse, will react to this because they sense everything that comes from you.

At other times, the work is more about personal coaching, helping you become a stronger leader for your horse, or guiding you to take on specific challenges or exercises that you haven't felt brave enough to face before.

The Connected Ones

On the word *"to connect"*: *"To link two or more things or areas together. For example, using a bridge, a transition, or a medium, allowing for the passage of liquid, electric current, or communication."*

And the word *"connected"* is defined as: *"To be grateful and devoted."*

It wasn't until *after* I had already named a specific type of relationship between horse and rider *"The Connected"* that I looked up the meaning of the words. As I read the definitions, they resonated deeply, right down to my soul. In all the years I've been working to help horses and riders, I've only rarely seen the kind of bond I call *"The Connected"*. This is a partnership in which horse and rider merge—becoming one. There's no one above or below. No hierarchy. No emotional imbalances in the rider that spill over into the horse, making it suffer.

Of course, every human being brings some form of baggage, childhood wounds, heartache, longing, betrayal, and broken trust. In spiritual terms, we might refer to this as *karma*. But the difference is this: a person in a truly connected partnership does not unconsciously allow the horse to carry that emotional weight for them.

And yes, this can happen even when the rider feels better simply by being with their horse, without realizing whether the horse is absorbing their worries in return.

A connected relationship can begin when the human dares to *admit* something is hard, aloud and directly to the horse. I often hear riders *unload* on their horses, walking into the stable, burying their face in the mane, whispering confessions into the horse's ear. They say things like, *"You're the only one who understands me,"* or *"You're the only one who's there for me."*

But genuine connection also requires that the rider, after that moment, can set their own emotional needs aside. To not only take in what the horse offers, but to give back equally. To be filled *by* the horse and to *fill* the horse with presence, calm, and love.

Suppose the horse is the only one carrying the weight, soothing the grief, filling the space, then the scales between horse and rider are not in balance. The horse compensates but doesn't receive the same level of energy and affection in return.

With *The Connected,* no physical imbalances in either the rider or the horse go unnoticed. And if they do occur, the rider is quick to recognize them, always seeking treatment or support. The rider knows that if they don't care for their health, those issues will inevitably be transferred to the horse. Their misalignments, their blockages, their pain, the horse will carry it. If the horse experiences discomfort or needs help, the rider senses it immediately. They may feel the pain in their own body, have a vision (sometimes even in dreams), or *know* it when standing next to the horse, acting immediately on that intuition. In this way, many problems are caught early. The horse is taken just as seriously as the human. That's what a truly equal partnership looks like.

In the interaction and training itself, I've both witnessed and coached riders and horses to understand that if they want a better connection and stronger partnership, the rider often has to set aside their own needs and ambitions, in other words, the ego, until the horse is at the same level physically, muscularly, in training, and mentally. Both partners must share a common ground in terms of needs, desires, and ambitions to maintain a balanced relationship. Of course, this can shift continuously for both horse and rider.

If you have a horse with a playful spirit, a *Child at Heart*, who doesn't enjoy what it experiences as *boring dressage training* four times a week, you might find that after four months of intensive training, the horse simply isn't interested anymore. It loses its spark and motivation. In this situation, as part of *The Connected*, you will sense this immediately and change your training approach, take a break, or introduce more playful elements.

Once you see that spark return to your best friend's eyes, you can gradually return to more structured training. The same goes for the rider. If your horse senses that *you* are becoming unsure or demotivated by something *it* enjoys, the horse will instinctively lower its energy to protect you.

Many riders have told me: *"I feel like my horse is protecting me."*

I've seen riders who can breathe deeply together with their horses. I've coached them to find a calm, resting pulse, even during training, to ensure the horse never senses anything to fear. Because if you, as one half of the team, suddenly tense every muscle, stop breathing, and your heart rate spikes, you are also implicitly telling your horse: *"There is something to fear now."* And because you are connected, you're saying: *"There is something* we *need to fear."*

Among *The Connected*, I've rarely had to correct much when it comes to balance and seat alignment. These riders already understand that the horse shouldn't be doing all the work to carry both of them.

I've encountered numerous situations where the rider receives body-work while the horse stands nearby, and the horse begins to lick, yawn, blink slowly, and exhibit deep relaxation. In those moments, it's clear to me that horse and rider are fully intertwined—that they've become a *we*.

Similarly, if you're truly *Connected* with your horse, you may begin to absorb some of your horse's pain, tension, or discomfort. I often see riders suddenly become very tired while their horse is being treated, even though they aren't the one on the treatment table.

I observe the same phenomenon when two horses stand side by side, with only one of them being treated. Suddenly, the *other* horse starts to respond as well, even though I haven't touched it or come close. This happens because the two horses are also connected. I work for, and look forward to, seeing increased riders and horses create this kind of connection: *The Connected*. And truly, *everyone,* and I mean everyone, has that possibility.

It only requires that you, as the rider, be willing to:

- **Meet your horse where it is**—mentally, behaviorally, and in its training
- **Understand your horse's personality** and hold space for it
- **Know that your horse's personality** has nothing to do with you, nor is it a personal attack
- **Take yourself seriously**, both mentally and physically
- **Take your horse's wellbeing seriously**, both mentally and physically
- **Have a genuine wish that the two of you become one united being,** both on the ground and in training
- **Never let your ambitions exceed your horse's**
- **Learn to breathe with your horse**
- **Understand that your body becomes your horse's body,** and your horse's body becomes yours, when you are truly together

All of this starts with *you*. The horse is born exactly as it is. Only if it has experienced deep trauma or has unresolved tension locked in its nervous system will it display unhelpful or reactive behaviors.

But if you take a step back and notice that your horse shows up, ready and willing to be with you, you might realize that there's no greater declaration of love than that.

When the horse senses that *you* are letting go, both physically and mentally, it will let go too.And together, you may reach a state of freedom and inner joy.

The Masters

Over the years, I have worked with horses, and I have only encountered a few on very few occasions who were spiritual masters and had owners or riders who understood the kind of energy they were dealing with and were able to handle it. The relationship between the *Masters* differs from that of the *Teacher and Student*, where the horse is the *Teacher* and the rider is the student, in that the *Masters* work with a high energy that is equally distributed and becomes universal and deeply spiritual between horse and rider.

When the horse functions as the *Teacher*, it can act as a kind of protector for you, the student. Or it may want to teach you something because it has progressed further in its development than you have. It can also help guide you in training. It looks after you in its way by teaching you something. It may unconsciously choose to do this in a very pedagogical and patient way, or it may do so in a more intense manner. It may present information in a more specific or forceful way because it has one of the dominant or majestic personality profiles, such as *Princes and Princesses* or *Kings and Queens*. Alternatively, it may act this way if it feels it cannot reach you. In such cases, as a rider, you may feel insecure if you don't realize that the horse is trying to teach you something. And through that, you may hopefully come to understand that its behavior becomes a declaration of love from your horse to you in the form of personal or spiritual growth.

With the *Masters*, I see a horse that is so at peace with itself that I find it hard to categorize them under the personality profile *Kings and Queens*. These are usually the born leaders. But in a true *Master*, your horse has no interest in leading a herd. It is at peace within itself. It may appear passive, reserved, or withdrawn. It may even seem shut down entirely inside because it does not noticeably react if a dominant horse, such as the *Prince* or *Princess*, tries to move it in the pasture. A few of them do want to show other horses and humans both their spiritual and inner strength, so that they may come across as a bit overwhelming in their energy.

The horse as *Master* is deeply grounded in itself, so it also expects you, as its owner or rider, to be the same. It has no interest in *educating you*, teaching you something, teasing you, dominating you, or any of the everyday needs that horses may have in their interactions with you. The *Master* simply *IS* with you.

As the owner or rider, you may start to feel uncertain about whether your horse even wants to be with you. Most people misinterpret these horses. They are often labeled as lazy, rigid, stupid, unintelligent, aggressive, overly dominant, and many other things. This is unfortunate because it is a true honor to meet a *Master*. But only in humility, gratitude, and dignity within you as a human being will you be able to discover the horse's hidden talents and the immense energy of love it can send to you when you understand it correctly.

The relationships between horse and rider that I have seen and would categorize as true *Masters* consist of two independently thinking beings. Two equally powerful individuals. They do not try, like *The Connected*, to merge into one. They simply want to BE, and by just BEING, they are *ONE*.

To become one with your horse, you must be one with yourself.

To be one with yourself, you must feel whole. And you can only feel whole if you love every part and side of yourself. When you can do that, you become capable of loving others. At this point, there will be no projections, prejudices, anger, irritation, or other negative thought patterns toward others. You will rest within yourself. Therefore, others around you are allowed to be just as they are, because it no longer affects you. This can be interpreted as indifference. Some might even think that you or the horse at this level do not care. But nothing could be further from the truth. Can you imagine reaching a place in life where nothing disturbs you anymore? And the reason is that you are resting in simply BEING here on Earth.

You are at peace with yourself because you love yourself deeply and no longer concern yourself with whether love can be measured or compared to anything else. You are, therefore, an independent being and soul who can stand alone because you are filled by and within yourself.

It is human nature to want to be part of a herd, a group. A place to belong and to be mirrored. The moment we feel we have to stand alone; we may become insecure. It could be the first day we're dropped off at daycare or with a child care giver. It's natural for us to feel separation anxiety. And this will likely continue throughout childhood.

We may feel excluded if we are bullied or if no other children invite us to play with them. In adulthood, we seek a mate, a partner, a life companion—not just to reproduce, but also to complete the circle of finding a mirror and a sense of safety. In this, I believe we return to what we were born for—to be ourselves with another and be loved for who we are.

In situations where we must stand alone, and therefore will naturally feel unsafe, uncertain, anxious, or fearful, a defense mechanism may arise within us. It's there to help us *survive* the situation—a situation where we feel left out, rejected, or excluded.

In my opinion, whatever feeling we encounter when standing alone is anxiety-provoking, because as herd animals, we may feel we've been left to die. And in that lies existential loneliness. A loneliness that is as fundamental and existential to all humans as the experience of freedom, isolation, and death. It's a feeling I believe most people are familiar with and have experienced at times. And it is also a feeling that frightens many when they encounter it. Yet in that loneliness, there is a learning to relate only to yourself and to learn to love yourself and your own company, without noise or outside stimulation.

The feeling of being utterly alone in the world. To feel lonely and lost. And in that feeling of being lost, I believe there is a small death. A sense of being dead inside and unable to find joy or a spark within yourself in the situation. So often, we act our way out of it because it feels unbearable. This action might be *doing something*. Others get stuck in the situation. This reaction, of course, depends on who we are as individuals. However, what we all share is that we have mechanisms to cope with something that feels truly terrible to us. We may either react outwardly or inwardly. Both types of reactions can be self-destructive and ultimately damaging to our self-love and self-worth.

The survival mechanism can manifest as projection. We tend to dislike the *ugly sides* of ourselves but find it easier to point them out in others. These traits may include things like being power-hungry, pompous, arrogant, overly confident, taking up too much space, selfish, loud, or dramatic. These are typically unpleasant traits in us. When we project onto others, we avoid facing these parts of ourselves that are considered forbidden and therefore *ugly*. They are often deemed forbidden because of our upbringing, where it was *not allowed* to be that way. Or it could be social norms or something we picked up that isn't welcomed when moving among others. And the ironic and challenging part of all this is that we long for connection and being part of a group. That means we cannot avoid projections wherever we are. We either project, or we are projected onto.

The survival mechanism can also take the form of numbing the feeling of insecurity, fear, or anxiety. We may turn to means that soothe the discomfort within us. This could be eating sweets, drinking alcohol, overeating, using drugs, engaging in excessive sex, and so on. All of these are ways of escaping inner pain.

In my work as a therapist, I see more young people who are struggling emotionally and in life. They feel lonely and become self-destructive. Some turn to substances or other addictive behaviors—even sugar. Others, in their self-destruction, attempt to exert control over something. They want to control either themselves or the pain they're experiencing, often through self-harm. This may involve cutting, also known as *cutting*. It may manifest as eating disorders, and others develop OCD —obsessive compulsive disorder—a mental condition involving compulsive behaviors like counting, hand washing, needing everything to be aligned, or that numbers must be even rather than odd.

To avoid the fear of being completely alone, some people attempt to create a sense of belonging in a group, so they don't feel isolated. They may speak in *we language*, saying things like, *"I know that Mrs. Smith also thinks you were out of line. There are several of us who feel this way about your behavior."*

This may come across as childish or even threatening when someone resorts to this technique to create a *club*, turning it into *us* versus you. It's a subtle form of adult bullying, where the person using the technique may not even realize how hurtful it can be to the recipient. And it ends up making the other person feel wrong and utterly alone in the world instead.

When it comes to projection and the *club-forming technique*, it often stems from the sender being unable to bear the feeling of loneliness and thus passing it on to others. In compassion, I understand the person who uses this as a defense. It's rarely a conscious act. However, going forward, try to notice how many people use these techniques, often without even realizing it.

In the face of fundamental and existential fear of loneliness, some people put on a *facade* and armor themselves to stand alone. They toughen up. And so, they may appear convincingly independent. Their belief often sounds like: *"Fine, I'll manage on my own!"*

People with this defense mechanism often appear outwardly to be incredibly strong and independent. But beneath the armor and the heavy iron visor lies an inner fear of truly being alone in the world. With all this in mind, it is therefore both surprising and overwhelming to me when I meet another soul who is truly able to stand alone without it being a defense mechanism. I have only encountered a few so far.

The horses, as *Masters*, possess a calm and a sense of wholeness. They rarely suffer from illness because they stand and heal themselves. They have come to understand and feel that they are, in fact, capable of self-healing. They have no desire to discipline other horses in the herd or the stable, because they know that each horse has its unique learning process to undergo. They feel no need to take on their human's worries or help them with their burdens when their owner or rider buries their face in the mane and tears run down their cheeks and into the horse's coat.

The horse simply *IS*, and with all its strength and inner peace, it sends out enormous waves of pure energy, which is love, so its human is immediately affected by the calm and the love. And in that moment, you as a human feel better the instant you meet a *Master*, even though you cannot put into words why.

When you, as a rider or owner, understand that you have a true *Master* in your horse, that energy will also influence you. For you to achieve an equal relationship as *Masters*, it naturally requires that you are at a stage in life where you accept this truth. The moment you let go and find acceptance and thus see your *Master* as they truly are, that is where you meet them. When you love your horse for the way it is in the world, and thus also love yourself, you will be able to achieve the same high self-worth that your horse possesses. You may not be a *Master* yourself in the beginning. Perhaps you're a bit puzzled when you take over such a horse, one that is so at peace with itself. You might even misinterpret it. But as you get to know the horse and discover that it continues to remain calm no matter what happens around it or to you, you will subconsciously absorb so much of its healing power and love that you will become able to reach the same level it is on.

When you let go of the ego—the need for your horse to do something for you, and accept that it may simply *BE*, then you are compassionate and inclusive in its presence. In that partnership, there are no ambitions that the other does not also share. There is a mutual understanding when one says, *"No, thank you,"* without the other reacting with childish offense or feeling rejected. In this way, a relationship is formed between two independent individuals and souls who accept each other exactly as they are, without needing to think the same, feel the same, or be the same at the same time.

Only through this, when one is a whole soul, can one become part of an entire organism. Imagine your own body. If you have a broken arm or a damaged cell, then you are not whole. You can compensate. You can continue living with a broken arm that will slowly heal. But in that moment when something is broken in you, you are not whole. Therefore, you cannot say you have an entire body.

When a cell or a soul is not whole within, then we cannot say we have a complete organism. If you choose to view everything around you as part of a greater whole, you might begin to understand or reflect on the fact that there is something much greater than yourself and beyond your comprehension. Even though we live in a small Scandinavian country, we know that there is a great deal of life on the other side of the world, where time is either ahead of or behind the present moment we are in. The Earth pulses, and there is life and souls everywhere—each with their own life, their learning, and their ways of seeking and giving love. I think it's a beautiful thought that we are all connected. There is an old saying: *"Treat others the way you want to be treated."*

It could also be said: *"Treat others as if they are a part of you. What you offer them; you also offer yourself."* Einstein also believed that our survival depends on our moving from seeing ourselves as isolated individuals to understanding ourselves as part of a larger whole. This whole includes all sentient beings, including animals. And that on this journey, we reach an expanded level of consciousness. If there's one thing I've learned and understood from the horses, it's that they think and live this way in the world. Whether they are with their herd or with their humans, they establish a connection with those around them and strive to find their place in the hierarchy, based on their personality and role in life, whether they are aware of it or not. They simply know that we are in this together and therefore belong together. They do not need to project any emotion onto others in the herd, because horses don't think about their behavior as forbidden, unwelcome, offensive, cheeky, or so on. They do what is natural to them. They seek leadership, take on leadership, or submit to leadership in the herd.

A few years ago, I had a vision that helped me understand what it means to be part of a greater organism. I just had to look at the ocean in front of me. The sea has no end; it has multiple depths and layers where some things can live and others cannot, due to factors such as oxygen and pressure.

The ocean can divide, but the ends always meet. There is no place on Earth where water does not connect around the land. Everything is connected in the ocean, and sound can travel far under water—so much so that some whales emit sound waves in one place, and they are picked up thousands of kilometers away. Under the sea, there are no national borders or obstacles that demand we divide the ocean. We humans have chosen to divide the sea into distinct bodies of water, naming them the Indian Ocean, the Pacific Ocean, and so on. But to the ocean, it means nothing. It simply is, and it merely exists.

Maybe it sounds far-fetched or overly spiritual? But I believe it is entirely logical and something we are all familiar with. We know that we all belong together because we share the same planet, Earth. And regardless of skin color, culture, religion, upbringing, social class, traditions, and so much more, we are all human beings. I look forward to the day when we begin to think a little more like horses do. Even though geography seems larger to us, because we understand the continents, borders, oceans, and scale of the Earth, we risk complicating the connection we share here on this planet.

If we think of ourselves as a whole organism, we will also understand and grasp that if another human being is suffering, then we are suffering. If you are unwell, either physically or mentally, then we, as a group and as an organism, are unwell together with you. And in that way, one might say that humanity still has a long way to go in its development toward a mindset like that of the horse—the *Master*. Because it requires us, as humans, to love all aspects of ourselves, and thereby also all aspects of others. It requires that we expect nothing from others for our gain or for them to meet our needs. These might be the need for recognition, the need for company, the need to be right, the need to be understood. Because on that level, you will rest in the fact that you can recognize yourself, enjoy your own company, know that you are right, and understand yourself.

At that level, you will be so grounded in your love for yourself that you will have enough love to give, simply by being yourself, and by loving yourself. And I believe that is what compassion is.

In times of crisis and disaster, we humans are capable of standing together. Whether it is when the Twin Towers fell during an attack in New York, when tsunamis struck vast regions, leaving many people homeless, when we collect donations for children with cancer or famine in Africa, or when these events are catastrophic enough, we truly act. An action is born out of the sense that *WE* must do something now. Not in December or during the annual UNICEF fundraiser, but NOW. No lifeguard, doctor, paramedic, or firefighter I know or have ever heard of enters such a caring and helpful profession and questions someone's skin color, race, faith, political views, or anything else when it is a matter of saving a life in the moment. They do not hesitate— they help immediately.

Sometimes I have the sense that, in addition to humanity's responsibility for the damage we are causing to the Earth, which we all live on and must leave to future generations, the universe also plays a role for all of us. That may of course sound very alternative, but I have a feeling that everything happens for a reason. Even in the most devastating natural disasters, a global imbalance is somehow being corrected. I feel that when the ego becomes too inflated and too many people are focused on money, power, hatred, recognition, or other things that feed the ego, then, unfortunately, major global events must occur. Perhaps to help us all remember the compassion and love we have for one another as human beings.

It is only because I pay attention to energies and have a continuous curiosity about my spiritual awareness that I notice such things. This is also part of the greater spiritual evolution happening all around us, whether we see it, believe in it, reject it, or not. And again, the horses help us stay grounded, find our connection to the Earth, and sense when the world within us or around us is out of balance.

Spiritual Development

We have, unconsciously, used horses as work animals in the fields, for transport, and other *hard labor* in the past. But as we have progressed in our personal development, we have also shaped horses to follow along, using them to create a space of freedom for ourselves or to help us gain recognition, for example, through competitions, where most people want to win something to feel that they have done well.

Humans, who have a developed neocortex in the brain, are capable of creating, imagining, and evolving through the mind, but that same part of the brain also becomes our greatest enemy. It allows us to dwell in the past, be present in the now, and—most of all—live in the future, at least in our thoughts.

Imagine living solely from what you feel in your heart, with an awareness of the collective—not just your ego or your *self*? Then you would sense energy, feel atmospheres, notice what felt good and what didn't. You wouldn't think your way to it. You would feel it. And that is why horses are a gift to us humans, because they force us to become capable of this, if we choose to feel honestly.

How does this become part of a spiritual development? I believe the meaning of life is to become more compassionate, just like the level I described earlier in the section about the *Masters*. Through learning, we evolve. We can learn through joy, but also through pain. Imagine a painful experience from your life. Maybe you lost a partner. Perhaps someone you loved died. Maybe you were bullied in school as a child. Possibly you tend to meet the same type of partner, only to end up feeling hurt every time. Hopefully, with time, you will begin to realize that you can respond differently when these situations arise. Perhaps you've even chosen to look inward and discover what your role is in why the outcome often leads to the same painful feeling.

You can explore this by consulting a psychologist, entering therapy, joining support groups, seeing a coach, or consulting alternative practitioners like clairvoyants. You can also encounter the topic through leadership programs, self-help resources, meditation, and other methods. This feeling is what I, as a therapist, call your *theme*, and within the spiritual realm, I call it your *karma*. The common ground between these concepts is that it's a feeling you encounter repeatedly throughout your life when you feel hurt. It's a headline or a pattern you see repeatedly. It may even be the word you fear the most experiencing in life.

It could be words like:

- **Betrayal**
- **Mistrust**
- **Loneliness**
- **Lack of attention**
- **And so on.**

I believe there is something greater than us. Some call it God, others call it the Universe, and some don't have a name for it, but they still feel its presence, even though we cannot yet prove everything. And I believe that there is a higher purpose for each of us. The purpose is to cultivate self-awareness and, through that, become more compassionate over time.

I also believe this evolution will take an incredibly long time, because although we can be loving, empathetic, and caring, no human being is 100% compassionate. Imagine only ever doing something for others—just because. Imagine never expecting anything in return and being completely at peace with that. That is also why I believe in reincarnation.

Reincarnation is a philosophical or religious belief that all life, the soul, can return in another physical body. This is also known as *rebirth* or *transmigration*. Reincarnation is a fundamental principle in many spiritual traditions, including Hinduism, Buddhism, and Sikhism. Even the ancient Greek philosophers believed in reincarnation, which they referred to as *metempsychosis*. The French geologist, Jesuit, and Catholic priest Pierre Teilhard de Chardin (1881–1955) developed this perspective on the evolution of consciousness in 1955, known as the *Omega Point*. It is a theory suggesting that the Universe is constantly evolving. He also developed the concept of the *Noosphere*—the sphere of human thought. He saw evolution progressing along a trajectory of increased consciousness, creating a mental layer encircling the Earth, generated by humanity's rising awareness.

The Canadian psychiatrist Ian Pretyman Stevenson (1918–2007) also became world-renowned for his research on reincarnation. He studied more than 3,000 children worldwide who claimed to remember past lives. He published both research and books on the subject, concluding that the children's detailed memories of names, places, and events not from their lifetime could be explained by reincarnation.

I believe I have lived before, and that my soul has moved on to a new chapter—today, as Ditte. I think this because I have witnessed it first-hand through regression therapy, meditation, and dreams. Some of these visions I've tried to verify—wondering if they were real or just my imagination. And in 99% of the cases, I have found names, dates, events like building fires, historical records of farms and locations, and much more. I've also sensed a sense of familiarity and comfort, both in Denmark and abroad. I feel a strong inner calling to certain countries, and deep down I know it's because I've been there before in a past life.

Some countries I've traveled to have felt incredibly familiar, even though I had never been there before. Other moments in my life have felt like déjà vu—like I've been in a place or with certain people before. That feeling comes when meeting people I feel strongly drawn to, whether as friends I want to spend more time with, people who make me feel safe, or in relationships. Don't you know that feeling yourself, when you meet someone, look them in the eye, and are sure you've seen them before? But when you both try to figure out where you have met, you must admit that you haven't met in this life?

That's the strong feeling I'm describing—the one only you can recognize deep inside yourself. The same goes for a country you feel drawn to visit. For me, it's Tibet. I know I've been there in a previous life. I also know it won't be easy to go there, but I feel pulled toward that place. The same may apply to you if you feel drawn to travel to Bali, and you don't know why. Maybe when you go there for a two-week vacation, you feel a strong resistance to leaving, and you can't explain it. You know, rationally, that it's not just *because it's a nice holiday.* You feel that you have to go back and explore more.

These are the powerful inner feelings that, I believe, come from our soul's longing for and recognition of something it once knew, and perhaps isn't finished with yet.

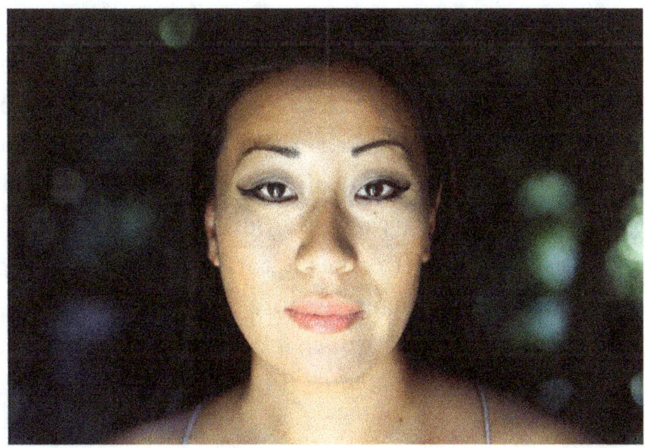

This also means that I believe that on the day I die, I will die as Ditte, and I will have to accept that this life—with all its relationships—is over. However, I also believe that my soul can move on to a place I don't yet fully understand and continue. I think I will meet some of the souls I'm close to today, those I'm connected with. But they may not necessarily appear as my family, friends, or partner. We belong to one large soul group, intertwined in many ways, and each person in my life is here to teach me something, just as I am here to teach them something.

I therefore firmly believe that life is one incredible journey of growth, where we are here to learn. I have seen it, heard it, and felt it for many years now, both in my own life and through the clients I have helped using clairvoyance, channeling, telepathy, and more.

Even many different religions point to the same thing: To be compassionate means doing something for another person purely out of love. You don't do it to get something in return. You don't judge, you don't point fingers, you don't get jealous or angry because someone else makes a different choice. You understand that every person has something they need to learn, and for that, you can only love them and the path they're on, even if you don't walk the same road or have chosen the same life.

So, how do horses come into the picture? They do because they are spiritually gifted, and it is in their nature to be part of a community. As a community, we, as humans, also seek to avoid the feelings of isolation or loneliness. A feeling, as mentioned earlier, that is existential for all of us. But often, we cannot bear to stay in that feeling. Even though everything we do tends to move us toward community, we seek friends who share our values, support our beliefs, and grow at the same pace. As a result, our ego also grows. And with that, a desire to stand on our own, to be independent, to be *our person*, something unique, eccentric, proud of accomplishing something extraordinary. But for what? Often, to gain recognition, whether from within or from the outside world. Horses have it right from the start. It comes naturally to them to be part of a collective, even with their humans, because they are herd animals.

When the human is not part of that collective, whether in training, mentally, or physically, the horse must protest and show you that you've stepped away from the shared *we* and the mutual understanding and respect. The horse is then, perhaps unknowingly, trying to draw your attention to love for yourself and the horse. It is trying to awaken your presence in the moment. The collaboration between you and the horse, where you and it become one, because you ARE part of something greater. You ARE.

Unfortunately, it often happens that a horse's protest is misinterpreted as *"Resistant to contact," "My horse doesn't trust my aids," "It's being naughty," "Disobedient,"* and so on. Sometimes, there may indeed be a conflict. But I will always recommend that you, as the rider, begin by looking inward. Ask yourself whether your horse, through the way it is in this life, might be trying to teach you something.

Ask yourself whether it is showing a behavior that you struggle to express in yourself. Whether it's a dominant behavior that feels somehow forbidden to you, or a hypersensitivity that you in no way want to connect with inside yourself. And if you can't see it in the moment, look at your horse's behavior afterward. It is precisely through this inner reflection that your personal and spiritual development occurs. This personal and spiritual development between you and your horse arises when you meet the individual soul for what it is and see both its soul and your own as part of a greater, unified organism.

The Spiritual Horses

I constantly experience moments with horses that move me, shock me, shake me, teach me, and uplift me. Time and again, I am amazed by the knowledge and extraordinary awareness that horses have toward us humans. This applies not only to those of us who are alive, but also to souls who have passed on to the other side. All horses are spiritual on some level.

The same goes for us humans. We are spiritual because we are connected, and we are all part of a greater process of growth and evolution.But the horses I refer to as *spiritual* are those with a much stronger focus on humans and a desire to help us in our learning, or they are especially receptive to activity from the spiritual realm.

These *spiritual horses* often appear as the generous and grounded leader horses that I call *Kings* or *Queens*. Or I encounter them when I meet a horse that is one of *The Masters*. Regardless of which personality profile I assign them, an encounter with a spiritual horse will always offer the human, whether the owner or the rider, some form of revelation. Often, they also help open up your spirituality even more. In such a revelation, you will often experience a moment or lesson that undeniably challenges your previous beliefs about what you thought you knew.

It may even create an inner conflict, because your left brain—the analytical mind—thinks, *"This can't be real."* But if you recognize this feeling, then remember: Your experience is your truth, regardless of whether others were there to witness it with you and your horse.

I have seen horses react with extreme intensity to spiritual activity in the places they were kept. Maybe you've seen or heard about horses who seem afraid of a specific corner of the riding arena or inside the indoor school. This is typical of the *sensitive* horses, the ones who respond to energies that others either don't notice or don't care about. I've visited places where the energy was so bad that the horses' hooves were falling apart, held together only with duct tape.

I've seen stables where horses developed ulcers, abscesses, or internal bleeding, one after the other. Veterinarians couldn't find a cause. The owners were beside themselves with worry. Riders were in tears. And the horses were euthanized in large numbers.

I can't describe all the episodes I've been through, but you can probably sense how intense and, at the same time, deeply instructive they have been. I've felt afraid going into these kinds of tasks, what we call *house cleanings,* because from the very beginning, I could sense how dark and heavy the energy was. I *knew* that what I was walking into was pure evil and darkness.

I've been in supervision repeatedly, trying to understand why I was receiving such assignments. Was there something dark in me, since I was being given these tasks? Had I inadvertently brought something evil along with me that was suddenly attracting these challenges? I always found peace in the fact that my work with animals was so pure and innocent. So why now these heavy, dark tasks—ones I still felt obliged to take on because I *could*?

Eventually, I found peace in the realization and in the confirmation that I was given these tasks because I was ready to learn more. As I became more skilled and my level increased, the difficulty of the assignments I received rose accordingly. I would like to share some of those experiences with you. Some of the less intense ones are described in this book. Others are available in video sessions on my YouTube channel, if you are curious to learn more.

I held a two-day supervision course for my animal communication consultants who work under my name on Funen. I had invited my colleague, craniosacral osteopath and physiotherapist Sidsel Sommer, as a guest teacher on the first day to teach my consultants about anatomy and the craniosacral structure of the horse. It was sunny and windy when we all arrived from different parts of Denmark. After finishing the anatomy part, we headed to the stables, where the consultants were to try out the craniosacral techniques under Sidsel's supervision.

There was a horse named *Ducati*, on which they were allowed to practice. His challenges were that he was a *headshaker* and had suffered from ulcers for an extended period. He had been detoxed, but continued to headshake, and no vets had been able to help. His rider still had no explanation for what was behind his behavior.

Each consultant placed their hands on him in turn, and he enjoyed receiving craniosacral therapy. At one point, I wanted to demonstrate a technique I use within the craniosacral system, and as I placed my hands on him, it felt like I was sending 350 volts through his body with both hands. Ducati shook violently all over, as if I were electrocuting him.

I have seen strong reactions before when blockages release, and the craniosacral rhythm begins to flow at a healthy pace for the individual horse. But I had *never* seen a horse react as if being shocked by my touch. I immediately let go of him and tried again, but the same reaction occurred. The consultants beside me stepped back in surprise, exclaiming *"Wow!"* in shock, and Ducati's owner looked at me in panic. I reassured them, saying that I'm aware I carry a lot of energy, and maybe it simply wasn't *me* who should be laying hands on him.

After a lovely dinner at the inn where I was staying, we each went our own way, and I collapsed onto my pillow after a long and fulfilling day. I was ready for another exciting day, this time with me teaching how I practice craniosacral therapy, blended with the telepathic techniques my consultants already know so well. When I turned off the light, I suddenly saw, in my mind's eye, a black snake lying on the pillow beside me. I was startled, jumped up, and turned on the light. No snake. I went to the bathroom, splashed cold water on my face, and then saw *two snakes* in the shower stall. I was terrified and thought, *"Now I'm seriously losing it. I must be going schizophrenic. I've got a full-blown work-related mental breakdown and can no longer tell fantasy from reality."*

That night, I didn't sleep a wink and kept asking my spiritual guides if I was going insane.

The answer I got was: *"NO."*

I asked them: *"Are these dark forces?"*

Answer: *"YES."*

"Are the dark forces directed at me?"

Answer: *"NO."*

"Then who are they directed at?" I asked. And suddenly, *Ducati's head* appeared clearly before me, just like when I telepathically connect with a horse through a photo, or from the other side, when a horse has passed away. I calmed down a bit as the morning neared and fell asleep, knowing this was something I had to address.

The next morning, we met again at the course location. During breakfast, I shared the snake story with some of the consultants. One of them asked if I had *seen the angel card of the day* by a woman, we all followed on social media. She lives in Hawaii and always seems to hit the mark for each of us. It was astonishing how she managed to give such precise and universally relevant advice. That day's card showed Archangel Raphael holding a trident wrapped in snakes. The message on the card was: *"FIGHT FEAR,"* followed by a long description about fighting darkness and opposing forces that day.

I smiled and looked around at the group, asking: *"Are you ready to drive out dark forces from Ducati today?"*

They were thrilled—none of them had ever done an exorcism before.

I hadn't either, not on a horse. But Ducati's reaction now made sense as the pieces fell into place.

We went to the stable, and after showing them how I combine craniosacral therapy with telepathy—which brought everything together for the consultants, we prepared for *the* actual cleansing of Ducati. We formed a circle, and I asked them to *be the light*.

We didn't touch hands, as Ducati didn't want to feel trapped by the circle. Still, each of us could feel the buzzing energy between our palms—the incredibly high vibration that the eight of us were able to create together through love.

I stepped into the circle and placed one hand on the back of Ducati's owner.

Then I began to chant and call on the dark energies to leave his body.

Ducati trembled, became restless, blinked his eyes, and yawned, even though I didn't lay a hand on him. He walked in circles, and I saw the darkness slowly lift and leave his body.

It clung to him, and for a moment, I had to focus on directing the darkness *back to the dark*—not to any of us. We stood there for a long time. Eventually, I placed a hand on his forehead. I continued chanting, as one consultant after another began to cry, overwhelmed by the extreme love we were creating, and the resistance from the darkness to let go.

When the darkness finally left his body, we were all able to breathe again.

Several of the women burst into tears, feeling grateful for Ducati's help.

He stood completely calm, his neck, head, and body at ease.

I placed both hands on him again to check whether he would react with shock, and to make sure the darkness was truly gone. He remained calm, yawned, licked his lips in contentment, and smiled at me with his eyes as I heard: *"Thank you so much."*

I bowed my head to him and whispered:

"You're welcome, Ducati."

We took a long break that day, completely overwhelmed by the experience. We shook it off, cleansed our energies, and then continued to help seven new horses with craniosacral therapy. There was something to be learned, both for Ducati and for his owner, who also received healing afterwards from one of my consultants. She needed to learn how to pursue what she truly wanted in life, to express it out loud to us and move forward, so that the *darkness,* which is fear and resistance, would not consume her. To stop being passive, to take ownership of her life, and stand by her dreams and desires. To understand that the universe was helping her by allowing the darkness to take over her horse was utterly overwhelming. It was a profoundly moving and beautiful experience that I will never forget.

Some months earlier, I had gone out to cleanse stables in the city called Taastrup, on the island of Zealand. It's not something I do often, but I do enjoy it. It's work that demands a lot of time because you must be thorough and make sure everything is cleared and that the energies are good afterwards. The previous month, I had performed similar work at a competition stable in the city of Herning, and before that, I had cleaned a large farm and its surrounding land in the city of Høsterkøb. So, some time passes between each place I visit.

Typical signs that a cleansing is needed include:

- **There's an unexplained heavy atmosphere** or bad energy on the property
- **The horses often become ill**
- **If children live there, they often suffer from night terrors,** sleep poorly, or wake at the same time every night.
- **There are areas, indoors or outdoors, where horses refuse to pass**
- **People feel watched** or sense someone standing behind them
- **The drains smell bad**
- **Things constantly break down,** like cars, machines, and electrical systems

I arrived at the location in Taastrup on a sunny day and was warmly greeted by three women, one of whom owned the place. They briefly told me about the many health issues the horses had been through, and it was extreme. Not just typical ligament injuries or some stiffness in the loins or pelvis. There were migraines, tumors, and more. It was intense.

I walked around the property and started in the paddock, where I asked the two horses that weren't sick where I should begin. The horse, which was the *King* of the place and thus the leader, looked at me and nodded slightly toward the shelter, saying calmly, *"start there."* The two horses explained that they hadn't gotten sick because they had the mental strength to withstand it. One was the *King*, the other the *Prince*, and they were the most dominant in the herd. Inside the shelter, surrounded by hay and horse manure, I suddenly saw many white souls who were *stuck*. I saw them holding their heads, swaying from side to side while moaning, *"Ohhhh, aaahhh, ohhhh,"* as if in deep suffering. I thought to myself, have I walked into a psychiatric ward for lost souls?

When I work this way, I see images within images. Similar to the film *Tomb Raider 2*, where Angelina Jolie opens the *Cradle of Life* orb and sees a glowing world around her, even though she is standing in a completely different location. It was just like that for me. I saw a round lighthouse, or something similar to it. It was empty inside. There was a dark wooden door, low and narrow, and stairs leading up to it—a wooden hatch with a lock. When I looked beneath the hatch, I saw the trapped souls.

They told me they were all girls, except for one—a younger brother who had been captured by mistake. A watchman had locked them up. He abused them, sexually assaulted them, and forced the others to watch. They cried as they shared their stories with me. They were humiliated, broken, and stuck in pain. I saw how the watchman, reeking and filthy, would attack them one by one, sometimes at night. Some girls wore nightgowns. He had something—ether or another substance—to sedate them. They would wake up in that tower, trapped, too weak from hunger and thirst to escape or resist.

I asked them how they had died. They showed me that the watchman eventually left in guilt, and they died of starvation and dehydration, still trapped in their suffering.

I stood in silence, listening to one soul after another tell their story, showing me the moments of their abuse. I contacted each one, sent them off into the light, kissed their foreheads while I breathed heavily in shock, trying to hold space for their pain. After I had helped everyone cross over, I double-checked that no one was left behind and then cleansed the area. I kept thinking that it must have been a guard, but my spiritual helpers corrected me and said no, it was a watchman.

I turned to the *King* horse again and asked, *"Where should I go next?"* He answered, *"To the water supply—the one that provides water for the horses, not the house."*

There, I encountered lower vibrational beings: trolls, nature spirits, mischievous energies that jumped around, laughing and trying to throw me off. In the spiritual world, as in life, there is both light and darkness. In this case, it was the latter. My guides, and spiritual helpers and angels, told me that the water contained too much metal and nitrate. Even though the owner assured me the water had been tested and approved, I kept receiving the same message repeatedly.

I shared the advice I had received: that the horses' drinking water could be energetically balanced by adding homeopathic drops to their buckets before they drank. Whether the owner chooses to do so or not, I do not know, but the information was delivered. After I had cleansed the area of the lower-vibrational beings, the horses told me to walk with the owners to a marshland a little further away. There, my spiritual helpers showed me that this had once been a battlefield where young men were prepared for war. I received the word *"civil war,"* which surprised me, as I didn't know we had experienced such a thing in Denmark. They showed me images of bows and arrows, arrowheads, and young boys running toward a field with loud cries. Many of these young men fell in battle and returned to the place that felt safest to them —the marsh.

About a month after I had visited, one of the women who had been present that day sent me a video from our national TV station, TV2. Just after my visit, a remarkable archaeological discovery had been made. A battlefield filled with arrowheads and flint weapons had been found two kilometers from the area where I had cleansed the marsh. It was an incredible feeling to have my vision confirmed, although the person boarding her horse there sounded a little shaken when she called me.

We returned to the paddock, and the two horses told me I should speak with *The Queen* of the place. She was in stall number three. I went out to her in the field, and she shared with me her psyche and spirit. She offered kind advice for her rider, who was the owner's daughter, and reassured them both that she would survive. Then I went into her stall. There, I saw a woodsman and his son. The man and the boy were dressed as farmer boys. The son had been very much left to himself. The mother had been mentally ill, but no one really addressed it at the time. She walked around crying, angry and screaming, but people ignored her. Instead, they tried to hide her away and talk her into silence, isolating her on the farm. The man was deeply frustrated by this, so he went out and chopped wood, pouring all his strength into the swinging of his axe to release his anger and frustration. The little boy just sat watching, too afraid to say anything. A sweet, blond-haired boy of about six or seven. That energy had become stuck in *The Queen's* stall, and I had to help them move on.

It all happened peacefully. The man was relieved when I told him that there was a better place where his wife would be waiting for him and that she would be well again, *healed*. I sent them both into the light. And every time I do that, I can breathe deeply into my lungs, and sometimes a tear rolls down my cheek. I then moved to the far end of the stable, where I saw an older man who had been an alcoholic. He had used the stable as a kind of workshop, and his drinking had greatly frustrated his wife. It had created a heavy atmosphere on the property. I helped him pass on as well, after reassuring him that the new owners would take good care of his place, keep it tidy, and treat it with respect.

I took a break halfway through the three-hour-long session. It was intense work, but also incredibly exciting for me to be part of. During the break, I received clairvoyant messages for each of the three women who were with me that day. They were very accurate. All three women were moved and laughed as they recognized themselves in the messages. I asked my spiritual guides what I should focus on next. Had I removed the primary cause of all the sickness and death at this place, or should I look for something else during the remaining 1.5 hours of my visit? Then I heard a voice in my head telling me that the core issue here was about unity. The horses had to fall, meaning they had to sacrifice themselves so that the people could come together. I was told that every time the barn community had to say goodbye to another horse being put down, they managed to come together, support each other, and be kind. I had to explain this to them in the most diplomatic and gentle way I could. Because, in essence, it was criticism—of the way they welcomed new horse owners and riders, and also of the overall way they ran the place.

Thankfully, they received it well and understood what I was saying. They were self-aware enough to recognize their own behavior and to realize that it might have contributed to the horses getting sick.

We made a plan for how they could become more open toward others and more inclusive as human beings. And they were to throw the biggest summer party of the year for everyone at the place, to start fresh. I really hope they stuck to that plan. A couple of months after my visit, I received word that the energy was still calm and the atmosphere at the stable was positive. That truly warmed my heart.

At one point, I had some supervision days together with two of my colleagues. One was Claus Toftgaard (again), and the other was the famous National Handball player Marianne Florman, who changed her career from the sports industry to becoming a horsemanship expert. We met to share knowledge from the different worlds we come from. But what we have in common, of course, is that all three of us help horses in our way. One time, we met at Marianne's beautiful place on the island Møn. I asked Marianne to help me with my deep fear of horses, which I had at that time. She taught me how she connects with a horse. She approaches the task in a much more physical way compared to the mental approach I use with horses. It was exciting and educational. When we were going to play with one of her horses in liberty, all three of us were supposed to play tag together. We were to catch him, and he was supposed to run in front. Suddenly, he stopped. He turned around, looked at me, and slowed down. I heard his thoughts. He said, *I'll slow down, Ditte. I can sense that you're struggling to keep up. That's okay. I will take care of you. You are a part of me and I am a part of you.*

Marianne was puzzled that he suddenly stopped while running forward because he never usually did that. I told her that her horse did it because he could sense that I had a ligament injury that not many people know about. I still struggle with it and therefore couldn't run very fast. It was a truly touching experience, and once again, I welcomed yet another intelligent and spiritual being, witnessing their shared understanding of the herd and their care for us humans.

Six months later, Marianne and I held a clinic together at the rescue center, *New Horselife,* on the island Funen. Almost the same thing happened there. We arranged a day on the horse's terms, where I started by telepathically communicating with the horse and understanding its personality, what it needed, and what it thought of the rider and key people around it. Then Marianne played with the horses based on what the horse had said it wanted. We worked with three different horses during the day, and each session was very different. The first horse healed all of us, and tears rolled down our cheeks. It was a compelling experience.

No one believed the next horse would want to play with poles when I brought it up to the horse, and suddenly, Marianne got it to do it to the horse's great enjoyment. At one point, one of the horses wanted to play tag with several of the participants, not just the owner and rider, and several people entered the arena to join the play. At one point, while they were standing at the other end of the arena, the horse ran toward us at the far end but suddenly slowed down and stopped. He told me, *"One of the women—he pointed to which one with his eye—just had her pelvis adjusted, so it would not be good for her to run."*

The woman at the other end could hear what I said because we had microphones and a sound system on the day. She was amazed when I told her what the horse had said. Because it was true, she had trouble with a bad pelvis and had just been to the chiropractor the day before to have it adjusted. Again, I saw how horses sense our physical and emotional challenges and take them into account, even during play, where they are thriving and motivated.

Horses help me understand what pure love is in its most valid form. When there are no expectations, only an acceptance of being as you are, and still being part of a herd, that is how the universe works. We are all part of something greater, and each one of us has a significant individual meaning. We cannot manage without one another, whether we are meant to be close in life or not. Do not judge, do not point fingers, do not hate, do not envy, but simply hold space for and love all people's differences and diversity. It sets us free.

Case with the Horse Fjola, Who Speaks About Her Health and What is Happening in the Future that Affects Her Mentally – In Collaboration with Osteopath, Physiotherapeutic Masseur, Acupuncturist, and Craniosacral Therapist Anne Tove Hansen

In this telepathic session, the Icelandic horse *Fjola* discussed her health and demonstrated her understanding and insight into what is happening in the future, which affects her mentally. Fjola's human, Helle, contacted me because she wanted to know whether Fjola was in pain anywhere.

Fjola had suddenly begun to show more aggressive behavior towards her other horse, Mani. And Fjola also didn't want to lift her legs. This case is an excerpt from my journal, which was sent to Fjola's human, Helle, in the form of what I call a *picture/remote telepathy*.

I reach out to Fjola and ask her to send me the topics she feels are relevant, through thoughts, images, and emotions. It is my primary task to interpret what she communicates accurately. I also write down the telepathy as a dialogue, as that is how it is shown to me.

I address the health issue first, as it takes up the most space. I need to point out that I perceive these things as energies in the present moment and based on the things that make a particular impression on Fjola right now. If things have happened to her in the past, or if she has sustained past injuries, she may not necessarily show them to me if they are no longer significant to her now. Since Fjola may not be aware of her future health condition, I unfortunately cannot guarantee that I will be shown what will happen to her in the future. If she shows me something that you are not aware of, I kindly ask that you verify it with a veterinarian or another qualified practitioner. I now begin to connect with her.

"Hi Fjola," I say and smile at her.

She comes right up to my face—to show herself and so that I understand that *ME time* is important to her. It's as if she just pushes straight into my *space* to say hello, and I can feel that she is happy, but concerned. She wants me to listen, and she is eager to make the connection.

"What makes you happy, and what makes you worried?" I ask her.

"I'm a happy lady, I'm happy with my life, but I'm worried that I'm no longer of use. Am I useless? The more useless I feel, the pushier and attention-seeking I become," she says.

"Shall we examine your health and evaluate it together?" I ask her.

"Yes, let's do that," she says, surprisingly upbeat.

The first thing Fjola shows me is that she feels she has tension headaches. I ask her where it comes from, and she points to her jaw joint, her hyoid bone, and her teeth. I ask her to show me everything in detail so I can be as specific as possible and so that you can pass this on to the right practitioner. And Fjola shows me that she feels she has a tooth bothering her in the upper right jaw. I believe it is a molar. She shows me that she then tenses up on the left side of her jaw, and the tension travels up into the skull behind her ears on the right side. She also tightens her jaw on the left side and in the neck. I have a sense that she locks up in the upper cervical vertebrae. She shows me that she feels her hyoid bone is slightly pushed to the left—just a little bit.

She shows me that she feels tired and heavy, particularly across her shoulders, and more so on the right shoulder. She is sore and feels locked up. She shows me that the discomfort radiates diagonally down to the left hind leg, and she feels she can't move it properly. It feels almost paralyzed, like when someone presses on your sciatic nerve and your leg might potentially give out. I have the impression that this is due to her sacroiliac joint (SI joint) being locked, and that she is unable to bring the left hind leg forward as a result. Her strongest and most muscular side is her entire right side, as I interpret her as having been born with a right-sided dominance. When she turns, she creates a right-sided banana shape, or the letter C, if you view her energy along the spine from above. She therefore carries most of her weight on the right side. But it's also her right side that she tightens the most in. I also want to note that this can cause misalignments in her chest and sternum, if it is indeed correct that her SI joint is also locked.

I sense that she feels her stomach is heavy in the lower region, and she feels tired after eating because she needs to use energy to digest her food. She shows me seaweed. Is she being given seaweed, I wonder, since Fjola sends me such an image? If not, I would recommend giving it to her based on what I'm sensing, but in a smaller dose.

If she is getting it, she shows me that it is rich in protein but also gives her this feeling of heaviness inside. I sense that she feels oats harm her digestive system. Her stomach feels heavy in general when I show her starchy products. She shows me that she feels her abdominal cavity is very large. When I ask further, she shows me that she just feels bloated. I get the impression that this is related to the feed.I ask about her organs and other soft tissue. She shows me that her liver is not functioning as well as it could. She would like it to be activated so that it can detox and work more effectively, which would also help her maintain healthy skin and coat. I don't have the sense that there's anything seriously wrong with her liver. It feels more like an imbalance in the liver meridian, where a detox treatment in the form of supplements in her feed would benefit her.

I ask if there are any other things, such as minerals or feed, that she's missing. And she points to the seaweed again.I ask her why you, as her owner, have difficulty lifting her hind leg.

She shows me that she feels locked up in the hip joint at the back, and the feeling I get is almost like an arthritis-like condition or tendency. She feels *stiff* in her hindquarters.

She shows me that she does not want to lift her hind leg because it hurts in her hip joint, and now I feel bones grinding against each other. I would recommend that you contact your vet or chiropractor to have this verified. What do you need for that? I ask her. *"I need my seaweed, and I would also benefit from thistle oil and aloe vera,"* she says.

She shows me that she drops down onto her hind legs to demonstrate that she does not want to lose contact with the ground. She is steadfast about getting that point across. And she is being kind to you, because with the level of pain I'm sensing, she could be reacting far more severely.

"Is it mischief or a matter of principle for you?" I ask her. *"No, I'm in pain, especially in my left hind leg and my right front leg,"* she says.

And this also explains why Fjola does not want to lift her legs. When she is locked in the SI joint and cannot carry herself properly on all four legs because of that, it would of course be very anxiety-inducing for her. Imagine walking on one leg because the other is broken, and you only have one crutch to lean vaguely on. Would you accept someone taking that one crutch from you? Or even removing the other leg you were supporting yourself with?

"What you need to know about me is that I've always tended to lift more through my left hind leg and at the same time down toward my right shoulder. So those are the sides that have carried the most weight, but they are also the most worn," she says.

"I know you've had a massage therapist and a chiropractor in. What makes the most significant difference for you in terms of treatment?" I ask Fjola.

"It's the massage, and I enjoy that too. The chiropractor just manipulates me, but as long as my owner tends to collapse into the seat on the right side and down toward my right knee, she can treat me from here to hell. It doesn't remove the cause," says Fjola.

"So, what is the cause? What needs to happen?" I ask her.

"Well, I was born this way, slightly crooked, you could say, when I push my right shoulder more forward, and the same with my left hind leg. So I

understand the use of a chiropractor, but if you bring in an acupuncturist next time, you'll help me much more, because I need everything to settle and find peace gently," she says.

"Could craniosacral therapy be a solution?" I ask her, as I know it can also help address the causes rather than just the symptoms.

"Yes, that would definitely help too, with my hyoid bone and my hip socket, but no treatment can stand alone if you don't look at the arthritis-like pain I have," she says.

"And acupuncture could also activate my liver by working on the liver meridian, so I prefer acupuncture and massage," she says.

"And preferably every fourteen days," she adds, laughing, because she knows she sounds demanding now, but I can feel she truly needs it.

"I've heard that nettles are good for joint pain. Can you use that?" I ask her.

"No, get thistle oil instead, that works better for me," she says.

"I also need to tell you that your owner finds it a bit unfair, I suppose you could say, that you want all the attention when the horse Mani also needs some of it. Do you understand that?" I ask her.

"I do understand that, but Mani is the one she can ride much more, so I just want more contact. It's a way of compensating," she says, as if it's the most obvious thing in the world.

"It would suit you to be a more dignified leader, Queen Fjola," I say to her with a smile.

"Suit me? It's not a beauty contest, Ditte," she snaps.

I can't help but laugh. She's so wonderfully direct.

"But what do you think about the behavior I see when you bite and kick at Mani?" I ask her. *"I think that little shit is asking for it, Ditte. That's honestly what I think. He shouldn't come so close to me. He needs to respect my personal space, and he needs to stay far away from my hind end. I'm nervous he'll try to climb on top of me or pretend to mount me,"* she says.

"But he doesn't do that", I tell her.

"No, but I've been honest with you and shown you that I have a major weakness in my hip and pelvic area, and that's why I fear he might do something. He just wants to play. That kind of shit—I'm too old for that. So, of course, I chase him off," she says.

I'm thinking that in this case, attack is the easiest defense to fall back on.

"Okay, but if you're treated based on what you've said, would you then stop chasing, biting, or kicking at him, and become a better leader?" I ask her.

"No," she says.

"Why not?" I ask. *"And what would it take?"*

"It would take knowing that I have my mom forever," she says, and now she becomes sad.

"What do you mean?" I ask her.

"My mom can't do very much, and I've always filled her up. But now I don't feel like I fill her up enough anymore. Others do. There was a time when only we animals could fill her up. Now humans can do it too, for

fuck's sake," she says, and now she shows me a child. I can't help but wonder if you have small children in your immediate family, such as grandchildren. And if not, then I get a powerful sense from Fjola that a small child is on the way to your family.

"And that makes me anxious about losing her. I miss the connection between us, and I know we have a good bond, and she loves me, but I don't feel like I fill her up anymore," she says.

"Have I then served my purpose?" she asks me, as if wondering whether that means she's supposed to die now.

"No, you certainly haven't. There are many good years ahead of you, and you're meant to live and stay here on earth, continuing to be a gift. But you're a much greater gift as a calm and grounded leader than when you come across as so grumpy," I tell her.

"I just want to be one of a kind and know that I'm good enough and that I have a purpose. To fill someone up," she says sorrowfully.

"Fill yourself up, so you don't make yourself dependent on others to fill you up, like your owner!" I say to her.

"You don't understand? I saved my mother's life. I saved her from a depression, Ditte. Now she's better. She can take care of herself... so where does that leave me?" she asks me again.

"You're exactly where you've always been. Right in the middle of her heart. But is there something I should ask your owner to do, since I can interpret between you?" I ask her.

"Yes, tell her that when she comes out to see me and meets me each day, she should whisper in my ear that I have great value, and that I just need to be calm and happy, because I still fill my mother up. And that means I have something to bring meaning to my life. I just want to feel that I'm important and that I have a purpose," she says sadly.

"I feel like I once was the only thing my mother had to live for. Now I'm not that anymore," she repeats, still sad.

"But regardless of whether that's true or not, because I don't know that Fjola—it's a GOOD thing if your mother feels that way in her life now. Can't you see that? What was the alternative? That your mother should be walking around feeling awful?" I ask her.

"No, I can see that," she says, and thinks about my words.

"Then feel it, and know that you saved her, and that's something to be

proud of. And you should keep being the proud horse you are, but in a calmer way. That way, it's easier for your mother to continue being proud of you. Negative attention isn't the same as positive attention—do you understand that?" I ask her.

"No," she says.

"Oh, for heaven's sake," I think to myself, and whisper, *"the stubborn lady"* and chuckle to myself.

"Well, then let me explain it to you again. The calmer, sweeter, and more lovely you are, the easier it is to love you and give you the attention you deserve. That's how people understand you. We can't always see beyond what you do. No one has the energy for that. We, just like you, horses sometimes, respond to what is shown. What you show is what we think you mean. Do you understand that?" I ask her.

"Yes," she says.

"So, when you show aggressive behavior, what do you think we make of that?" I ask her.

"That I'm angry?" she says.

"Exactly, and you're not. You're playing a game, which I didn't think was possible for a horse. Or maybe I now think it's become a defense mechanism within you. But do you understand that now, Fjola?" I ask her.

"Yes," she says.

"So, what will you do about it starting today?" I ask her.

"I will try to show a calmer and more loving side of myself," she says.

"Is that a deal?" I ask her.

"Yes," she says, laughing too, because she feels like she's been tricked into this deal by me, and I can also think that deep down, she's relieved inside.

So, she has a massive defense mechanism, which it seems takes time to break down and through.

"Then I would like to express my sincere gratitude for taking the time to talk to me."

"Thank you, Ditte, it helped," she says and smiles calmly.

And then we say a polite goodbye to each other.

Owner Helle recognized everything, and Fjola stopped chasing Mani in the field after our communication. The funniest part was that on Christmas Eve, the owner was told there was a little grandchild on the way. I'm always surprised by the horses' insight into the future.

Cranio-Sacral therapist, physiotherapeutic masseuse, and acupuncturist Anne Tove Hansen from Norway shares her thoughts on my work:

"Journal from January 12, 2016: **Treatment of Fiola:** *Finds restrictions in the return of the right hind leg (SI joint), sacrum, and down the left side; the left hip is locked and heavily strained due to the right front leg, and the shoulder is locked. The left breastbone is locked. This means there's a twist in the thoracic spine; the horse puts most of its weight on the left side. The lower back is locked on the left side. The right neck is locked at numbers 1 (atlas), 5, 6, and 7. The left neck number 2 (axis) is also locked. The primary strain sits on the left side because her right front leg has restrictions.*

I think it's fantastic to read Ditte Young's conversation with Fiona through a pictorial telepathy. I received this after the treatment. I am impressed with how direct and accurate the messages she receives in her communication with the horse are. I am thrilled to be able to collaborate with her, because she is a fantastic person and therapist."

Chapter 7

See You In Heaven

"My home is in heaven. I am just passing through the world."
– Billy Graham

This is a profound and reflective passage, touching on some of the most profound aspects of life, death, and the connection we share with animals. It's hard to avoid the inevitable truth that life is fleeting. In the case of our beloved animals, we often find ourselves in a position where we must make difficult decisions on their behalf, especially when they reach the end of their life. The way you describe the instincts of animals to seek solitude as they approach the end is poignant. It reminds me of how they often, in their way, know when it's time for them to move on. In the wild, they would follow their instincts, but in our world, where they depend on us, we become the stewards of that final journey.

The search for a peaceful end in a familiar, quiet space, whether that's out in the pasture or seeking solitude, is something that many pet owners will recognize in their animals' behavior when they begin to sense their time is near. It's as though they can feel the change in their bodies and the world around them, even before we fully understand it. *Is this something you've experienced with animals you've known? How do you process that transition?*

When We Say Goodbye To Our Horses

The most challenging thing about losing a horse is when it's a final goodbye. Never again will you see your best friend, touch them, sit on their back, be with them, breathe together, and simply be present in the moment with them. Many who have experienced the loss of their horses have described to me that they feel as though their horses are still present in the stable. Sometimes they aren't sure whether they are in their old stalls because they suddenly smell their horses. Some riders have even told me that they are convinced their old horses are teaching their new ones. They know their horses are watching over them, like guardian angels from another place that we can't see with our naked eyes.

For many years, I've been asked if I would help as an interpreter between the horse and its owner or rider before, during, and after euthanasia. There have been times when I've declined. And many times, I've said yes and felt honored to be part of a process where a horse transitions beyond. In a sense, I've always thought it's a big responsibility, while at the same time, I've been very grateful for the opportunity to interpret between two souls who need to say goodbye.

I've always been highly aware of the high moral and ethical standards required in my work when being part of such a *journey*, where it's vulnerable, sensitive, and sorrowful for all parties. I've always been cautious not to play the role of a judge in life or death. What I can do is describe what the horse feels and experiences; ultimately, the decision is up to the horse's owner, rider, and veterinarian.

I've found that most horses with a health issue are ready to die. It's natural for them if they feel extremely weak inside, or if they know that the problem they have will never get better. The last situation I saw was a horse that had suffered a concussion and was leaking fluid from the dura around the brain, causing it to always feel a paralysis in its hindquarters. Animals, like many humans, also want to leave this world with dignity. It is we humans who are afraid of death, mourn for a long time, and struggle to let go, even though death is natural and one of the two things in life we are certain of. We are born, and we die.

When I debate death, whether on social media, my blog, or through sharing videos on the topic on YouTube, I see that it is a highly controversial topic that sparks great debate and often divides opinions.

One group of people is frequently opposed to the idea that horses want to be euthanized if they don't believe they can live a dignified life. These are usually people who don't think horses have an opinion, and therefore, in principle, shouldn't be asked.

The other group of people knows that horses want to leave this world with dignity. These are often the people who are very focused on their horses' well-being and want to hear from them.

Of course, there are also cases where the horse is dangerous to itself and its surroundings. It could be because it has been *coded* wrong, throwing the rider off the saddle and being completely unwilling to cooperate, thus needing to be put down. It could always be debated whether the horse should have been let loose in the field instead, so at least its life would have been saved. I secretly agree. But my job isn't to have an opinion; it's to interpret and speak to the hearts of humans so that we can do the best we can for the animals, at a pace that each individual can handle. I need to keep this in mind so that I don't cross boundaries, either for the people or animals I assist, during their process, but instead simply hold space and understand both parties.

What makes death such a delicate topic, in my opinion, is that it's something we don't want to talk about. We encounter our fear of death. And it's also a topic that, if one is not careful, can make alternative healers seem like executioners concerning animals. *When should they live and when should they die? What's right and what's wrong?* In my opinion, the final decision must be up to you, as the horse owner or rider, to determine the fate of your horse, since it is ultimately your horse. Then, it's essential that the vet also provides advice that makes sense to you and feels right so that you can find peace with the decision.

If what you're told doesn't make sense, find another practitioner or ask for a second opinion from another vet. In Denmark today, there is freedom of choice, which applies to both clinical and alternative practitioners. For some people, horses are working animals, while for others, they are their best friend and most cherished possession. For some, they are both, or something entirely different.

When I assist horse owners and riders during a difficult time when they're unsure whether their horse should live or die, because they want to know what the horse itself thinks and feels inside, I distinguish between the ego and the heart of the rider I am working with. Regardless of which side I encounter, I don't think there's a right or wrong, but rather a journey between horse and rider that may end in one way or another. We are all on our journey, and each of us exists in the world in our own unique way. This also applies to our goals, ambitions, desires, needs, and many other aspects of our lives.

Some riders must decide to euthanize their horse based on economic reasons. It could be questions about whether the horse can reach the goals set for the day or whether it's being used. Questions like whether the rider can truly achieve the recognition that drives them with this horse. Essentially, it's assessed whether the horse is usable/applicable or not, and whether it should live or die. So, there can be a kind of business logic involved, or whether it would be profitable to keep the horse. *What purpose was the horse bought for? What is its fate with these particular people and riders? Is this right or wrong?* It is what it is on the journey they are taking together. No one can judge this, regardless of morals, values, understanding of animal welfare, or pure business sense. Ultimately, only the rider and the horse must feel and experience what is happening within themselves during that process.

When some riders decide whether their horse should be euthanized or not, they will always have to feel what they believe is the right thing to do for the particular animal, regardless of their feelings. What do you think as a rider? Is it a dignified life for your horse? Do you have a horse that can cope with and accept being put out to pasture? Do you, as a rider, have the resources to keep a horse that is having a good life but can no longer be used as a riding horse? Is this right or wrong? I don't think you can set it up like that, but I know that many people have an opinion about what the other person is doing and can sometimes seem judgmental. Because again, what works for one person doesn't necessarily work for another. The economy one person has, another may not, and the heart one person has, another may not have either.

I can establish contact with horses that are on *the other side*. The method is the same as for regular telepathy, but I also feel like I am working on a different frequency, or the vibrations are higher. My eyes can blink faster, my body may slightly shake, and I can feel as though I'm being drawn into a parallel world when I communicate with them, even though my consciousness knows that I am physically present here and my body hasn't moved.

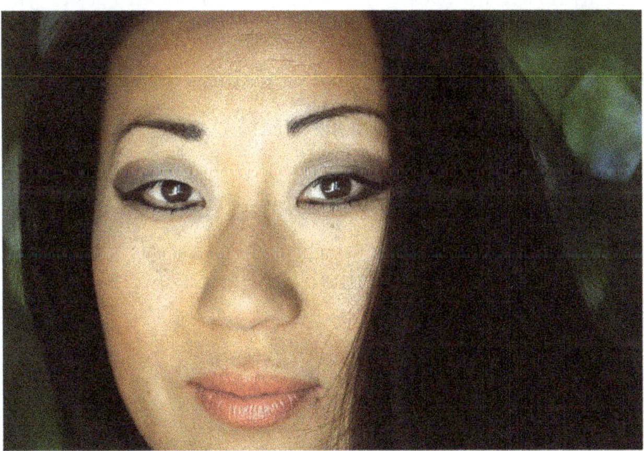

It works the same way as with regular telepathy. Some horses are faster to connect with than others. This may be because they are preoccupied with something else, are on a different frequency, or simply more selective about who they want to connect with. Or it can be situations where you can't just barge in without sensitivity. In such cases, the horse responds more cautiously when interacting with a stranger. This is also how I sense whether the animals I see in a picture are alive or have passed away. I always ask the animal whether it is alive or dead, and if the animal is not aware of its state, I then sense how far I need to extend my energy to establish contact. If it feels very far away, I know I am communicating with a deceased animal.

Sometimes, I feel I need to push the energy through to reach them, but I always ask for their permission before they come to me. I do not want to disturb or bother them if they are busy with something else. I have never experienced being rejected by a horse during telepathic contact. Much of this also comes down to using the proper questioning techniques and coaching methods to ensure it works every single time.

A horse that is hesitant or skeptical in its contact with me also reveals something about its personality. I meet the horse where it is and allow it to be wary. I don't take it personally or feel offended. I know that the horse's behavior is likely influenced by its personality or past experiences. It may be related to its encounters with other humans and usually has nothing to do with me. Most of the time, I sense that the horse relaxes in its sympathetic nervous system when I *set it free* this way by allowing it to be just as it is. I convey this to myself in my thoughts, in images, and through the energy I transfer from me to it. And it responds. At that point, we are already in communication. We have created a new present moment together and a safe platform for the horse to express itself.

I always ask deceased horses the same kinds of questions I would ask if they were alive, but I phrase them in the past tense. *What did you think of your rider, and what resources did you have when you were alive? What motivated you? What health issues made an impression on you, and did they impact your well-being and training? How did you die? What was it like for you to step into death? Are you okay where you are now?* And then I ask them to show me their version of heaven. Often, their owners or riders also have questions they want me to ask. It could be things like: *"Did you understand that I did everything I could and tried to save you?"* or *"Were you in pain before you were put to sleep?"*

Most of the thoughts from the owners and riders revolve around their grief and guilt, even if they may not have any reason to feel that way. How their horse passed is something that profoundly affects them, along with the health problems that often led to euthanasia.

Letting Them Go Is Also An Act Of Love

Sometimes the greatest act of love we can offer our animal, and even other people, is to set them free and say goodbye. Holding on to another soul can often be more for our own sake than for theirs. For animals, it may be that they no longer see a reason to stay. They may feel they have fulfilled their life's purpose with us, often due to old age. Or they may be in pain and hope we will help them end their suffering. For humans, it might make more sense to separate than to hold on to a broken relationship. Perhaps the future holds more joy, learning, and happiness for everyone involved.

Of course, it is painful for a horse owner to carry the grief that comes with saying goodbye to their animal, their best friend, their dreams, their hopes, and much more. However, I know that if you tune in with your entire being, you will know when it is time. Holding on to an animal longer than necessary is usually for the human's sake, not the horses. In such cases, unfortunately, it may be driven by ego and internal needs. Most horses are never angry at their owners for waiting too long to let them go. But they do experience a sense of relief when the decision is finally made, as long as the horse is truly ready to die.

The horses I have spoken to just before euthanasia are also the telepathic connections I remember best because each of them touched my fear of death, something I have worked intensely with. None of them were afraid to enter death, but they feared dying alone. That means they had a strong desire for their owners or riders to be physically present with them when they were put down or received injections from the vet.

I remember once being called by a young girl, crying over the phone, telling me her horse was about to be euthanized. She asked me to go to the riding club in the city of Holte, where the horse was, and be present during the process. When I asked if she would be there too, she said no. I declined to go alone to a horse I had never met before, and I told her, *"If I'm going to be there, then you must be there too. We'll do this together in honor of your horse. I'll give your horse a voice, and you can say goodbye properly. I'll be there to support both of you."*

She couldn't bring herself to go through with it. It was too emotionally painful for her. However, after hearing from all the horses who have told me they were scared to die alone, I firmly believe that owners and riders must be present if the horse requests it. They are the ones the horses know and trust. I would only be a temporary comfort, a translator. Would the horse find peace by telling me about its final thoughts before closing its eyes? Absolutely. But only if I could deliver those messages directly to the owner. And if that's the case, the owner might as well stand there physically with us, even if it's hard and sorrowful. Being present through life and death is part of the journey of having an animal.

The moments I remember most vividly are the ones involving horses right before euthanasia. These are the ones I will describe in this book. I have spoken with many horses about this topic, but only a few stood out because they provided me with such profound insights. One horse that left a deep impression on me was a large and proud gelding. The owner asked me to travel to South Zealand to help them say goodbye before euthanasia. The gelding told me about his life, being a riding horse, how proud he was of himself and his rider. He had lived a good life. He knew the injuries he had were irreversible, and he knew he could not be saved. He had made peace with the fact that he was going to die and communicated all of this to his owner and the daughter, the rider, who stood beside me in the stable.

The revelation for me was that, at the time, I had not yet discovered the spiritual gifts of horses. I had been focused on finding the difference between telepathy and clairvoyance during my early years. I had spent a great deal of energy separating the two. I never imagined that the horses I telepathically connected with had guides or spiritual helpers who might suddenly chime in. That made me realize how important it is for us, as humans, to act as their protectors and advocates.

This horse, on what was essentially his deathbed, suddenly began to tell me that he wished the daughter would be less uncertain about her education path. I remember stopping in silence. The daughter started crying because neither of us expected her horse to know these things, and none of us thought the session would turn toward her future. The gelding told me that, of course, he knew about her doubts, because she thought about it often when she was with him and riding him. Naturally, he picked up on her thoughts. He had usually comforted her and told her what to choose, but she had never listened. She had never managed to pick up on his signals.

Her choice was between an academic program that would formally qualify her to work with animals or a program she was genuinely passionate about, but which would not offer the same academic prestige. The gelding was clear: she should follow her heart. The girl was shocked, relieved, and cried all at once. I was also surprised that the horse could discuss her educational path, especially since she hadn't mentioned it to me in advance. It was a massive eye-opener for me to realize how much the horses can pick up telepathically. I questioned how a horse could understand what an academic or alternative education was. These are not concepts that exist in their world.

What I discovered was that the horse picked up on her thoughts and, most importantly, her energy. There was energy built up around both choices, and from that, the horse interpreted what would be good or not good for her. Because emotions and energy don't lie, when you are true to your feelings and listen with a pure heart, you cannot be conflicted by ego or others' beliefs. In your truth and love for yourself, you can't be driven by a desire for external validation. Your low self-worth or ego may try to confuse you. But your heart cannot. We just need to learn to feel it and stay true to it. That way, I believe we will make fewer compromises in life and simply be present in the now, just as the horses are.

The horse then moved on to give messages to his human mother. He said to me in thought, *"She has to end the affair she's having."* I fell completely silent and said nothing. I remember thinking I had no idea how to communicate this. A thousand thoughts raced through my mind: *"How does he know this if he hasn't seen it? What should I say to the mother? I can't say that in front of her daughter. What if it's wrong? What if the mother lashes out at me and says it's none of my business?"* So instead, I asked the horse what I should do with these thoughts he was picking up inside me. And I still stood there, saying nothing, with the mother and daughter beside me in a cold stable on a winter day, while the thoughts flew silently through the air around them, unnoticed.

The gelding looked at me and smiled calmly, bowed his head, and took a step toward me. I could feel the warm air from his muzzle and nostrils. And I became calm. Then he said to me that I should tell the mother out in the parking lot when I was about to leave, when the daughter was no longer by her side. He assured me that what he was saying was true, and the reason it was so crucial for him to deliver this message was because he knew he would no longer be able to protect his (human) mother once he was gone. It was crucial to him that she knew she had to make the right choices in life, to take care of herself.

I promised him I would do what he asked, and then I continued speaking as if nothing had happened, while the mother and daughter were still present. They were able to say a proper goodbye, and we had a touching moment, all four of us crying together. He was one of those who didn't want to enter death alone. He was very focused on both being there during the euthanasia. When we were done, I said goodbye, kissed the gelding on the forehead, and was deeply moved.

When we went out to the gravel parking lot to settle payment and say goodbye, it was only the mother who accompanied me. That's when I told her that her horse wanted her to end her affair. She looked at me, fell completely silent, and then threw herself into my arms and began to cry. She said she already knew it, but she couldn't stop. She was living in an unhappy marriage and felt utterly lost. Her husband wasn't affectionate and didn't understand her. She had fought for years trying to get him to listen and to be more loving and devoted in their relationship, but she couldn't reach him. She was so unhappy and afraid to divorce him. So, she did what many people in her situation do: allow themselves to be filled up by someone else who can give them what they desperately long for in that moment, whether it's the right thing to do or not.

I hugged her, comforted her, and said that her horse had passed on the message for her to stop, and it was now up to her to decide what to do with her own life. There was a gift in this confrontation, where her secret had been revealed. She could choose to face the decision, even though it was hard. The choice could be to stay and find peace and happiness in that, or to leave and find peace and happiness in that, and at the same time, explore what the fear of leaving was about inside her. She thanked me for delivering the message while we were alone. Anything else would have been completely unethical, so of course I waited.

Driving back to Copenhagen on the highway, I thought for a long time about what had just happened. I was utterly shocked that a horse could stand there and tell me these things. And suddenly it dawned on me that the thoughts we humans have often come to us when we are in a state of calm. When there is space to think, and that usually happens in the company of horses. That's what most horse owners tell me: that their horses heal them. They become de-stressed by their horses. And the horses listen to your thoughts. They act as good listeners and therapists for you without you even knowing it. Of course, they know what's going on inside their humans. It has nothing to do with clairvoyance. It's simply that horses pick up the thoughts and energy around them. And they hold it, tolerate it, and carry it. Horses have no secrets from one another or you. They are so honest, and they know what is good and what is not.

Unlike other types of animals I communicate with, such as cats and dogs, I repeatedly find that horses understand the consequences of the choices we make. Even though they shouldn't have the ability to foresee the future if you look solely at the neocortex of the brain, that tells me that many horses also possess a spiritual insight that goes beyond ordinary understanding and brain capacity, and that makes them highly intelligent in my eyes. I will never forget this prince of a gelding. He provided me with a profound understanding of his insights. And it was then that I began to understand what great teachers they are, if we listen to them.

Another episode that made a strong impression on me involved one of the horses I spoke with, who had already passed away. It was also a trip to South Zealand many years ago. I arrived at a home where the daughter wanted to connect with her deceased mare. The mother and father were home, and her boyfriend was also present for the session. They had set a table for coffee, and we all sat down on their black sofas around the coffee table. I explained how it would work, and when I was ready, I was passed a photo of the deceased mare and a piece of her mane. I described the mare's personality and all the things I typically cover during a telepathy session. The daughter smiled and nodded in recognition at every word I shared. We were all touched. And there was something beautiful about creating that connection between the two of them, allowing them to communicate during my time there.

I knew nothing about the mare before I began. That's how I prefer to work. Both to avoid any doubt about what I do or don't know, and because I get too influenced by what owners might tell me, which can confuse me during the session. I prefer a blank canvas to work from. If there's something I need to know, I either ask the horse or the owner, if the horse doesn't answer me. This cozy moment took a different turn when we reached the point in the session where the daughter wanted to ask her mare if she knew what she had died from. I still hadn't been told anything and was curious to hear how the mare had experienced dying. At the same time, I felt humble and honored to pass on the messages from the mare to the girl.

The mare showed me that she was standing in the aisle of the stable, and a vet was going to examine her. She was nervous and had been ill for a long time. She had trouble supporting herself on her right hind leg because of an injury. She showed me that at the moment the vet was about to examine her rectally, two things happened simultaneously. First, the vet pushed her tail in a way that pressed on a nerve running to her right leg. She showed me a sensation that the leg gave out, and she collapsed right there in the stable aisle.

Second, an artery ruptured, and she bled out in the middle of the aisle. The mare told me she was scared and remembered people screaming around her. She felt it was important to say that it wasn't the vet's fault, and the artery would have ruptured regardless. But to an outsider, it could appear as if the rectal exam had caused her to bleed out. When I told the family this, the daughter suddenly stood up in the living room and screamed. She covered her mouth and screamed with everything she had while tears streamed down her face. Her boyfriend ran around her, unsure of what to do. Her parents sat still on the sofa, clearly in a state of shock. In situations like this, I'm also grateful to be a trained therapist.

I stood up calmly and walked over to her. I placed a firm hand on her lower back and told her just to let it out while I held her and gave her a sense that she could fall apart and I would catch her. She screamed and screamed, and I held her hand. I looked at the photo of the mare and asked her for help as well. I was worried it might be too much for the girl, but the mare assured me to let her release it. When she was done reacting, she sobbed uncontrollably for a while, and then it slowly subsided. I looked compassionately at her parents, and occasionally at her boyfriend, who, in truth, was the one I was most concerned about in all of this. It looked pretty intense.

When the girl was finally able to speak again, she told me that what I had said was exactly what had happened, and she had never understood why. She had always blamed the vet for what had happened, even though she couldn't make sense of it. She had been in desperate need of closure. Especially to find some release from the shock and trauma of witnessing the violent death of her mare, bleeding out in front of her in the stable aisle. The rest of the session was about the mare describing what her heaven looked like and letting her know she was at peace now.

Of course, I remember the episode, because it was so traumatic and intense. The revelation I received through this mare was that she had known all along during our conversation that the girl needed to release her grief. And that she needed clarity about how she had died. What this taught me, and what truly dawned on me that day, was that sometimes, as the voice of the horse, I have to communicate things that are not easy to hear, because it will make sense afterward. And most importantly, it can be healing for the person receiving the message, even if it may seem too much or too harsh. But who am I to judge that? Isn't it true that if I withhold something, I am not being faithful to the animal?

The art for me lies in how I deliver the message. Not holding it back because I assume it's too much for the recipient. I must never project or assume anything I don't know, and that's what this mare taught me that day. I trust that the horses know what their people can handle hearing, and how they need to hear it, meaning, in what tone, and with what words and phrasing. When I pause and hesitate about something the horses want me to share, I always ask them if their people can bear hearing it, when I'm in doubt.

Gislinge Church

"I belong to a Christian church, but I also know that any religion claiming to be the only true one is wrong and dysfunctional. God loves all people. The most important message is one of compassion and understanding that we are all interconnected. Just as it will never be possible to prove that God and heaven exist scientifically, it will also never be possible to prove that they do not." — **Eben Alexander, MD, American neurosurgeon and author of the book *Proof of Heaven***

Through my work as a therapist and clairvoyant, I have observed a growing interest in people's desire to discover themselves and develop self-confidence. They no longer want to be mere extras in a movie where the framework has already been set. A traditional, authoritarian, and in some ways outdated way of thinking, especially regarding faith, has changed and evolved rapidly in recent decades. In its place has come a desire for each person to play the lead role in their own life and, importantly, to define the framework for how that life should unfold.

When it comes to faith, I grew up with the Danish National Church as a natural part of our family life. My father was on the parish council at the church located just a few meters from my childhood home. I was a regular presence in the church every Sunday—a church where I was both baptized and confirmed. Later, I joined the church choir and sang hymns every Sunday during services in the ample, beautiful space with Jesus hanging above the altar and the ornate lamps in the ceiling. I earned some of my pocket money by delivering church newsletters around the neighborhood. I also read through them to ensure I knew what I was handing out to people in my community and at the church.

Over the years, I have spent a lot of time reconciling spirituality, existentialism, psychoanalysis, body therapy, and, not least, my Christian faith in a way that makes sense to me. In the various methods and belief systems that were part of my personal and spiritual education, I chose to take the best from all worlds. I explored where they agreed and where they differed, creating a belief system within myself. I read both the Bible and parts of the Quran. I immersed myself in the works of great philosophers—from the Greek philosopher Socrates to the Danish philosopher and theologian Søren Kierkegaard. I read about Buddhism, Catholicism, took an interest in New Age movements, and was fascinated by what makes people believe, or not believe. What drives the human need for faith? What is it that allows the people I help today, whether in therapy or through clairvoyance, to leave my sessions feeling lighter after just 60 minutes, having rediscovered faith in and insight into themselves?

Why does it sometimes take another person to reveal this to them? Where is their faith in themselves and within themselves? Is there a longing in all of us that, when we finally believe in ourselves, we feel whole? Could it be that many animal owners, consciously or unconsciously, feel that their animals accompany them on this journey toward a higher understanding of themselves? And what happens to us when they are with us, and when they are no longer here? These are some of the topics I discuss during the lecture *We'll Meet in Heaven*, a talk I've given all over the country, which has generated significant interest from many animal owners.

In October 2015, pony mom Dorthe Thaulov contacted me for the first time. They had a pony named Davidoff, which her daughter Amalie rode. They wanted to understand his behavior better, and their goal with him was the Danish Championship in dressage. Our first meeting arrived, and they were impressed by my abilities, recognizing everything I interpreted from their pony, whom they called Doffi. In June 2016, I helped them again with the pony, and Amalie was now preparing to find a new owner for Doffi and move on to a horse, as her pony years were coming to an end. That session also went very well, and everyone was pleased.

In March 2017, Dorthe contacted me again—this time in her role as the parish priest of Gislinge Church. She asked if I would come and give a talk in the parish hall. The lecture would focus on what happens to animals when they die. Many of her churchgoers had asked her for guidance, and she wanted to share her knowledge and experience with them. Since Gislinge is a *"happy dog town,"* the lecture would cover all types of animals and what happens when they cross to the other side. We agreed that I would give the talk in the parish hall on June 1, 2017, with the approval of the parish council. Dorthe asked how many attendees were needed for the event to take place. I replied, *"If you can gather 30–40 people and there's space in the hall, I'll come."*

I had a feeling this might be a bit of a controversy. I felt I needed to approach this assignment more humbly than usual and focus on communicating with a group who might be more traditionally minded than those I'd previously spoken to. I hoped it could be time to start building a bridge between the church and spirituality—a bridge and space that could be created through information, existential questions, and insights from my work. I was proud and grateful to be invited by a parish priest—a priest I also knew as a mother and client, with whom I had a warm and close relationship through my work with Amalie. Still, I had no idea how controversial it would become.

I arrived about an hour before the lecture to review the final details with Dorthe and verify the PowerPoint, screen, microphone, and all technical equipment. Attendees began to arrive, and soon 130 people were standing outside—a number neither Dorthe nor I had anticipated. We were both delighted to see such great interest in the topic of what happens when animals pass away. Even a journalist from the local newspaper turned up and followed the evening's events. At the last moment, we decided to move the lecture into the church itself, where there were enough pews to accommodate everyone.

When I stepped into the beautiful Gislinge Church, I felt a calm come over me—a sense that here, in this space, the ceiling was high, both literally and spiritually. I went behind a backdrop and screen to prepare. I looked at the baptismal font to my right. The audience couldn't see me from where I stood, so I knelt by the altar and folded my hands. I prayed to God to give me the strength to be a good communicator and to help those who had found a connection with themselves, their hearts, and the departed animals that would show themselves during the lecture. I felt a sense of peace, and I was grateful and humbled to stand in God's house, in a sacred space.

The lecture began, and I started sharing my experiences with animals crossing over and what happens on the other side. I spoke about how humans need nature and animals as living beings, and how, through my work, I've come to realize that they do not have guardians and guides watching over them in the same way we humans do. My calmness and voice filled the space, echoing gently as I spoke about our responsibility to care for these incredible creatures who, in many ways, care for us.

Although they are in some aspects more primitive than we are, I share the belief that we are mutually dependent—animals and humans. And I believe this is precisely why Noah was commanded by God to build an ark with his family and the animals, to escape the great flood. A belief that by simply existing, animals help maintain balance within and around us here on Earth, in the eternal present they embody.

I did two live demonstrations with selected participants who had brought photos of their animals. I didn't know them or their deceased pets. It was a beautiful evening, filled with good spirits and a fantastic atmosphere.

The following day, I saw an article about my lecture on our National TV stations' website. A local reporter from a newspaper, who had been present in the church and written a nice little piece about the lecture and how joyful it was to see *"an animal clairvoyant draw 130 people into an otherwise empty church on an ordinary weekday evening,"* apparently had their article shared with other media outlets. That article then spread like wildfire, and for the next two weeks, priest Dorthe Thaulov and I gave an average of 4 to 8 interviews a day. We were inundated with calls from every single newspaper and TV station in the country. The story went viral. What started as a feel-good story about a cozy evening in a whole church turned into a significant debate about what one is allowed to lecture on in Danish churches. The bishop temporarily suspended Dorthe Thaulov while the case was investigated. It caused a great stir. Ignorance, miscommunication, and misleading headlines didn't make the situation easier in the following days. On social media, there was significant support for Dorthe, who had invited me and, as a parish priest, was open to hearing about other people's experiences.

On a personal level, I was outraged, furious, and heartbroken that Dorthe was suspended and effectively silenced. I kept wondering how this evening had suddenly become a media storm and a battlefield. A debate that, for me, turned into a minefield full of discussions about whether animals have souls. A debate about what is and isn't allowed in the church's space. Arguments about how pasta services and rock concerts are permitted, but it is not allowed to shelter refugees, speak about reincarnation, or have a priest invite someone to discuss what happens to animals when they die. Questions about whether priests are the only ones who can *"call God directly,"* whether people would leave the Danish church, and whether we should be burned at the stake in front of the church—these kinds of sentiments swirled around both Dorthe and me every day during that time. I felt an enormous sense of guilt towards Dorthe for being a contributing factor to her situation, even though I knew I wasn't solely responsible since I had only been invited.

Still, I was part of the debate, and with that came a guilt that felt like carrying a four-ton brick on my shoulders. I felt like Dorthe was standing alone in a minefield, having to stay still to avoid stepping on any more mines around her. In my guilt, I saw myself as the mines and her as the one trapped. And amidst all this stood a pony mom to Amalie, whom I cared deeply for, and who was now at risk of losing her home, parish house, and position as a priest if she were dismissed. To me, it felt like being invited to a cozy evening in a warm and loving home, only to be thrown out the front door so forcefully that the echo of the wooden door slamming still rang in my ears.

After recovering from the shock of being thrown out, I turned around and looked at the house. A house I had once grown up in and believed in, now with closed doors, boarded-up windows, and a large iron gate in front of me. I sensed that I was no longer welcome due to my beliefs and work. I wondered what the problem was with withdrawing 130 people into a church from the parish hall when there wasn't enough room for that many people there. Why wasn't the church open to this kind of debate, especially when interest was so high, and so many churches stood empty across the country? If the interest in alternative perspectives is so great, why try to silence those who want to help inform others? To me, it's every person's responsibility to judge whether the information is suitable for them individually. I wanted to share that in heaven, as souls, we withdraw and do not judge one another. Our perspective becomes broader. Amid the media storm, I chose to follow what I believe in: to move through it without a reflex reaction fueled by anger. Instead, I aimed to present a reflective response. I stayed quiet and withdrew, while feeling an extreme tension between the church and spirituality. An energy I wasn't sure could be brought into balance or whether it would explode, with Dorthe being the first in line if it did.

On a professional level, I completely understood that it would stir things up to have a clairvoyant speak about deceased animals in a sacred space like a church. I thought that the debate about whether animals have souls might stem from the biblical interpretation that *"man is above animals."* That humans have personal lives and consciousness, and are the only beings created by God. At the same time, animals possess a *"life spirit,"* but not to the same degree of consciousness or personality. In Genesis chapter 1, verse 30 in the 1871 edition of the Danish Bible Society, it says:*"And to all the beasts of the earth, and all the birds under heaven, and to everything that creeps on the earth, in which is a living soul, I have given..."*

In the 1992 edition, the text was changed to:*"To all the wild animals and all the birds of the sky, yes to everything living that moves on the earth, I give..."*

The word *soul* was omitted in that edition. The word soul in the Bible's original language, Hebrew, indicates that a soul in biblical terms is a living being. A living being is, therefore, a soul. The word is used for humans, for God, and for animals. And God can restore the soul, the living person, through resurrection to either an earthly or heavenly life. I thought it might be interesting to debate the word *"soul instead."* In the Jewish faith, Jesus did not distinguish between the soul and the body but instead focused on the resurrection of the flesh. In Egyptian mythology, there were distinctions between various souls, such as a name-soul and a shadow-soul. And in shamanism, there are distinctions between several types of souls. Hinduism speaks of *atman*, which is the soul of a human that can merge with the divine force *"brahman."*

Despite my curiosity about exploring the commonalities between religions and belief systems, and despite my strong disagreement with the bishop that animals do not have souls, I had to hold back my wonder and quest to understand the entire debate. I understood that it had to have some form of consequence in a traditional Lutheran institution, that a priest had not considered how such a lecture might appear too *hippie-like*. And I thought to myself that I also understood the bishop's need to hold things together so that the church didn't spiral into chaos over what is permitted in a holy space.

I thought long and hard about what this debate might mean for future efforts to bridge the gap between Christianity and spirituality. It felt like one tentative step forward and twenty steps back in my emotions and frustration over Dorthe Thaulov being silenced. I also knew that in previous cases, priests had been asked to issue public apologies and retract their belief in spirituality to keep their jobs. Was the church a fortress with excellent and closed doors that would remain shut forever? Was the fear and control in the whole *Gislinge case* really about avoiding a church without doors? A transparent sacred house with airy, see-through walls where traditions and doctrines could flow out through the windows and walls?

Might it one day be possible to create bridges after this debate? Two very different doctrines within the church, which, to me, are ultimately about the same thing: loving your neighbor. At the same time, I understood that perhaps the time was not yet right, even though many churchgoers today also practice yoga, receive healing, believe in the universe, and more. These things do not contradict belief in God. They are an expansion and support of faith in a Creator and, simultaneously, in oneself as an individual.

I was invited to an interview at our national radio station in connection with the whole *"Gislinge Case."* I was asked to conduct a live telepathy session with a horse I had never met before, to gain insight into what had caused such a stir in the church. I was given a photo of a horse, as mentioned, with which I had no prior knowledge, and then I was to communicate with it while the horse's owner joined by phone to provide feedback. The interview went well, and the live demonstration proceeded smoothly. The horse's owner was very pleasantly surprised by all the concrete tools and information she received about her horse, which she recognized. The journalist was impressed and amazed by what he had just witnessed, mainly because the horse was in Southern Jutland while we were sitting in the warm studios in Copenhagen.

As I left the studio, a newly appointed bishop arrived for the following interview. I listened on my mobile phone as I drove out of the radio station. There, I heard the bishop being asked: *"So are you saying that people like Ditte Young are not welcome in the Danish National Church?"* And to my great surprise, I heard her reply, *"Yes, that is what I am saying. We need to be able to help churchgoers into the church ourselves. We need to gather people within the church space, create grief groups, get them to talk to the priests, and fill the church."* I smiled as I listened to her words. And I thought that if this debate could also help us think differently about how we can use the church space in the future, then it would all make sense. Could the next step in a bridge-building effort be that the church one day would leave the closed doors slightly ajar? And could we meet on a bridge in the middle, where there would be room for something more meditative and therapeutic for everyone?

There has been room for perception and rich renewal movements throughout the ages. For example, monastic orders, cloister movements, and other church-affiliated institutions have allowed space for healing work in line with confession and the Lutheran interpretation. Could we meet to discuss the typical traits I see in some monastic and nun movements that practice the solitude of monastic life? In a silence and calmness that seeks life's highest purpose. Where can you find both prayer and meditation? Could this search be compared to the very popular and not least expensive yoga trips to Bali or India, where people choose to live in silence for a few days? Can we have a debate about whether it is right or wrong that, within the Christian faith, people find peace by holding the hand of Jesus Christ in their search? While many Buddhists Walk the path entirely alone, without anyone to guide them in their spiritual search for nirvana. A state where salvation is achieved without suffering? And where, within spiritual work, does the learning lie in working with one's karma to attain what is called *cosmic consciousness*? Can we have an open discussion about an individual's faith and their journey toward eternal life? And whether there is a truth about what lies on the other side?

In the reflective aftermath, perhaps the church, following this debate, will work more to create a community and an open space where all those churchgoers who are lonely or lost have a place to be, just when they least expect to find comfort inside the church. I dream of a church that one day will open its gates and doors, instead of creating an isolated house where strict control is exercised over what may be debated inside. And perhaps make an existential space within a framework where the ceiling is higher and there is room to discuss the concept of correlation, allowing for a connection between the two individuals' spiritual journey and faith, among serious people.

Spirituality could perhaps one day be an expansion of faith, rather than an opposition to it. And maybe the Danish National Church could one day be a building with doors and windows that can be opened and closed as needed. But at the same time, a house that allows people to build bridges between religions across regions and around the world. Because after all, we all live on the same Earth. I wish we could strive for true inclusiveness—not just church inclusiveness.

What Their Heaven Looks Like

When it comes to the horses' heaven, I have come to understand parts of how it works, what it looks like, and how it feels. And yet, there is still so much I do not understand. Heaven is endlessly vast, beyond my comprehension. But I will try to share the information I have received so far. Knowledge, I have gained together with the horses and their owners, through the images and states they have shown me, and allowed me to feel.

The horses that pass away peacefully, having lived a long and good life and having made peace with dying, enter directly to what we call the other side—heaven. The horses who are aware that they are injured and cannot stay on Earth also seem calm as they step into death. I sense from them that they are entirely at peace with it. They do not fear death. They know they will find peace.

The horses that die suddenly due to a traumatic event or accident and don't have time to realize they are dying can sometimes get *stuck* on Earth. That is, the soul leaves the physical body, which is dead, but the soul does not know where to go because it still believes it belongs here with us. Horses whose owners struggle deeply with grief and continuously *call for them* by lighting candles, looking at their photos, and being heartbroken for an extended period, may also have a hard time letting go of Earth and their humans. They can end up in an inner conflict, knowing deep down that they are supposed to move on to another place—heaven—but being so loyal and devoted that they do not want to leave their person behind. These are often the cases where people say it still feels like their horse is standing in its stall or walking around the stable. They can simply sense their horse's presence without being able to see it physically.

I have not yet encountered horses who are stuck in what I call the *gray zone*, the state between Earth and heaven, by their own doing. This is something I sometimes see in humans who have taken their own lives, when I do clairvoyant sessions. If I see souls stuck in this gray zone, it becomes my primary task to help guide them into heaven. This is also what some may have heard about in connection with mediumship and spirit clearings, the kind of thing people often refer to when they say a place feels *haunted*.

I have also never experienced horses in what some would call *hell*, which I see as a state of mind and feeling, not a physical place with a man holding a pitchfork. I have, however, seen that humans can feel or experience what might be described as hell. But like everything in life, no emotion lasts forever if one is willing to grow. Based on what I know now, I don't believe that anyone ends up in hell forever. From what I've seen and felt, hell is a feeling; pain, grief, loneliness, low self-worth, guilt, and much more, that doesn't end just because life on Earth does. It is, in that sense, simply an energy. A part of the greater whole and part of spiritual consciousness. And it is also a lesson, the realization that learning continues on the other side.

The reason I sense it is called heaven is that it feels like that. It is a state and an energy—a presence of peace and love that is indescribable. You could compare it to a feeling of joy rushing through your veins and arteries, through your breath and heartbeat. A sensation of warmth washes over your body, where you feel like you're about to burst from bliss. The difference between feeling this on Earth and feeling it in heaven is that, here, it's not constant. In heaven, it is. It's a heavenly state, which is why the word *heaven* makes so much sense. When I have *tuned in* to the frequency where heaven exists, and animals or departed humans have transferred the energy and feeling to me, I've often thought: *"God, this place feels so good. I want to stay here a little longer."*

It's a place filled with love and peace, where the horses can appear however they wish, eat whatever they want (even though they don't feel hunger, thirst, or the passage of time), and choose what their surroundings look like. It's a kind of dreamlike scenario they live in. Heaven is right here, right next to our world, and they can enter our world at any time. But it seems like they exist on a different frequency, in a kind of parallel world, making it impossible for *normal* people to pick up their signals, and vice versa. It requires a gateway, someone with telepathic or clairvoyant abilities, to open a window through which communication can happen. This kind of work is energetically demanding, and in my experience, it is possible to work with it for only 4 to 6 hours per day at most.

The day after I've done intense telepathy for 4 to 6 hours, I get headaches and feel like I have a hangover. My head feels heavy, and I can't make decisions. This also happens when I communicate using telepathy with living horses. That means I can't work unlimited hours in a day because I take care of myself. Since I am the tool, I have to care for that tool; otherwise, I can't help anyone, or I can't be the window and interpreter people ask me to be. Most horses' version of heaven is in nature, on vast green meadows without borders. Tall trees may frame their space on one or both sides, or by hills, valleys, or bodies of water like rivers. But the space continues endlessly behind, ahead, and around them. There is a physical sky—no sun—but it is very bright, and the sky is blue and lit by white light. Some fields may have flowers, and there may also be other animals: cats, dogs, other horses, birds, and so on. There may also be humans, if the horses want them there. The horses are placed together with other souls they knew in life or with other horses they can learn from in their version of heaven.

In heaven, they are allowed to land and acclimate, to get used to their new surroundings. They enjoy themselves doing whatever brings them comfort. That might be watching birds or walking calmly down a hill. From my perspective on Earth, from another frequency, I might observe them walking around for an hour. But for them, time doesn't exist. They just feel like they've stepped onto the hilltop and are gazing out over the valley. They are simply in a state of being, and in that state, time doesn't exist. Sometimes they need to learn something. That made sense to me when I saw it, because everything is a process of growth and everything is constantly evolving. So, they, too, are asked to reflect on something they must learn in heaven. They know in a different way, not by sitting at a school desk, as we do. Instead, a voice appears inside their mind and asks questions they must reflect on in peace. For example: *"What do you think you can do to understand patience better, and how does your lack of it affect the souls around you?"*

The reason this is a learning moment, and a tricky question is that it requires the horse to gain self-insight and search for the answer within itself, because the horse is only allowed to answer in a single sentence that sums up all the situations where it has acted impatiently or restlessly in its life, with people or other horses. When I try to explain how heaven works and how the entire universe is structured, I explain it like a kind of school, but not like the schools we know today. When horses have fully understood the questions, they've been asked, and there can be several, it may have taken hundreds of years. We know that time in space doesn't function the same as here on Earth. When we send humans into space and they return, we've aged more than they have. To reincarnate, for both humans and animals, means that we are reborn in a new body. The soul is reborn. When we—as souls, whether human or animal—reincarnate, it depends on how long it takes to reflect on the questions and lessons we're meant to learn. It also depends on how soon we wish to return to Earth.

In some cases, I see and hear that the beings asking these questions are more evolved entities or souls. It may be God. It may be a council of spiritual guides. What I do know is that it's not the deceased horse asking itself these questions, because they tell me during telepathic communication that the questions were asked, and that they've been thinking about them for a long time. They find the questions very difficult and don't have the answers right away. Once they find the answers, they also realize that their soul's goal is to become more compassionate and spiritually aware. After that, they can choose to revisit that lesson or theme. A theme is what I've previously referred to as karma. Let's take patience as an example. On Earth, this horse may have chased others in the pasture, causing injuries and bringing grief to other horses and their owners. The horse may also have had the personality I call *The Playful Child*, with a short fuse, trouble standing still, easily restless in the stable, and more. When the horse reaches an understanding of whether that behavior was compassionate toward those it lived among, it may then say: *"I want to learn to be more patient."* The karma this horse brings into its next life would then be summed up in the word *patience*.

This is a fictional but realistic example, based on the many telepathic sessions I've had. I've encountered this theme multiple times. Then the horse would be born into a foal's body, placed with particular horses and humans who would unknowingly test it on patience. If the horse had been impatient and now must learn patience, one task could be that everyone around it stresses it out, so it must learn to breathe through it. In this way, it grows more tolerant and patient.

Let's take a rider as an example. The horse may learn patience by having a rider who is very impatient during training, expecting the horse to perform flawlessly from day one, and who thinks the horse isn't doing well enough. This rider might place unnecessary pressure on the horse, driven by their ego or ambitions, which are also shaped by their karma. The horse has no choice but to live and work in those circumstances. Its only option is to find a balance between its impatience and growing patience, unless the rider chooses to look inward and take responsibility for their lesson. A horse's nature is, as mentioned, to flee, to fight, or to freeze. Based on its personality, it will respond differently in the same situation. That means some horses will fight their rider, and the rider may interpret this as being *difficult*. Other horses will shut down and become somewhat depressed in those settings.

Based on their karma, they will also act differently in the same situation. This horse, who has asked to learn about patience versus impatience, will stay in the conflict until something else happens. Another possibility is that the rider finally listens to themselves and considers the cooperation or lack thereof that unfolds between them. Other horses might be sold and get a new owner, who will have to learn the same things but will be handled differently by their humans. Therefore, I have come to understand that I cannot generalize about horses or riders, for that matter, because multiple layers play an essential role and factor when we consider karma and the way we choose to learn something in life, whether we are horses or humans. Thus, learning something in life becomes more complex, even as I find it very simple. The point in sharing all of this, both in its simplicity and complexity, is to convey the knowledge that everyone has chosen to learn something in life. And therefore, we cannot be judgmental or say that something is right or wrong. Because the lessons in life, in joys and pains, are something we have chosen for ourselves. In other words, the rider has chosen to learn based on the challenges they face in life. And the horse is available to the rider during that learning process, regardless of whether it is proper or reasonable, from an animal welfare perspective. There is often a higher meaning in why exactly a particular horse and a certain rider are together. In this way, it remains a mystery to me how the universe manages to create the lessons and challenges that we have all requested. Maybe because like attracts like? And perhaps because we all truly belong together, this will come together in a higher unity.

I have seen the same processes, the same questions, the same learning, and some of the same things happen for people in their heaven, but much more complex than for the horses. Heaven, as part of the universe, is a vast collective energy in which one can exist. So, everyone is connected in the same energy. But just like in the human body, where everything is interconnected and belongs together, there can be an independent cell, muscle, or body part. Therefore, there are also independent *cells* in heaven, meaning several celestial fabrics that are part of something greater. In heaven, one can always make contact with another cell or another's heaven and thus come together in a meeting, in the present, and in community, then withdraw again, still being part of a community. Therefore, no one in heaven feels lonely. No one is ever truly alone *there*, even though they may initially appear alone in their heaven. Several horses have told me that when they show up alone on a green meadow, they know they can just call out to the herd, and then other horses will appear from the sides along the trees in their vicinity, allowing them to socialize and interact with them. They can also choose to say that now the other horses should go, and then those horses leave this particular horse's heaven, so it is again just with itself. I have been asked many times if I believe that horses have a collective spirit.

And yes, I feel that several animals do. They have an understanding that we all belong together. However, I also think that each animal understands that they have an independent thinking *I* with an *I-need*. At the same time, they are part of a larger community that influences and affects each other's energies. I know that the same applies to us humans, but very few today understand how our actions affect each other down to the smallest level and in the most minor details. From the thoughts we think, to what we feel, to what we send out, to what we create here in the world while we are here together.

Will I Meet My Horse Again In This Life?

Many horse owners have asked me if their horses will *come back down* so they can experience each other again in this life. And I must say that, unfortunately, it is rare for horses to come back so quickly, because time does not exist on the other side. We know this from astronauts who venture out into space, as I mentioned earlier. Time stands still for them, and that is how it feels for the animals on the other side. So, even though 50 years might pass for us, it may feel to the horse as though only 1 month has gone by. I think the movie *Interstellar* (2014), starring Matthew McConaughey, illustrates this very well. Both the parallel world and the time lost when you are out in space or the *other world*.

Horses often stay on Earth for a few months after they have passed.

They keep an eye on the place where they stood, their owners and riders, and other horses that they feel responsible for, for a time after they have passed, much like deceased humans. Some horses, especially the lead horses, continue to guide the other horses in the pasture if they were the leaders of the herd when they lived on Earth. They also give minor signs to their humans that they are there. This can range from moving buckets around (which requires a lot of energy), starting the music on the radio in the barn aisle, or blowing air into their humans' ears or on their cheeks so they feel the horses are right there. It requires patience and an expansion of the senses for humans to notice and feel these things I am describing now. However, you can be assured that the other horses in the barn will sense the presence of your deceased horse. Often, we humans are more open to the beyond during times of grief because, through sorrow, we are automatically in touch with our emotions.

However, you should know that if you have a horse you had to say goodbye to, imagine the horse's head in front of you. Look into its eyes, even if you feel emotional or sad, and remember to take a deep breath. If you can see your horse in front of you, almost coming to life, either because its head is imprinted in your mind's eye, no matter where you look, or because it moves in front of you, then trust that you are now in telepathic contact with your horse from the other side. The same applies to living horses. This is how, among other ways, I make contact with the horses and also know that I am truly connecting with them.

For the deceased horses, they describe this contact in the following way. They are standing in their own and experiencing heaven when they suddenly look up towards the sky. There, they can see their human's face clearly in front of them, as if it were painted in the clouds. A wave of love and energy comes over them from the celestial body, and they know then that it is their rider or owner sending them thoughts and thus *calling for them*. Just like when you go out into the pasture and whistle for your horse, it is also not in doubt about your sounds, your way of moving, your thoughts, or the energy you send out. When they sense that their humans are sad because they feel the vibration of energy you are sending toward them, they can send comforting thoughts back to you. They can also become sad themselves because you are sad.

Once they have completely crossed over and are in their heaven, they are at peace. If they have just *arrived* there, they need a moment to get used to being in a body that doesn't exist but is a form of matter so that we humans can recognize it as a horse when we make contact. In this body, they feel no pain, discomfort, irritation, tension, or any injuries they had before they were euthanized. Even in their bodies, there is a form of ecstasy and peace. A feeling of love and calm pervades their mental and physical state.

When your horse senses that you, as its human, are sad and your horse doesn't feel that it can reach you with its comforting words, your horse often experiences sadness for a moment. But exclusively on your behalf, not on its own. Your horse wants to be there to comfort you, just as when you were physically together. Those moments when your horse looked deeply into your eyes, laid its head on your shoulders, tugged on the strings of your jacket to make you laugh, opened stall doors, and laughed to itself because your horse could make you smile. It blew air into your hair with its warm breath, filled with the love energy from its heart. It nuzzled you on the head with its muzzle, leaving a prominent woolly tuft on top of your head. It leaned its muzzle against your mouth and kissed you in the way only you two did. All of these moments, your horse can convey to you. And if you're fortunate enough to be one of those who can sense them, know inside yourself that it is your horse sending you this.

Horses have many ways of showing tenderness, care, and love, and I know that you, as the reader of this book, have felt this yourself. From the moment you release your thoughts to your horse, your face disappears from its heaven, and it returns to the now it is in, no longer dwelling on memories, thoughts, sorrows, or worries about you, or about the time you had together. These emotions do not exist in heaven. Instead, it can consider learning what you had together that was fulfilling and developmental for both of you, and how it can elevate this to a higher level and consciousness for itself the next time it is on Earth.

Eternal Life

Now I have written about horses and death, and I know that some of you reading this book may have cried your way through that chapter or at least been moved by it. This is because you carry a deep sorrow from having lost a horse at some point. You know how painful it is, and the thoughts of never meeting again can be overwhelming. Some of you hope to reunite one day, and I promise you that you will, although perhaps not in this lifetime, because time does not exist in the universe.

Therefore, you must trust that when *the time* is correct, you will meet again. Horse owners and riders who react this way when they lose their horse do so because they have seen the personality in their horse and know that it cannot simply be replaced. They could have three other horses, perhaps already do, but it is never quite the same. Other riders who react similarly are those who are transitioning from riding ponies to riding fully grown horses.

They know that the pony learned with them, taught them, and helped them gain all the knowledge and skills they now have. They may have won many competitions together and shared many emotions and joyful experiences. And as always, it is difficult for many people to move on from something familiar to something new and exciting that is unknown. You know what you have, but you do not see what you will get. Can a horse become a human? Or what does it become when it dies? I do not sit with the ultimate truth, but I believe that everything is part of a development toward a higher consciousness and a greater sense of emotional compassion. This means that for this development to take place, a refinement of character must also occur, which we achieve through education and learning. Through that, we grow and expand our horizons.

I believe the process of development may be that we evolve from being a basic organism, to a plant, to a monkey, too, for example, an animal with a sense of community and a sense of self. It could be a dog, a dolphin, an elephant, a horse, and so on. When we, as souls, have undergone that evolution, we can develop into something even more spiritual, and the tasks can become increasingly complex. We can then evolve into becoming human. And from there, we can help on a higher level to develop others and pass on the messages that may come to us. As humans, we can share knowledge, question things, but also overcomplicate spiritual awareness more than it is. Horses, of course, help develop their herd and their people, but being human is both good and bad. It can seem complicated because we are equipped with a brain.

The brain complicates so many things for us because we want evidence for everything, and we want to understand. This also causes us not always to trust or feel the things we sense within ourselves or around us. The brain is our strongest resource for development and for passing on messages, whether through mobile phones, the internet, or other human-made devices that help us share knowledge and increase awareness of our interconnectedness. That same brain can, of course, also complicate or exploit this ability when driven by power, money, and the need for recognition. Instead of using our knowledge to share, inform, and enlighten the societies we live in, we can end up destroying each other. For example, through war and devastation, without recognizing that when we destroy something for one part of our shared world, we also destroy it for ourselves and for those we care about.

I always feel very honored when I am asked to come and help interpret between a horse and its owner before euthanasia. Of course, it is emotionally heavy to be in that space because death is a delicate and often complex topic for most people. It is very different from when an owner simply wants to know how their horse is doing, or when I am helping to change a behavior in a horse, which of course always depends on the rider being willing to change something in themselves or the environment the horse lives in. But being there for the horse and the owner, when both are either calm, crying, or grieving together, is one of the most beautiful things I know.

I think it's admirable when people ask me to be there and genuinely want to hear what their horses have to say. They want to know if the horses are ready to die. They want to say goodbye one last time. They want to be sure it is the right decision. I often think about what I should do if the horse disagrees with being put down before I undertake such a task. However, in the few instances it has happened, I have always stayed true to what the horse says and tried to buy it more time to explain why, if I sensed that the horse did not understand why it had to die. Horses often convey caring messages to their humans. They want their people to feel as much peace and calm inside as possible, if euthanasia is the right choice. Most often, it is the horses that comfort their humans.

One summer, I was in a city called Tune interpreting between a horse and his human mother and her daughter, an hour before the vet was scheduled to arrive and euthanize him. He told me he was ready to go. He comforted the mother and daughter. He comforted his pasture mate, whom he knew would miss him and struggle with being alone.

He showed us in detail what would happen during the euthanasia and how quickly he would pass on, already with the first injection. The mother later told me that the process happened exactly as he had shown us, down to the smallest detail, and that it was comforting because she was prepared for something complicated. I gained yet another insight and realization that even though he had never witnessed a euthanasia himself, he somehow had a vision of what would happen. His name was *Don Pedro*, and I had previously used him in a major horse show. I already felt like I knew him a little, which made it even more emotional for me to stand there. I felt like I was saying goodbye to a friend.

What surprised me the most that day, beyond his calmness and efforts to comfort everyone around him, was what he said about what we humans need to learn. He had the clarity to say he didn't understand why humans have to resort to violence to feel heard. He thought it was wholly unnecessary and even a little pathetic. He felt sorry for us that we hadn't figured out another way. He also wanted us to become better at understanding the gray areas and not view everything in black or white terms. Only then can we become more accepting people and simply be in our being and our existence.

And that is what life is all about. When we understand that and can practice it, we are living in love. These are the kinds of messages I hear from the significantly *evolved* and spiritually aware horses, and it only deepens my desire to keep working toward equality for them, so that they, too, may have rights. Some horses are wiser and more compassionate than many people I know. They deserve to be protected and heard, regardless of their purpose. They have heart, soul, and intelligence. They have a right to be heard.

I know they are not going to vote in parliamentary elections or demand *mare rights* the way we women have fought, and continue to fight, for equality. By rights, I mean the respect to listen to them, to consider their thoughts, their preferred ways of learning, of training, of relating to others, and to meet them as best we can, even while they remain in captivity under our care. But I don't feel that horses themselves experience this as captivity. They live in the present moment, focused on feeling safe in their surroundings. It is in their nature to be part of a herd, whether that herd is made up of two horses, a human, or a companion pony makes no difference. They are not alone and abandoned, and in that way, they are no different from us humans. Our deepest needs are also about being seen, being heard, and being mirrored, and that helps us never feel entirely alone in this world.

When we have a friend who understands us, when we find a life partner whom we love and who loves us, when we have a horse with whom we feel we can be completely ourselves. Or when we have a colleague at work who fights for the exact causes we do, when we are with others in social circles and seek those with whom we share something in common, rather than those we feel we don't, in all these ways, we seek security and belonging. A belonging that is larger than we can truly comprehend, and that we long for, though we may not even notice it in our daily lives. Perhaps because many of us are preoccupied with us.

Nurturing and developing oneself is also necessary to find inner peace and contribute to the growth of both oneself and those around us. Nothing is random, and everything happens for a reason. I find peace in trying, every day, to let go of control, to be present in the now, and to remember that the universe has a plan. I can throw balls into the air, and then it is up to something greater than me to decide who will catch them, or where they will land. There is tremendous freedom in living that way.

Eternal life lies in the knowledge and belief that the soul continues. Whether you are a human, a horse, a dog, a cat, a plant, or any other living being, some researchers once conducted an experiment in a school where they placed two large green plants. The students were instructed so that half of them would speak negatively to one of the plants—essentially, to bully it. The other half of the students were to speak kindly and lovingly to the second plant every day. Within just a few weeks, the plant that had been spoken to with negativity began to wither. Its large green leaves started to fade and die. The other plant, the one receiving kind words each day, grew taller and developed more side shoots and leaves. Regardless of whether a plant has intelligence, it has been proven that all growing life reacts to energy. Believing in eternal life also means embracing, or accepting, the concept of reincarnation. A repetition of what you've already read: you are born here on Earth, whether as a human or a horse, with a purpose to learn.

A desire to evolve even further as a soul, with the hope of becoming more compassionate. Throughout life, you will learn and grow through complex tasks, which will often feel challenging and painful. This is your karma, which you chose *on the other side.* One day, when you die, you will arrive in heaven, where you must face yourself and the choices you made while living on Earth. You can reunite with your loved ones simply by thinking of them. Because we are all connected, those you love will also be by your side and one with you in heaven. This applies to people you have known and to your beloved animals whom you have said goodbye to. You can choose to be together. You can also choose solitude.

When you are ready to learn more again, you will be sent *down* once more to Earth (or to other places where souls can live) and you will have the opportunity to learn all over again. And thus, life goes in cycles and circles. Everything is in motion. And I do not believe that when we die, that's it. That everything simply goes dark and ends. Nothing else in life lasts forever. Not even flowers—not even the bulbs we plant in the ground, which by logic should die in the winter frost. Not even waters that dry up, not even fallow fields. Not even Earth itself ended during the Ice Age. If you look at nature as its force, it will always find a way to restore itself. Only human-made interference with the planet disrupts this.

If you look at us as humans in human bodies, these too can restore themselves. If you get a wound, it heals. If you shave your head and your hair grows back, it will return. If you cut your nails down to the root, they too will grow again. There will always be life, as long as there is a soul. I have met a few horses who still do not know what awaits them in heaven and who are uncertain about what it looks like, or what it means to cross over to the other side.

One of these beautiful horses was the black Friesian mare, whom I affectionately call *the Queen*, a trait of her personality that made her a faithful lead mare, Tsjitske, also known as Tjiller. I met her during a clinic I held in Hellerup on a cold winter day. It was called *When Telepathy Meets Craniosacral Therapy*. The focus was on how horses can express where they wish to receive treatment. Since both telepathy and craniosacral therapy work with energy, the synergy was powerful, something I continue to work with today and which I want to explore much more deeply.

Case with Tsjitske from the City of Sønderlade – Also Known as Tjille, When it Was Time to Help Her Cross Over to the Other Side.

Clara Galler was born in 1994 and had always been passionate about horses. Among others, she had Danish Warmbloods and Danish Olden-burg horses. In January 2014, Clara bought the mare Ruby. At the end of February that year, she fell off Ruby and was severely injured. After the fall, she became slightly afraid of getting back on a horse, but she didn't give up. She gathered all her courage and traveled to Jutland in

March to inspect several horses. Many of them could perform a range of medium-level dressage exercises and were well-trained for competitions with Clara. But among all those horses, there was one in particular, a Friesian mare who only knew the basics: walk, trot, and canter. On the way back to Copenhagen, Clara couldn't get her out of her head. There was *something* about her. After a few days of careful consideration, she decided that the Friesian mare had to undergo a pre-purchase examination and be brought home.

Just a week after their first meeting, Tsjitske arrived at the small private farm Selsmarken in the city of Allerød, north of Copenhagen. Since no one could pronounce her name, Clara changed it to Tjille. In the time that followed, Clara began riding and training her in dressage. It went smoothly, and Tjille progressed quickly and easily. She learned to go out into the forest alone, and their connection grew day by day.

In August 2015, I met Tjille for the first time. Clara had called me because she couldn't clip her legs. Tjille tried to strike out and panicked. She kicked if anyone even approached with the clippers. Even just thinking about the clippers without holding them triggered a reaction in her. When I entered the stable, I was greeted by a true *Queen*. She stood there, regal, and I wasn't sure whether I should curtsy or simply stand tall in my light and meet the energy that faced me. I showed Clara some exercises they could do together, and after that, it became much more tolerable for Tjille to accept the clippers. I developed a special fondness for Tjille. I had only met a few *Queens* at that point, and they nearly took my breath away every time. I've described horse personalities in my book *Understand Your Horse.* But briefly put, Tjille was one of those Queens, a lead mare. She had great awareness, demanded respect, and loved to be admired. She needed to have a purpose. She was a working horse and only wanted to be around people who were worthy of her presence.

She found anything else unserious. That made her a mare who was easily misunderstood. Some were afraid of her in the stable. Some thought she was spoiled. And others didn't even see the brilliant light she radiated—the same light that took my breath away and deeply attracted Clara to her. She picked up on every energy, both positive and negative. Among the negative energies was jealousy, that she was such a beautiful horse and received such special treatment. To us, she wasn't just a horse. She was an old soul, a teacher, and in a way, a wise, instructive old lady.

In November 2015, she began to act strangely. When mounted, she reacted as if she had girth pain. She bucked and wouldn't stop until the pressure was released and the rider dismounted. She was then taken to a veterinary clinic in North Zealand, where the vet believed she had a bent rib and was suffering from azoturia. Tjille came home, rested for 8 weeks, and received treatment. When Clara started riding her again, the same symptoms returned. That November, Clara called me to try to understand what was going on in Tjille's body and mind. We agreed to meet in January 2016. In December, Tjille was taken to a vet clinic on Funen for a scintigraphy scan. It showed she had inflammation around two spinous processes and was diagnosed with kissing spines. She was treated with Tildren and prescribed 3 months of rest.

In January 2016, I visited Selsmarken to help Tjille again. I asked Clara to change her feed and explained that Tjille didn't feel comfortable where she was, which was why she kept returning from the paddock to her stall. She didn't like the other horses. Tjille told me, *"I don't like the way they look at me. They think I'm different. And I feel different because I have a different kind of energy, more majestic than theirs. I want to be recognized for that, but I'm not. That's why I don't like them."* From then on, we affectionately called her *Aunt T*, like the old stories of Aunt Green and Aunt Lavender. I felt as if I were standing before a dignified lady who set the rules and made her displeasure with the world known.

She also didn't thrive in that place because she wasn't doing what she wanted. She couldn't understand why she had to stand still. At the same time, she sent me the sensation of burning pain throughout her body—like fire under the skin. I felt a fiery, restless discomfort that made me not want to be touched unless it was done firmly. She hated being brushed at that time. I sensed that giving her pure aloe vera to drink might help, and it did. About 14 days after starting it, she was more accepting of grooming. It made a big difference in her behavior.

I told Clara that Aunt T wanted to work. She was happy to have found Clara. She didn't see it as Clara choosing her, but the other way around. She felt it was her purpose and her mission in this life. She was saddened that she couldn't fulfill that purpose, that they couldn't ride together at that point. And that they couldn't pursue the shared dreams they both held.

After that, she was sent to Healthy Horse in Skibby with Sandie Bregnager Kjær for one month of aqua training rehabilitation. When Clara brought her home, she began to ride her again, but she still wasn't fully recovered. Clara then moved her to the private stud farm Straight Horse in Allerød to fulfill Aunt T's wish to live somewhere she would enjoy more. They focused on groundwork and lunging. Aunt T showed joy and satisfaction at the move.

Unfortunately, at the end of April, the symptoms returned—not as intensely, but she was uncomfortable. She was sent back to Healthy Horse for aqua training. She stayed for three weeks and was gradually reintroduced to being ridden. I visited her there, as I work on-site once a month. I could see that Aunt T was thriving and had made friends in the paddock.

After the three weeks passed, Clara was excited to get started again. However, after riding her twice for just 15 minutes, she developed lameness in her left front leg.

Working with a vet clinic in North Zealand, she received joint treatments every two weeks for 8 weeks. After that, she was put on a 24-hour turnout to encourage joint movement. This lasted about a month until the end of July. At first, she didn't understand why she wasn't allowed in the stable. But after a week, she adapted—she discovered there was grass and found companions who liked her. She started to relax.

One morning in late July, Aunt T suddenly wouldn't walk. Clara called me immediately. I visited them five days later. Clara hadn't told me why she needed me to come, and I didn't know the full extent of the medical history. She only told me she needed urgent help due to *an ongoing issue*. As soon as I stepped through the door, I knew why I was there. The heavy, sorrowful energy hit me—from Aunt T, from Clara, and from Clara's partner Morten, who was there that day. I began by tuning into her health, which was always one of the first things I looked at with Aunt T, due to her history. In our communication, I saw she had pain in her left shoulder, like arthritic pain. It felt as though something was missing in the joint, or as if the bones were grinding against each other with no cushioning. She was in severe pain and was lame because of it.

Otherwise, she felt generally well where she was, but the pain overshadowed the joy she felt about being in a place she liked. I told Clara that the new feed, following the diet change, suited her well. She had become a generally happier horse, but I also sensed she still couldn't understand why she wasn't allowed to work. "*If she couldn't work,*" she said, "*then she didn't want to go on. She didn't want to be a pasture ornament, not as the Queen she was.*" Everything Aunt T said made perfect sense to Clara, who was devastated and helpless, not knowing what to do anymore.

Aunt T herself brought up the possibility of euthanasia. I was somewhat surprised because I remembered that she wanted to do things and be seen. In the communication about euthanasia, she expressed a wish: *"That she wanted to be put down somewhere other than on the farm. She didn't think it would be dignified for the other horses to see her lying under a tarp until she was picked up. She didn't want to show her weakness as the Queen she was. She wanted them to remember her as the dignified Queen, not the weak horse under the tarp."* She also said: *"That she didn't want to be euthanized at Straight Horse if Clara got a new horse, because then she was convinced Clara would always remember that Aunt T had lain dead somewhere there. She didn't want Clara to have those memories."*

She sent me the thought that she would like: *"For Clara to be present during the euthanasia, holding her and being there all the way. She wanted a huge bucket filled with carrots and apples before she was put down, because that must be what heaven feels like. It should be filled to the brim so she couldn't eat it all. Because she had suffered from kidney failure, she hadn't been allowed apples for a long time, and she missed them."* Aunt T said, *"And then I want my heaven to be a big field with water in front of me and green grass as far as the eye can see. There will be peace, and I will be at peace, and it will be warm. It never rains, and I am never cold,"* she said. And I described this heaven to Clara, who also thought it sounded like a lovely place for her to be. In her heaven, she was alone and at rest. She knew there would be another gelding somewhere, whom she could call upon. There would be tall trees on her left side, like the edge of a forest stretching as far as the eye could see.

She wanted a few days so she could take in her surroundings and say goodbye. She needed to prepare the others for what was going to happen, and in doing so, she would also come to terms with it herself. She told me in the stable aisle how her heaven should be: *"With a field with big trees."* I was amazed and found it insightful to think it might be possible to shape your heaven. But since more horses had shown me this, I was once again reassured that everything starts with a thought and an intention. Both here on Earth and on the other side. When we later went out to the pastures, which I had never seen before, I was captivated and had tears in my eyes. Out in the pastures, I saw exactly the scenery Aunt T had described to me. It was precisely the pastures she had been on in her final time. A piece of land that was her home and her kingdom.

A little unexpectedly, and to everyone's great surprise, something happened: I suddenly saw someone who had passed away. First, a soul lit up in front of me, gradually becoming more transparent and more precise in my mind's eye. In the end, I saw a man standing in front of me, and I described him to Clara. She once again had tears in her eyes and stammered that she believed it was her late father. He said, *"Now I'd like to see the nag you're so proud of and have fought so hard for."* A choice of words and a sentence Clara instantly recognized as her father's. He said he would take good care of Aunt T in heaven. Clara's father died in December 2012 of cardiac arrest at just 56 years old—a deep sorrow Clara still carried with her.

Aunt T said that she was at peace with leaving now because her task in this life had been to bring Clara safely back into the saddle, and she felt she had completed that. So now she was okay with it, even though she had never been in actual training. She told Clara that she needed to go out and find a new horse quickly, because otherwise, Clara would never get one. She would remain stuck in grief, and Aunt T didn't want that. Again, I felt like I was communicating with an energy that resembled a very dignified old grandmother, issuing orders as she sent out her thoughts and energy. *"It has to be a mare. It must not be a gelding. She didn't think Clara was a gelding rider. She shouldn't get a street boy.*

That would be too boring and undignified." Aunt T believed Clara should find a Princess. Aunt T knew that Clara would never find a horse as dignified as herself, so she more or less commanded Clara to find a horse that ranked just beneath a Queen. It was a massive emotional rollercoaster for all three of us that day. We cried our eyes out and, at the same time, laughed ourselves to tears over the orders Aunt T issued. She gave us a sense that nothing was left to chance. There was a bigger plan, and Clara felt that Aunt T was in control of it, even without knowing what the plan or the future held. And I was stunned that Aunt T could see into the future or had a broader overview than the rest of us in that moment, even though she was the one in pain.

Four days later, Clara drove her to the veterinary clinic in North Zealand. At home, she got a strange feeling—like something was utterly wrong with Tjiller at the clinic. Clara drove back to North Zealand and saw that Aunt T was panicking in the stall. Clara called me in tears, completely panicked, and explained that Aunt T had gone into a panic during her final day. She asked me to sense what could be causing it. I sensed that Aunt T didn't want to be there alone. The surrounding stalls were empty, and there were no companions near her. I also sensed that she just needed to be somewhere familiar on her final day. Clara had her moved immediately. That was not how Aunt T should remember her last day. Aunt T spent one night at Straight Horse, and the next day, Clara drove her up to the vet again. We met in the parking lot, where I had agreed to be present for the euthanasia.

We went into the stall with Aunt T, and she was utterly calm and entirely herself. She knew now that she had friends with her and that she was not alone. She seemed very at peace. Clara had brought a bucket filled with apples and carrots, which had been Aunt T's final wish, and almost more like an order. The vet came to meet us by the stall, and the three of us—Clara, her boyfriend Morten, and I- led her out. I explained to the vet that Clara and Aunt T needed five minutes alone together before he brought the injections. During that private moment, Clara wanted to talk to me because she wasn't sure whether she should hold her during the euthanasia. She was uncertain whether it would be too overwhelming. I sensed that Aunt T had *surrendered* to the situation, and I felt that it would not be a violent experience at all; she wouldn't resist. I sensed that Aunt T would lie down quietly after the second injection. I also felt that Clara should only cut her tail once she had passed. Aunt T was afraid of going to heaven without a full tail, that wouldn't be fitting for a Queen.

We called the vet back and asked him to proceed. He came out with three syringes, which is standard in case the horse resists. I assured him that she would let go after the second injection and wouldn't fight. She was ready to move on. The vet was very kind to all three of us and especially respectful of Aunt T and Clara's wishes in what was a challenging and sorrowful situation. He had followed Aunt T for a long time and gave Clara a pat on the shoulder for making the right decision, since everyone had fought so hard for her.

We went behind the clinic, where a small paddock had been made with hay bales. There, the vet gave her the first injection. I felt tired and dizzy. I felt myself begin to relax, like when receiving morphine after an operation. I felt a bit disoriented, but safe. I knew I was sensing Aunt T. I described everything I thought to the others as we stood close together, still feeling the warmth of Aunt T's body. Then she received the second injection. She folded at the knees and lay down calmly. There was nothing violent about it. We stood very close to her when she fell. When she went down, the vet took over and held her in case she had reflexive spasms. I explained during these reactions that she had already crossed over while her body was simply reacting. I knew they were reflexes because I saw her soul standing beside us while the vet still had a hand on her. First, I noticed a white glow in the corner of my eye while I stared at her physical body. I turned my head to the right and saw Aunt T's soul standing tall and dignified before me—a presence I knew so well. I quickly looked back at her physical body. I saw the light disappear from her eyes, and suddenly there was just a body lying there. The vet pronounced her dead, and Clara had a moment alone with her. Aunt T's body was still warm, but there was no pulse and no energy left inside. Aunt T looked at us from the side and smiled and said to me, *"I'm not in pain anymore, Ditte. I feel a sense of freedom and peace in my body. Tell Clara."* She looked at us with a smile and with warmth and love. I heard her whisper in my inner ear, *"I am so grateful for all the time Clara, and I had together and for being listened to. And most of all,*

I am proud that I completed my life mission of bringing Clara back into the saddle. Even if we weren't meant to train high-level dressage, just being together was enough," she said, which I of course passed on. Her soul was bright and lit up the whole area, even on a cold autumn day when the sun was shining.

Clara asked me if she could cut a piece of her tail to have a piece of jewelry made from it. I turned to Aunt T's soul, who was still with us, and asked her if it was okay to cut some of her hair. Aunt T smiled and calmly said, *"Yes, you may. I won't need it anymore. But just don't take it all. I still want the other horses to see how beautiful I am, like the Queen I am,"* she said proudly and calmly. I didn't explain to Aunt T that she would have a different form of body where she was going, and of course, we respected her wishes and only took hair from the inside of her tail so that she would still look dignified.

That day, I learned even more about heaven and, for the first time, saw a soul leave the body and remain on our frequency on Earth, knowing that Aunt T was at peace and understood she was heading toward the light—to a frequency and a heaven that few can see, but one we always. I mean, honestly, always have access to. Because it is part of where we are now, it is a part of who we are. And the horses we say goodbye to will always be a part of us, in our hearts, in our thoughts, in our memories, in our cells, in the air, and in the energy around and within us. We all said our goodbyes to her and found peace in knowing she was well on the other side. We touched her, stroked her, and kissed her before we left.

To move away from the grief and honor Aunt T's wish, Clara quickly began looking for new horses. She asked national elite rider Bo Høstrup to assist her in her search. With every horse they looked at, Bo and Clara could only conclude that Aunt T had been right. None of the geldings sparked Clara's interest or touched her heart. One day, Clara went to the city of Fredensborg to see a horse, and suddenly, a black Friesian Princess walked into the arena. Her name was Imperial—a mare they hadn't even planned to view, mainly because of her high sale price. Clara fell head over heels for her and had to try her out. They fell for each other, and five days later, Imperial was in the stable after a vet check at The Hørsholms' Veterinarian Clinic. When Clara's job at Straight

Horse ended, she moved Imperial to a private boarding stable in Slangerup.

In April 2017, I visited them because Clara had asked me to communicate with both Imperial and Aunt T on the other side. I sat with a piece of her tail in my hand and a photo of her. When I connected with Aunt T, the first thing she said was, *"We need to talk about children!"* She was very insistent, and I didn't feel like I could get a word in—I had no control over the direction the conversation took.

Aunt T said, *"Clara needs to step up and get started on the project of having a baby. No ifs, ands, or buts!"*

A project that no one knew Clara and Morten had secretly discussed. Clara's jaw dropped when I told her, laughing. Aunt T said, *"It'll take the time it takes, and you mustn't stress about it. It will happen when it's meant to. Three children are waiting for you in the universe. The first will be a girl. Shortly after, you'll have a boy. And then there's another girl, if you wish to have her. The opportunity is there. But now that I'm not around to teach Clara more things, she'll learn the next lessons when she becomes a mother. So, get started!"*

Clara laughed. It was utterly surreal. She hadn't spoken to anyone else about it, and here Aunt T was revealing one of their biggest secrets. Even from heaven, Aunt T still had control over her life and everything in order.

The next time I saw Clara was in September 2017, when I was giving a clinic at the Hillerød Horse Show together with para-rider Stinna Tange Kaastrup. Clara was working for the event organizers and was showing me to my backstage room.

Clara hugged me deeply and whispered in my ear, *"Ditte! Aunt T was right."* I had to stifle a scream and threw my arms around Clara, giving her a big hug. I knew it meant she was pregnant.

In January 2018, Clara had her first scan and, of course, was told they were expecting a girl. Even from the other side, Aunt T was right.

Clara told me this when I asked whether it had all been worth it and if communicating with Aunt T had made sense: *"It gave me an enormous sense of peace and a feeling that everything was under control during the whole process. I trusted Aunt T's decisions the entire way. She taught me to trust my intuition. She did that by telling me and signaling that there was a reason behind everything. If I trusted the decisions I made, things would unfold as we had hoped. There's a greater purpose to everything, even if we can't see it.*

The peace also came from knowing, both when she was alive and through the contact after, that she had control over my life as if I had a guardian angel watching over me.

She gives me a sense of security. Of course, I have grieved her, but because Aunt T was involved in planning her passing, it gives me a kind of satisfaction knowing I did my best, and I can rest in that decision.

Over time, I've learned to trust Aunt T's guidance. She's always been right. Every time she communicated something through you, Ditte, it either gave me a more relaxed Queen in her behavior or her body. I am entirely sure that, on a personal level, she has more influence over my decisions than I do sometimes. If I'm in doubt about something, it feels like I can ask her what she thinks. I know she has a broader perspective than I do. And she'll always answer with what she believes is best for me. Now that's love."

Clara had three bracelets made from Aunt T's tail hair—one for herself, one for her boyfriend Morten, and one for me. In this way, we honor her memory, and she will never be forgotten. And I am convinced that some part of her wisdom and soul will live on in Clara and Morten's daughter.

Closing Words

I am often captivated and surprised when people around me tell me that I make a difference. I don't understand it. I'm just doing what I feel like doing. Recently, someone said to me that the things I initiate through my work and by being who I am, *move things*. While I listened with a little giggle and almost blushed, she told me, *"It seems that the things you work for are on a higher level and move all of humanity. Both debates about people and animals, and I will keep on fighting."*

Of course, I am flattered when people tell me such things, but at the same time, I wonder and think that little old me can't possibly accomplish something so big and universal. In my humility, I just do what I believe everyone is capable of doing. Maybe I have been given a potent ability? I know I'm good at seeing details, especially regarding animal health issues, which are some of the most complex subjects to read as a telepath. If all people could breathe and put aside their egos, I believe everyone could sense and listen. Listen when it's quiet. When we listen inwardly, we can feel what is right and what is wrong without a noisy ego wanting recognition or power.

When we listen inwardly, we are also better able to listen outwardly. In the information we receive, we can better select what comes to us and separate whether it is projections, helpful advice, other people's anxieties, judgments, or ego, and thereby keep ourselves free from it. If we could do that, the world would be a better place. I often wonder if we can exist without an ego. I don't think we can. Otherwise, we wouldn't have been born on Earth. We would have been stardust or angels helping other souls around us. In the ego lies development and learning. I once asked my teacher in the therapy course: *"When does learning stop? Can you learn enough and then take a break?"* I asked her. It wasn't much of a surprise, but a bit of a disappointment at the time when she smiled and told me that learning never stops because development stops as well. And so, I keep going. I have long learned that all the people and horses I help carry a problem that I either have or have had in my life. Because I know that like attracts like. I also get solutions for myself if I look closely and listen quietly to the advice I give them. And so, we continuously provide something to each other.

Everyone I am in contact with teaches me something, and I teach them something in return. They do this by making me confront my issues and mirror what is happening in their lives in my own life, without projecting. See, this is my perspective: that we are all dependent on each other, and we teach each other something, both in pain, in laughter, and through love. I hope that next time you meet someone who does you harm, look at them as a gift. It might be that the *gift* is wrapped strangely in your eyes. But if you ask yourself, *"What has this person taught me?"* Instead, you are well on your way to listening to yourself and learning more about yourself. A lesson that will benefit you the next time you meet a new person who, in your world, might be interpreted as wanting to harm you.

In my work and in my quest to continually expand my spiritual consciousness, I often think about how we can help each other grow this consciousness and deepen our community understanding. How can we, in our daily lives, demonstrate that we belong together? How can we create curiosity and understanding that the division and separation between two minds is an illusion? There is no doubt. We are one. We can think independently and make free choices. But in the end, we are all connected. These are other words for the chapters you have gone through, such as *The We Connection, The Mirror,* and *The Connected Ones.* One of the ways I have found effective is to articulate and concretize the horses' energies, thus translating their non-verbal language into a completely down-to-earth level that most people can understand. It has been, and still is, an art to possess such excellent spiritual knowledge and learn to select the information when it needs to be shared. Perhaps through this work and this book, another small energy is awakened in you as a reader, prompting you to become more aware of the spiritual consciousness within all of us. And how something so complicated can also be straightforward when you see and feel yourself and your horse. I know that deep inside, you do not doubt anything about yourself and your horse if you trust more in what you think and what is thus the truth for you.

I know that I will continue to reach out to academics and laypeople. We need to create a form of bridge-building, even in the early stages, for the bigger picture ever to become a reality. I am committed to continually improving the quality and professionalism of my work, as well as that of those I teach. However, I have a great wish that academics and laypeople, who are skeptical about *alternative methods*, will also raise their quality and professionalism and cover as broadly as possible in the search for understanding on other levels. I hope they will explore, and measure based on different forms of evidence. And rise above preconceived ideas about how consciousness has behaved or should behave. The most common view of the brain within the scientific world is that the brain produces consciousness. But this has never been proven. It is a thesis. This means that you need a brain that functions to create consciousness. And how do you explain all the near-death experiences of people who were in comas or on ventilators? If this thesis were actual, then consciousness could not exist outside of the brain. Since we are different, our brains are too. If we are all part of one community on a higher level, does that mean there is only one brain?

Plato (427-347 BC) said: *"Our desire for and striving for wholeness is called love."* That is what the horses give you, and others, and me, included. They help make us whole by showing us the difficult things that hurt, as well as the joyful and heartfelt aspects. The things I struggle with in handling the horses are the same things I struggle with in my private life. After many years as a healer, I wanted to overcome my life-long fear of horses, which I had developed in childhood. I wanted to work with different horses in *liberty* and practice horsemanship. Primarily because I wanted to learn to feel into the other horse systems, about mine, and never be *lazy* or expect anything from them, as I had become accustomed to one of them. I wanted to learn to ride and get the basics in place. I believe that it is an ongoing process that will never stop, as this work can constantly develop, refine, and improve itself, regardless of the level at which you train or ride. This, without any helpers, except for a rope halter or cordeo around the horses' necks, while we train together in the arena with me on their backs. No stirrups and no whips. Nothing, except for my breath, my balance, my sense, my intention, and my heart.

It has been, and still is, an incredible journey where I discover every time that when I am with the horses, they mirror the issues I know in my own life. It can be anything from losing control and becoming scared to not wanting to dominate them and feeling that I am being dominant rather than leading them. And that feeling is almost forbidden, deep inside me. I've been more focused on checking if the horses are OK than on whether I am OK. Initially, when I encountered this issue, I thought it was a *professional hazard*. I am so used to positioning myself as a translator that I don't have an opinion and am more focused on how the horses are doing. That just doesn't work when interacting with them. Some horses become irritated due to a lack of leadership, and others become insecure because they don't feel that I have an overarching plan. Through my in-depth work with the amazing horses that make themselves available, I discover that the tools and learning I gain from them provide me with the means to become a more whole person —tools and knowledge that I will carry with me for the rest of my life. I pass them on to those I love and to those who find them useful. Because I know that when I heal, a part of you also heals. And when you heal, you are helping to heal me.

Bibliography

Battle
Source: http://www.mynewsdesk.com/dk/romu/pressreleases/ny-arkaeologisk-udgravning-i-roskilde-centrum-1499610

Kristeligt Dagblad
Source: https://www.kristeligt-dagblad.dk/liv-sjael/hjernekirurg-sjaelen-lever-videre-naar-krop pen-doer

Paolo Baragli
Source: https://www.ncbi.nlm.nih.gov/pubmed/28268877
Source: https://www.nature.com/articles/s41598-017-16729-z

To connect and the word *"connected"* is defined as:" To be grateful and devoted."
Source: *ordnet.dk*

Ugeskrift for Læger
Source: Melatonin's Effect on the Immune System and Cancer

Thank you

To all of you animal owners who reach out to me daily, seeking help to understand your animals and thus create a stronger bond with them: Thank you for recognizing that your animals have something to say. Even if you may not yet trust your abilities when receiving the nonverbal messages your animals send to you, I hope you will continue to rely more and more on all the things you feel, which are the truth for each of you, together with your horse, and just for you in your life.

A special thank you to my ghostwriter, Christina Obel, for once again being with me on this journey in the book. For helping to create a sense of wholeness, a space of the heart, and constantly supporting me in conveying the messages I hold dear.

Thank you to Muusmann Publishing for believing in me and my messages and for publishing my books.

Thank you to my regular photographer, Nadia Fryd, for being able to see the things I want to convey through the lens of the camera and always jumping in when I need you. Thank you for the beautiful pictures and the extensive post-editing work you've done on all the images in the book. I feel so secure with you, and you are just wonderful.

Thank you to my family and friends for always supporting me and giving me space and room to be myself. I know it's not always easy when I need quiet or to find inspiration and creativity and thus end up isolating myself. You should know that you are everything to me.

Thank you to Køgevejens Horse Pension and especially to you, Gitte Olsen, for allowing me to borrow your talented Friesian boy, Pourqui, for the photo sessions in the animal park.

Thank you to Charmaine Berdino for lending me Kazarro for the photo shoots and for the excellent training you've provided with him, which made it possible to create such beautiful images.

Thank you to Noreen Krogsgaard for lending me the beautiful and spiritual pony, Jolie, again. I love all the pictures with her, and not least the time spent with you.

Thank you to Dorthe Thaulov for being such an open-minded and accommodating priest and person. I look forward to more with you. You pave the way!

Thank you to Christian and Camilla Schou for letting us take pictures of Palle and include them in the book.

Thank you to Anette Munch Andersen for your story, and for listening to Nád.

Thank you to Clara Melanie Galler for letting me be part of your journey, both with Tjiller and in your life today.

Thank you, Helle Alice Popp Gad, for listening to your horses and for the experience with Fjola.

Thank you to Emilie Nordvig for letting us use your beautiful stables for the photo shoots at Ellemosegaard in Vedbæk.

Thank you to photographer Erik Kunddahl for the beautiful images in the book.

Thank you to all the horses I have ever encountered with and those I will encounter in the future. You are part of healing me and are the teachers I need on my journey.

See you out there 💗

About the Author

Ditte Young is an internationally renowned telepath, licensed therapist, animal communicator, clairvoyant, intuitive coach, and bestselling author who has dedicated her life to expanding human understanding of consciousness, connection, and communication, both seen and unseen. Born with a rare sensitivity to the spiritual world, Ditte possesses a unique ability to practice telepathy with remarkable speed and clarity. She has taught her methods to thousands of people around the world, helping individuals connect more deeply with themselves, their children, and their animals. Through her books and global work, Ditte continues to empower others to trust their intuition, understand behavior on a deeper level, and live more connected, authentic lives.

To learn more about Ditte's work, attend an event or telepathy course visit: https://ditteyoung.com